Images of Modern America

CHARLOTTE MOTOR SPEEDWAY

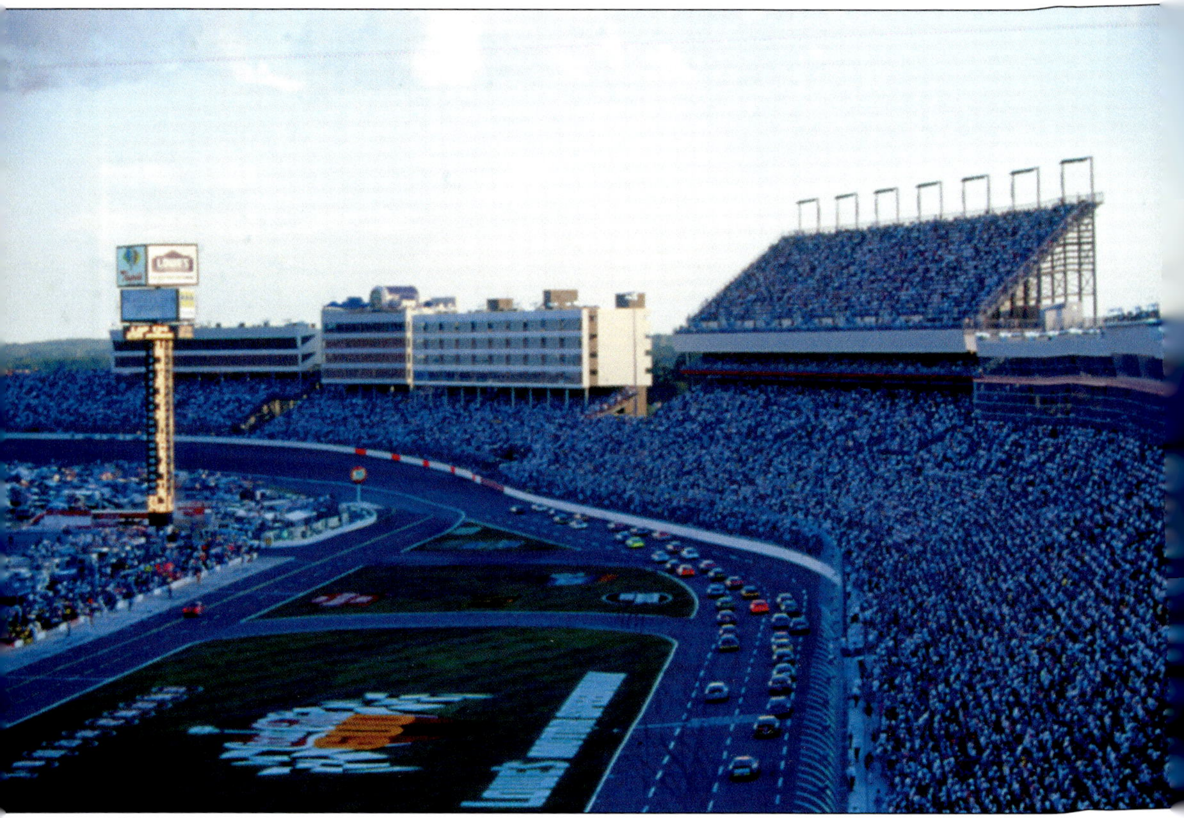

Charlotte Motor Speedway has continued to evolve since its beginning in 1960. Today, it provides first-class accommodations for its fans and garages for the competitors. Race weekends have become more than an event; they are now an experience. (Charlotte Motor Speedway Archives.)

FRONT COVER: Charlotte Motor Speedway owner Bruton Smith (right) congratulates Dale Earnhardt in victory lane following his first Coca-Cola 600 win. Four generations of the Earnhardt family have competed at Charlotte Motor Speedway. (Charlotte Motor Speedway Archives.)

UPPER BACK COVER: The dogleg-shaped frontstretch means drivers must often develop different passing strategies. (Charlotte Motor Speedway Archives.)

LOWER BACK COVER (from left to right): Legend cars are a popular way for people to race at a reasonable cost. Twice annually, series champions are determined at the track in the Winter Heat and Summer Shootout. (Charlotte Motor Speedway Archives, see page 64); Bruton Smith (left) interviews 16-time NHRA Funny Car champion John Force. (Charlotte Motor Speedway Archives, see page 95); The Dirt Track at Charlotte hosts numerous events. (Charlotte Motor Speedway Archives, see page 89)

Images of Modern America

CHARLOTTE MOTOR SPEEDWAY

DEB WILLIAMS

ARCADIA PUBLISHING

ISBN 978-1-4671-2636-6

Published by Arcadia Publishing
Charleston, South Carolina

Printed in the United States of America

Library of Congress Control Number: 2017932825

For all general information, please contact Arcadia Publishing:
Telephone 843-853-2070
Fax 843-853-0044
E-mail sales@arcadiapublishing.com
For customer service and orders:
Toll-Free 1-888-313-2665

Visit us on the Internet at www.arcadiapublishing.com

This book is dedicated to Bruton Smith, who through his enduring tenacity turned a tremendous vision into a state-of-the-art reality with Charlotte Motor Speedway. His commitments to hard work, innovation, and putting on a show have established a legacy of sports entertainment that has awed generations and will continue to do so for decades to come.

Contents

ACKNOWLEDGMENTS

While one person may be listed as the author of this book, I certainly did not create it by myself. Just as no person is an island, a book cannot be created without assistance from other people.

Unfortunately, many of them are no longer with us—they were the ones who had the foresight to chronicle the speedway's early years via photography. They also understood the importance of maintaining the negatives, slides, and prints. Their work is the reason all of the photographs in this book, unless otherwise noted, are from the Charlotte Motor Speedway Archives.

A special thank-you goes to the current employees of Charlotte Motor Speedway's communications department who were willing to help at a moment's notice, even while preparing for their hectic annual Media Tour. Not only did they assist in providing photographs and historical race programs, but in proofing copy as well.

Also, I am grateful to Johnny Bruce who took time to provide me with a photograph of his *Stroker Ace* poster autographed by the movie's director, Hal Needham. To John Davison, Frances Flock, Kim Wood Hall, Tom Roberts, and H.A. "Humpy" Wheeler, thank you for assisting with identifying people in various photographs or providing information on the images' content.

Personal knowledge, as well as old race programs, Greg Fielden's four-volume series *Forty Years of Stock Car Racing*, and the book *Charlotte Motor Speedway History: From Granite to Gold* provided the information contained in this book.

I hope seeing the photographs resurrects exciting memories for you and that you enjoy looking at them as much as I did selecting them for you.

INTRODUCTION

When Daytona International Speedway opened in February 1959, it signaled the beginning of a new era in stock car racing—the superspeedway—and Bruton Smith knew he wanted to build and own one in his home state of North Carolina.

A promoter at various dirt tracks in the Charlotte, North Carolina, area during the 1950s, Smith initially planned to build a high-banked, two-mile track south of Charlotte in Pineville, North Carolina. It would be named Charlotte International Speedway, contain a road course, seating for 75,000, a football field between the frontstretch and pit road, and would cost $2 million to construct. The Stanley County, North Carolina, native had selected Pineville because a beautiful superspeedway board track had operated in the area from 1924 to 1926.

On April 22, 1959, when Smith held his news conference announcing his intentions to build a superspeedway, NASCAR driver and entrepreneur Curtis Turner did the same. Only Turner's plans called for a 1.5-mile track to be built north of Charlotte on North Carolina Highway 49 and carry the name Charlotte Motor Speedway. It would cost $750,000 to construct, have 45,000 seats, and a one-mile road course. Neither man, however, possessed the money to fund his project. By June 1959, they had decided the only prudent thing to do financially was to join forces. They settled on 550 acres of hilly land saturated in rocks and boulders just inside Cabarrus County on US Highway 29. The property had at one time been owned by Nathaniel Alexander, North Carolina's first elected governor.

From the beginning, the two men were confronted with issues that escalated construction costs. The biggest problem was the half-million yards of solid granite discovered on the property that had to be dealt with before the speedway's first and second turns could be constructed. Turner said the core drill report had identified boulders on the property, so he negotiated a deal to remove the dirt and boulders for 18¢ a yard. When the granite was discovered, the removal cost escalated to $1 a yard, plus the dynamite. It required $70,000 in dynamite just to get through the first turn.

Construction costs skyrocketed, and in January 1960, the workers were put on two 12-hour shifts in an effort to catch up on the construction that was lagging due to more than 10 inches of rain in the last few months of 1959. More weather-related problems developed in March 1960 when an 11-inch snow halted all work on the project. Then there were two more snowstorms in the next two weeks. Construction delays forced the inaugural 600-mile race to be moved back to June from Memorial Day weekend. Even before the first green flag waved, Bruton Smith and Curtis Turner had accumulated $500,000 in outstanding debts.

Paving of the track was completed the morning that qualifying began for the first World 600, and that resulted in another problem. Holes developed in the turns during practice and qualifying, forcing patchwork to be done daily. The drivers took their own safety measures against the flying debris and installed large screens over the cars' grilles and windshields. Sixty cars started the race, which took slightly more than five and a half hours to complete. It was a phenomenal achievement for Smith and Turner, but it also left them with a tremendous amount of debt.

After the inaugural race, Turner approached the Teamsters Union about an $800,000 loan to bail the speedway out of debt. In exchange for the loan, the Teamsters wanted Turner to organize the drivers into a union and bring pari-mutuel betting into the sport. Turner abandoned the idea after talking with some drivers. Slowly, Turner and Smith were paying off the speedway's debt, but it was not fast enough for the creditors. In early June 1961, slightly more than a week after the second World 600, the board of directors removed Curtis Turner as the speedway's president and Bruton Smith resigned as vice president.

Turner returned to the Teamsters Union in August 1961 about acquiring an $850,000 loan that would bail Charlotte Motor Speedway out of its impending bankruptcy. The teamsters made the same requirements of Turner as before: Unionize the drivers and get pari-mutuel betting in the sport. NASCAR president Bill France Sr. quickly defeated Turner's efforts and suspended him indefinitely from the sport. Charlotte Motor Speedway found itself in bankruptcy. Smith left the area to pursue other business ventures, and Turner began racing in non–NASCAR sanctioned events.

By the time 1961 concluded, the speedway had more than $1 million in outstanding liens from creditors. A.C. Goines, a member of the speedway's original board of directors, and Richard Howard, a stockholder in the facility, raised the money needed to keep the track from being placed in a foreclosure sale. Instead, the track was placed under Chapter 10 of the Federal Bankruptcy Act, and the men began working diligently to make it solvent.

A Denver, North Carolina, native, Howard eventually became the speedway's president, and on June 1, 1967, he took nearly $300,000 to a bank in Newton, North Carolina, to clear the track of its remaining debts. Eighteen days later, the World War II–era marine held a mortgage burning for speedway officials and invited guests.

Howard continued to run the speedway until 1975, when Bruton Smith regained control of the track and returned to North Carolina. The years of financial conservativeness had resulted in the track needing several upgrades. Getting the facility out of bankruptcy and keeping it there had been Howard's primary objective. By the time Smith regained ownership and convinced H.A. "Humpy" Wheeler to join him in running the facility, the two men had to assess and prioritize the upgrades that were needed.

A self-described frustrated builder, Smith began a construction spree in the 1980s that left many people shaking their heads in disbelief. A new press box, VIP suites, offices, and the Speedway Club were constructed. The announcement to build trackside condominiums even made the late-night television show hosted by David Letterman. Race day was transformed into a spectacle with often lavish prerace shows. After years of merely surviving, the speedway was now being transformed into a state-of-the-art facility that set the mark for others to follow.

This book shows the birth, growth, and continued evolution of Charlotte Motor Speedway through photographs from its own archives. It is truly amazing to see how the speedway, its fans, and drivers have progressed through nearly six decades, thus providing a true glimpse into modern America.

One

In the Beginning

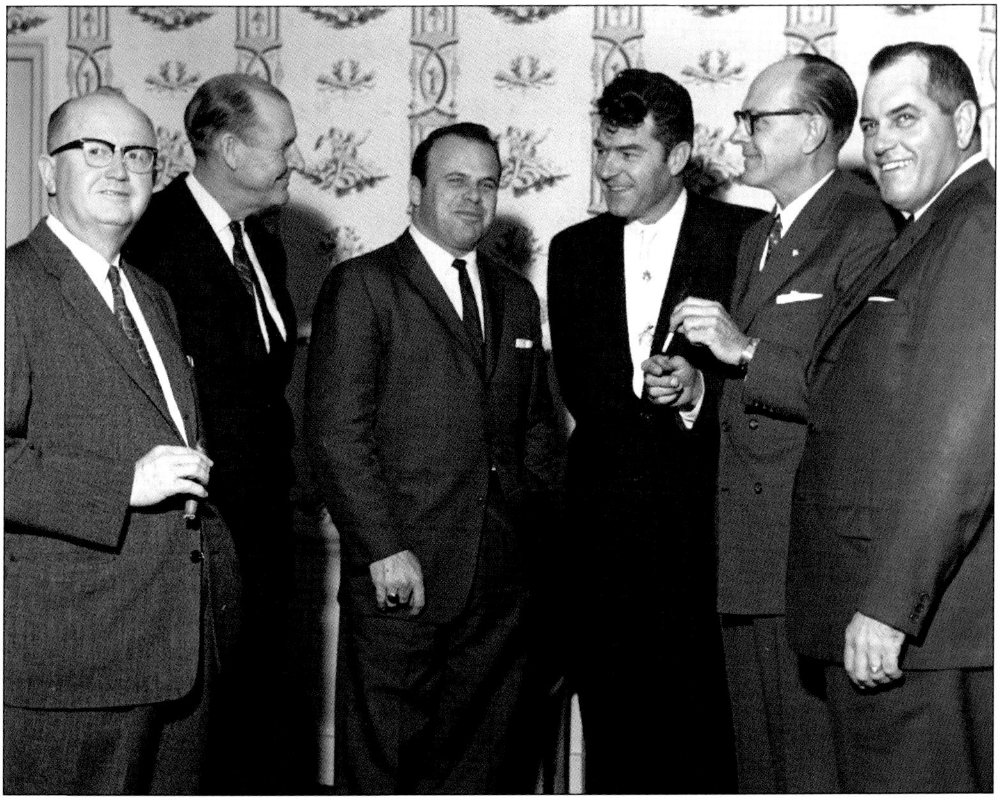

In June 1959, Bruton Smith (third from left) and Curtis Turner (third from right) joined forces to build Charlotte Motor Speedway in Cabarrus County, North Carolina. Initially, the men had envisioned separate speedways, but working together was the prudent thing to do financially. The board of directors were, from left to right, A.C. Goines, G.D. Smith, Jerry Ball, and G.B. Nalley. Absent from the photograph was Charles Crutchfield.

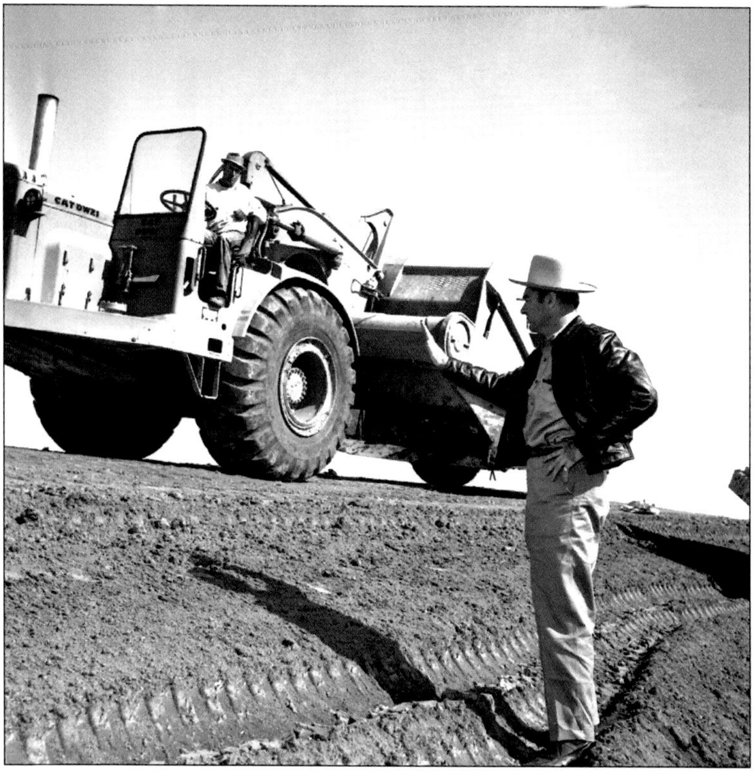

Ground was broken for Charlotte Motor Speedway on July 29, 1959. John B. Lippard calculated the tremendous amount of details that went into constructing the 1.5-mile track. The Belmont, North Carolina, native and North Carolina State College School of Design graduate said the speedway contained practically every known construction angle and elevation at one place or another. Lippard was 41 years old when he spent 18 hours a day on the project.

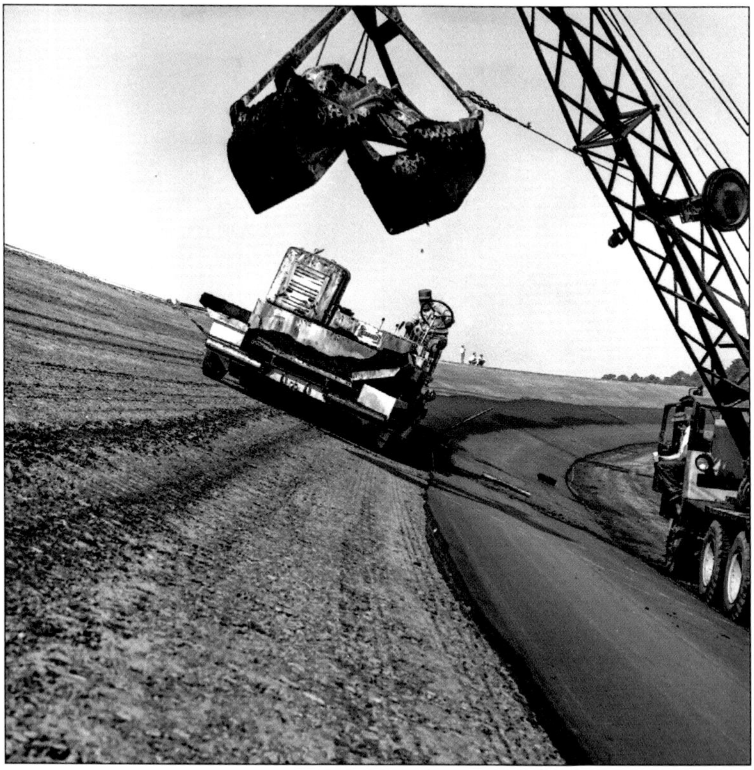

An 11-inch snowstorm in March 1960 forced construction on the speedway to stop. Two more snowstorms in the next two weeks followed. The inclement weather left the men with no choice but to push back the inaugural race from Memorial Day weekend to June 19, 1960. Paving was completed on the morning of the first round of qualifying for the inaugural World 600.

A yellow, two-story farmhouse located at the speedway's entrance served as the facility's first office building. Located near a pecan grove, the house had several walk-up ticket windows on two of its exterior walls. Eventually, a two-story structure known as the Goodyear Building replaced the old wooden farmhouse. It was located at a front corner of the property at the intersection of Morehead Road and US Highway 29.

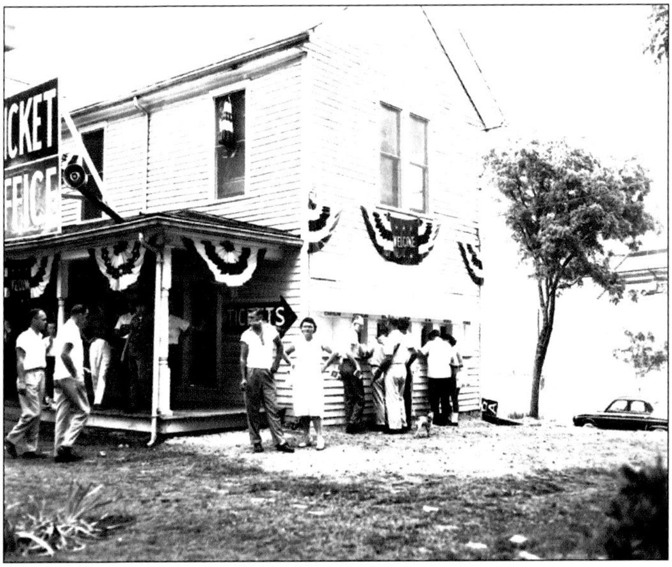

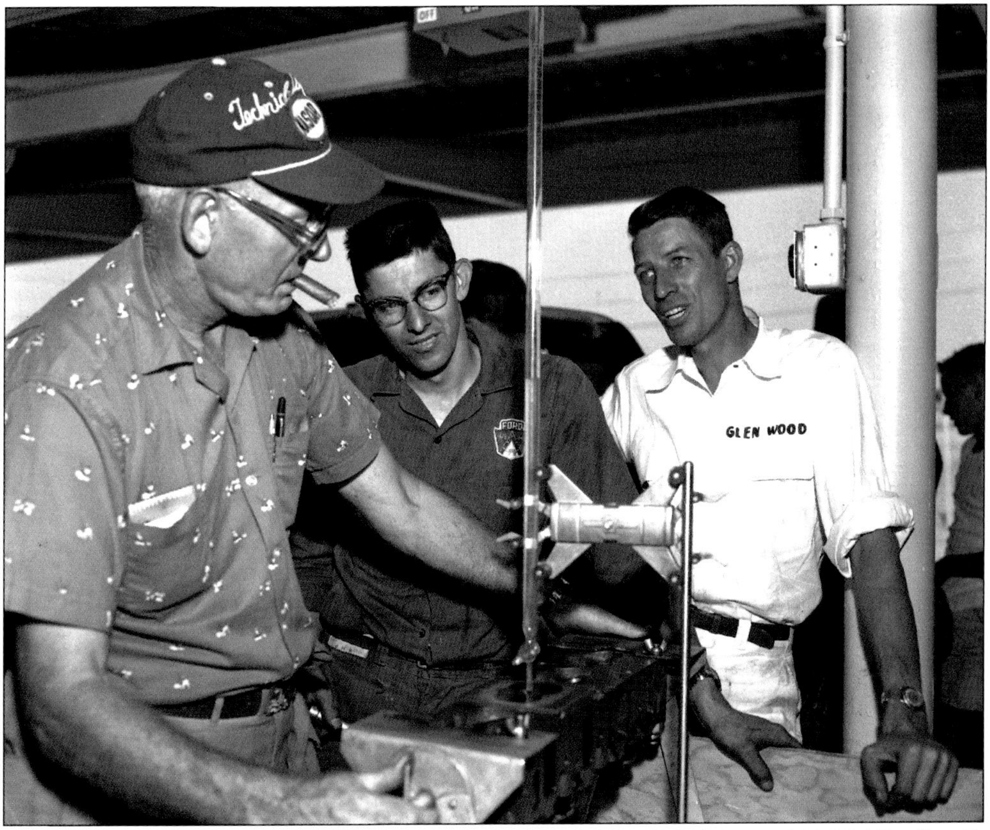

Glen Wood (right) and his younger brother Leonard Wood (center) observe a NASCAR official's work during the engine inspection process at Charlotte Motor Speedway. The Wood brothers, from Stuart, Virginia, have fielded one of the sport's most successful teams during their more than 60-year tenure in NASCAR. The Wood Brothers team won Charlotte Motor Speedway's inaugural fall race on October 16, 1960, with driver Speedy Thompson.

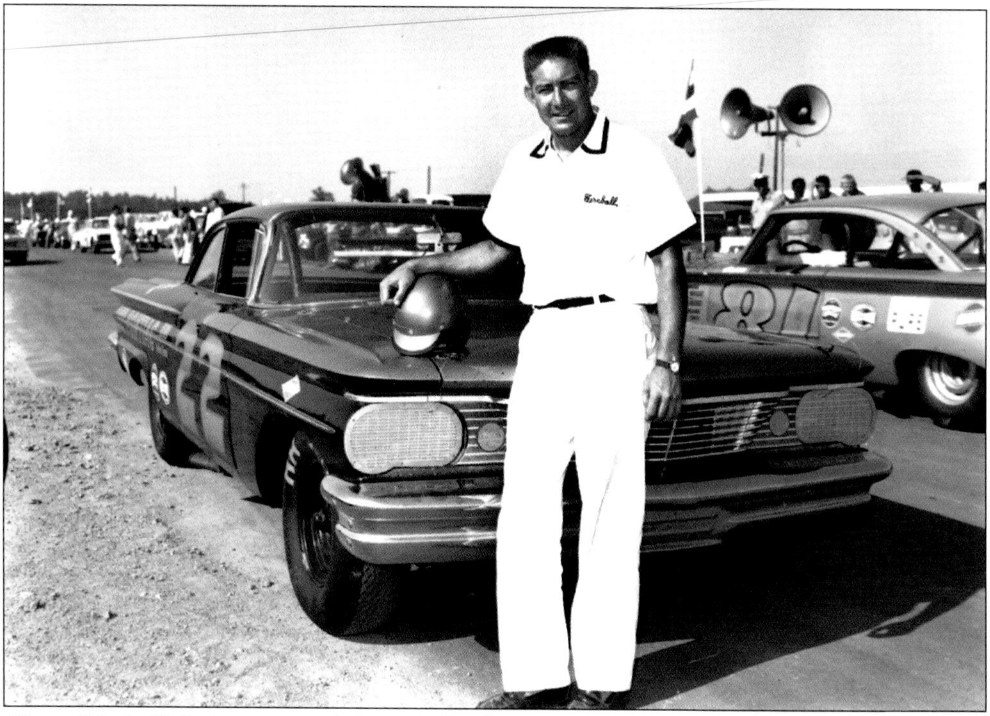

Glenn "Fireball" Roberts earned the pole for the inaugural World 600 with a speed of 133.904 miles per hour in a Pontiac. However, Roberts, who was given his nickname due to the speed with which he threw a baseball, had to settle for a 35th-place finish in the 60-car field. Four years later, he died of complications from severe burns suffered in an accident in the 1964 World 600.

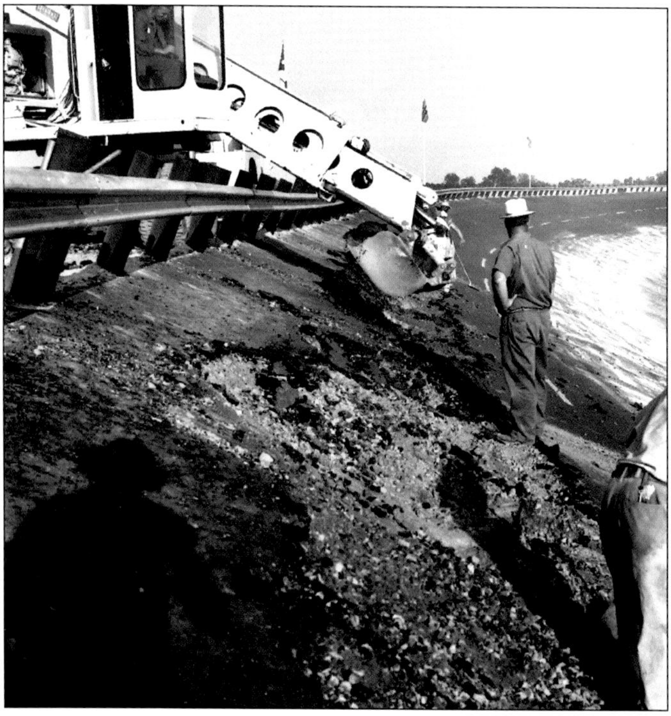

Due to the paving of Charlotte Motor Speedway being completed the morning qualifying began for the inaugural World 600, huge holes in the track's surface appeared in the turns. Patchwork of the track was done daily, but drivers still prepared for the worst. They put large screens over the cars' grilles and windshields to keep chunks of flying asphalt and rocks out of the radiators.

Bill Ward (left) of Charlotte's WBT radio was also a member of the broadcast team for the speedway's races. In the early 1960s, no radio network devoted to motorsports existed. If a track wanted to broadcast one of its races, it assembled a team and syndicated it. Ward was at the track for the inaugural World 600 and interviewed pole winner Fireball Roberts.

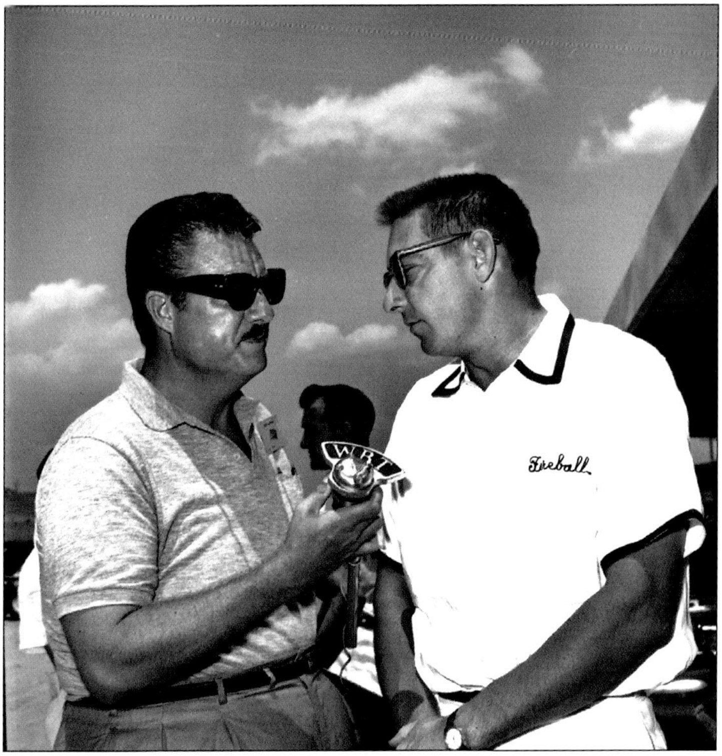

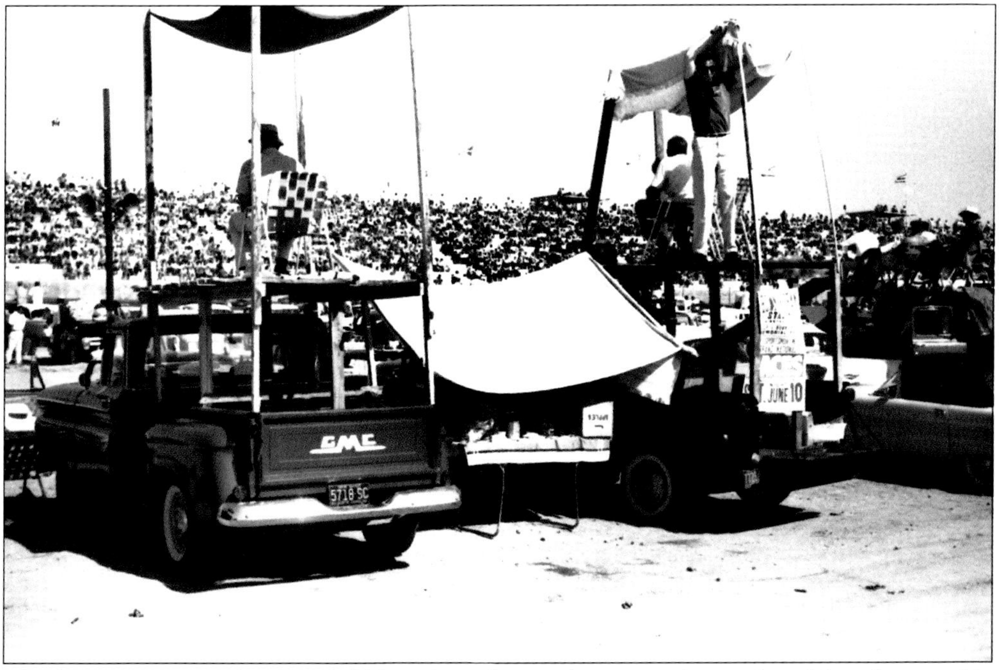

Charlotte Motor Speedway's infield has always been a favorite with race fans. Many fans quickly learned that building platforms and installing them on their pickup trucks gave them a better vantage point. Tarpaulins were used to provide shade and shield food from the hot summer sun that beat down on the speedway during the 600-mile race.

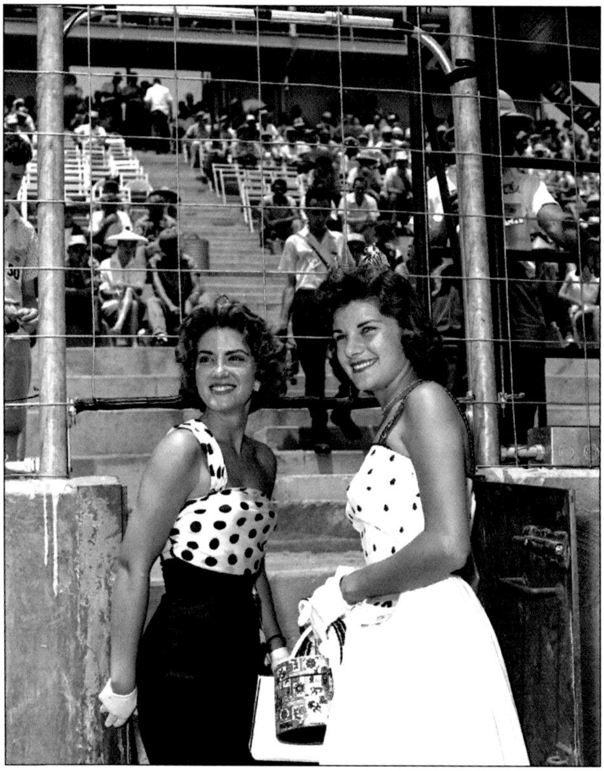

Ever since Charlotte Motor Speedway opened, it has attracted world-class athletes, glamorous stars, and Hollywood producers for its events. It has also been a favorite of politicians—not just local, but presidential and gubernatorial candidates as well. These VIPs have often played a key role in prerace activities and sometimes in postrace events. At left, appearing at the inaugural World 600, are Miss North Carolina USA Lyndia Ann Tarlton (left) and Miss North Carolina Judi Klipfel (right). Below, English model and actress June Wilkinson (center) attended the 1961 World 600. She visited with drivers during the weekend and posed for photographs in victory lane with the race winner. In this photograph, she is shown with NASCAR drivers Joe Weatherly (left) and Marvin Panch (right).

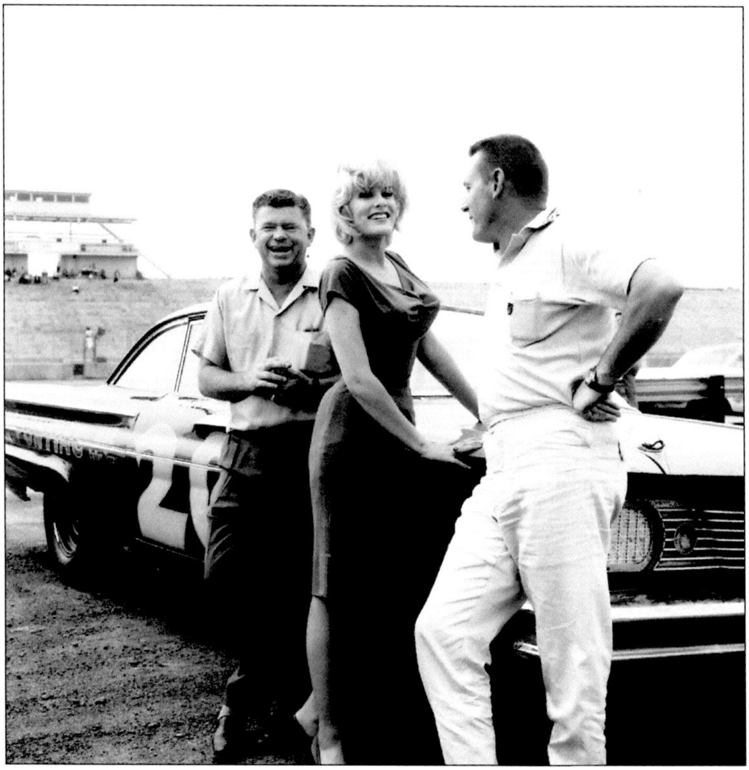

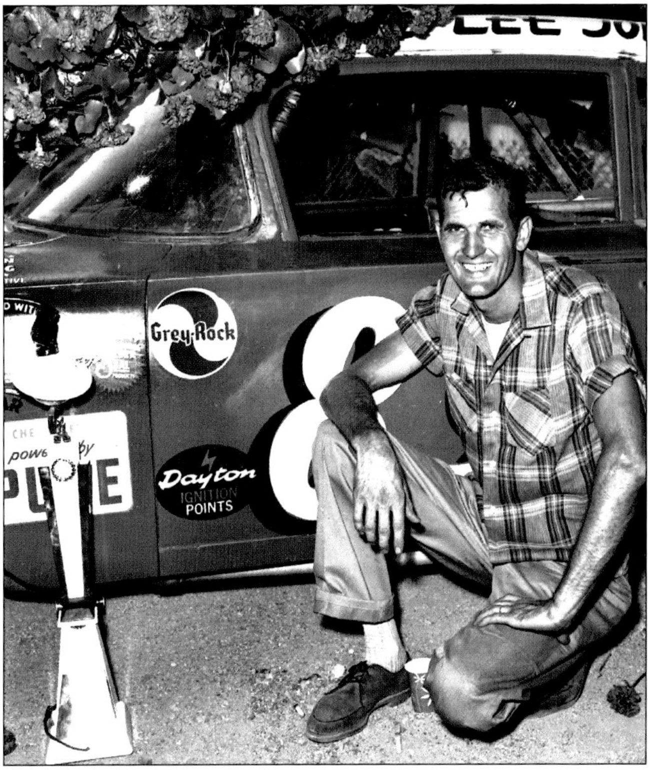

Joe Lee Johnson (right) came from five laps down to win the inaugural World 600. The 29-year-old driver took the lead in his Chevrolet after a chunk of asphalt tore a hole in the fuel tank on leader Jack Smith's Pontiac with 48 laps remaining. It was the second series victory for the Chattanooga, Tennessee, driver and the biggest of his career. He finished four laps ahead of Johnny Beauchamp's Chevrolet, which was piloted by relief driver Johnny Allen. A few days after the race, six drivers were disqualified for making improper entrances to the pits. They were Richard and Lee Petty, Junior Johnson, Bob Welborn, Lennie Page, and Paul Lewis. Below, Johnson's winning car was prepared by crew chief Paul McDuffie (left).

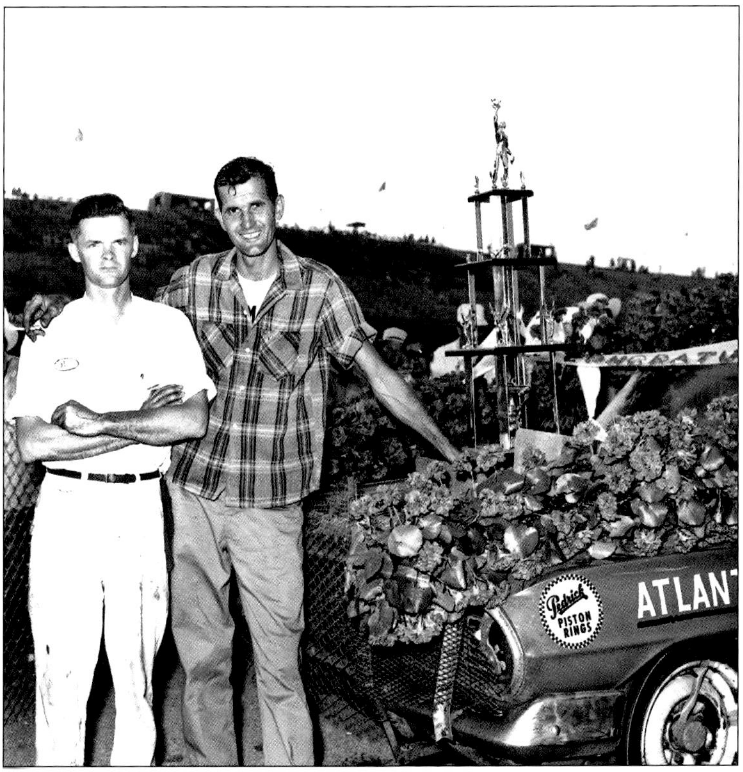

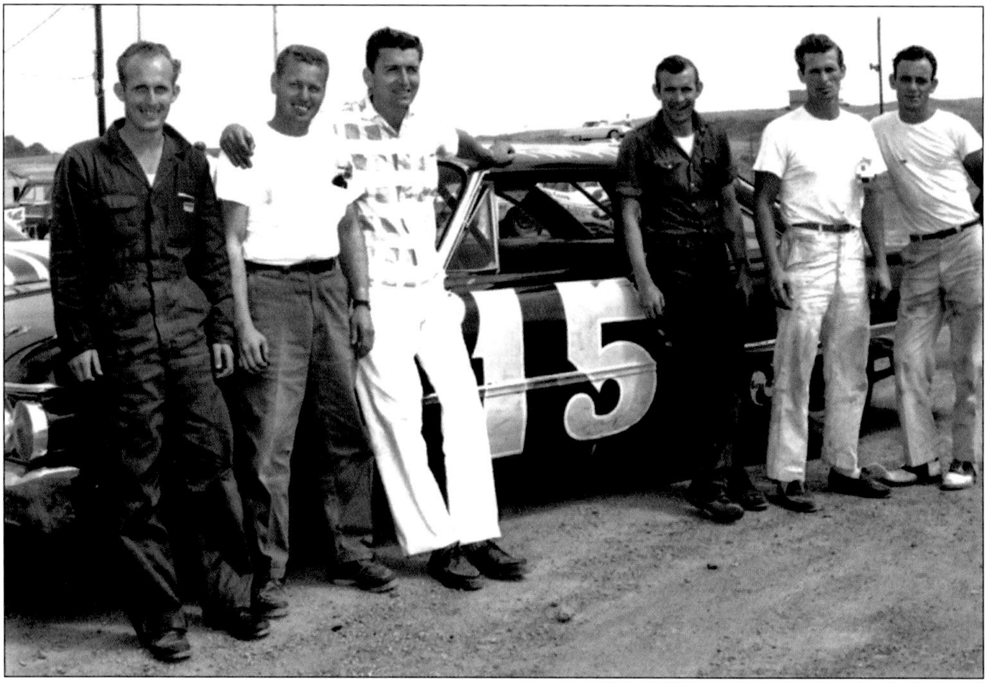

Tim Flock (third from left) competed in his final NASCAR race at Charlotte Motor Speedway in a Ford owned by Beau Morgan (second from left). Flock qualified 24th but finished 37th in the 1961 World 600 due to engine problems. He later was suspended from NASCAR for joining Curtis Turner in an attempt to unionize the drivers. Flock eventually worked in the speedway's marketing department until his death from cancer in 1998.

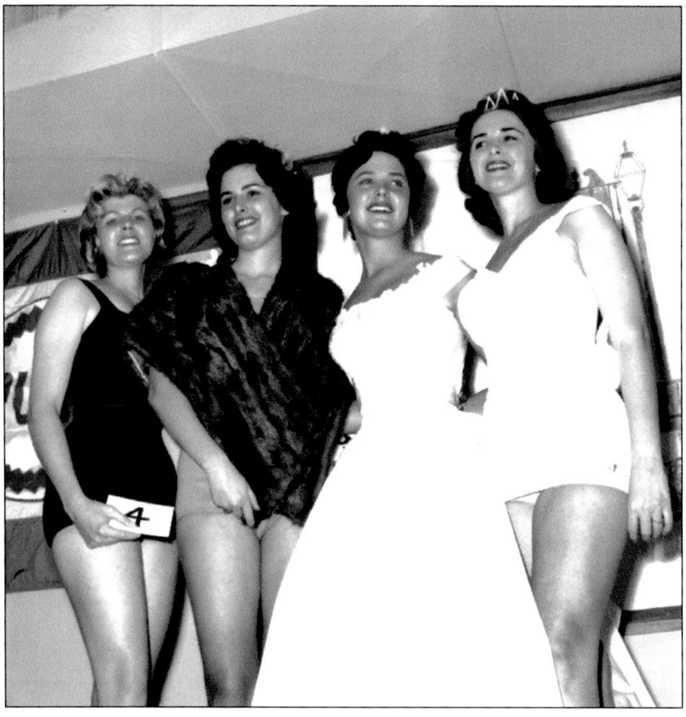

In the sport's early years, beauty pageants were often held in conjunction with a race to select either the event's or track's queen or the representative for an automotive product. The Miss Automotive World pageant was part of the World 600 activities in the early 1960s. Various prizes were awarded to the winner, including a fur stole. She also appeared in victory lane and posed for photographs with the winner.

Ralph Earnhardt (right) made his debut at Charlotte Motor Speedway in the 1961 World 600 driving a Pontiac owned by Cotton Owens (left). The father of Dale Earnhardt and grandfather of Dale Earnhardt Jr. qualified sixth and finished 11th. In six races at his home track, the Kannapolis, North Carolina, native recorded one top-five and two top-10 finishes.

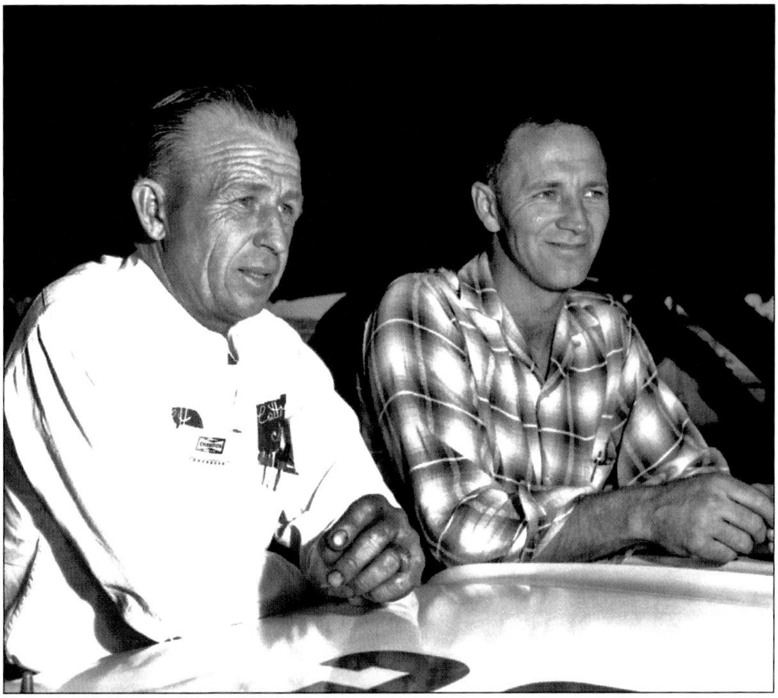

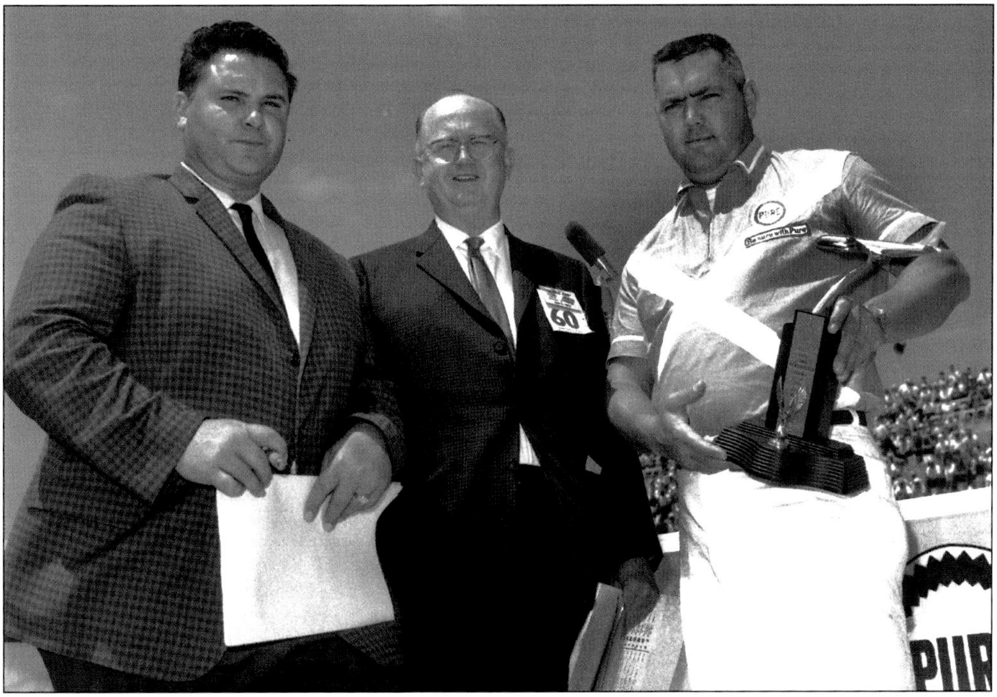

During Charlotte Motor Speedway's financially troubled years, A.C. Goines (center) was named the track's president and Richard Howard (left) its vice president and general manager. Howard eventually became president and led the speedway out of debt. In 1971, Howard partnered with Junior Johnson (right) to field a competitive Chevrolet, something that had not existed in the sport since 1963 when Johnson won the pole for the World 600.

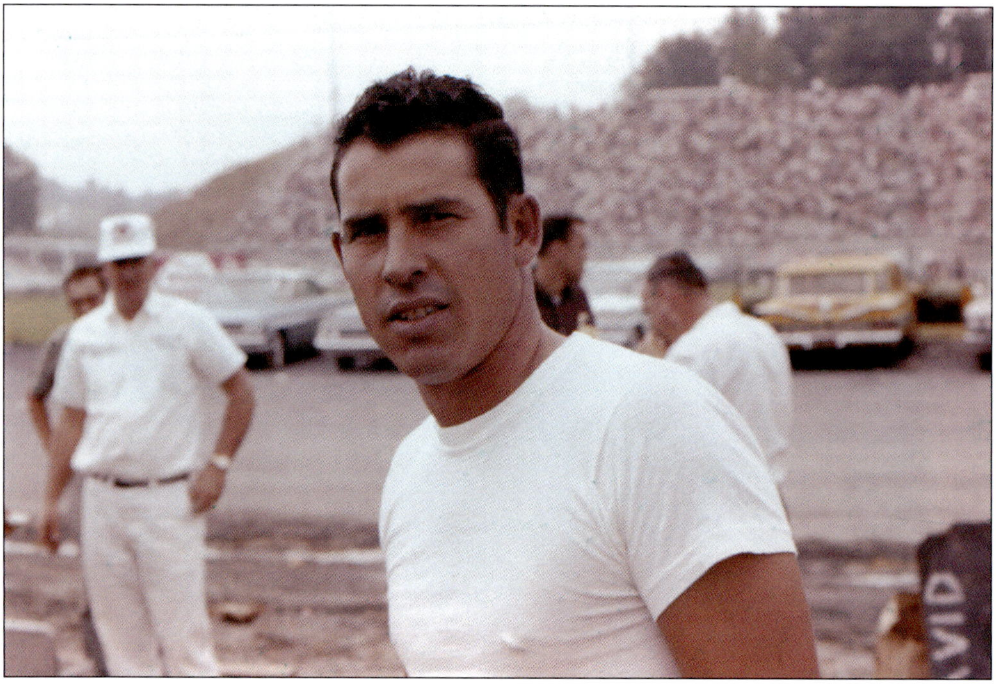

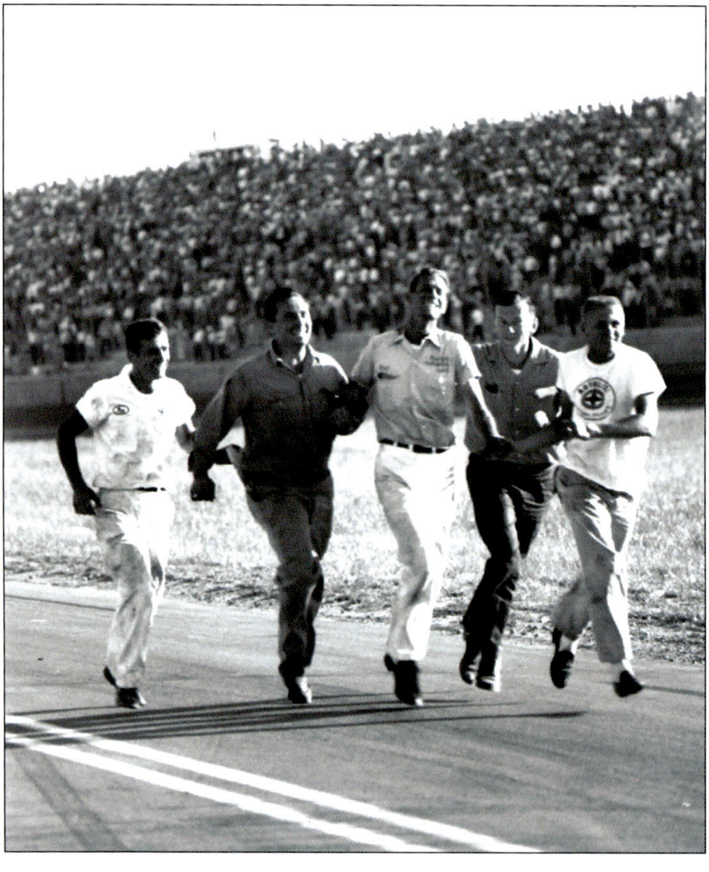

David Pearson (above) was hired by car owner Ray Fox the week of the 1961 World 600 to drive his Pontiac in stock car racing's longest race. The top rookie of the series in 1960 led the final 129 laps but had to finish the race on three wheels after cutting a tire with two laps remaining. Pearson still claimed a two-lap victory over runner-up Fireball Roberts. In victory lane, Pearson admitted he was so new to the team that he did not know his crewmen's names. The ride with Fox materialized after Pearson parked his own car due to financial issues. At left, Fox (center) and his crew run jubilantly down pit road after Pearson's stunning upset.

In 1962, nineteen-year-old Mamie Reynolds (right) became the youngest car owner on record. The daughter of US senator Robert R. Reynolds of Asheville, North Carolina, acquired a Ford from Holman-Moody, and Darel Dieringer (left) was assigned to drive it. Dieringer qualified 10th, but finished 38th due to engine problems in the 1962 National 400. Mamie Reynolds's car competed in 20 races before she left the sport with one victory, obtained by Fred Lorenzen.

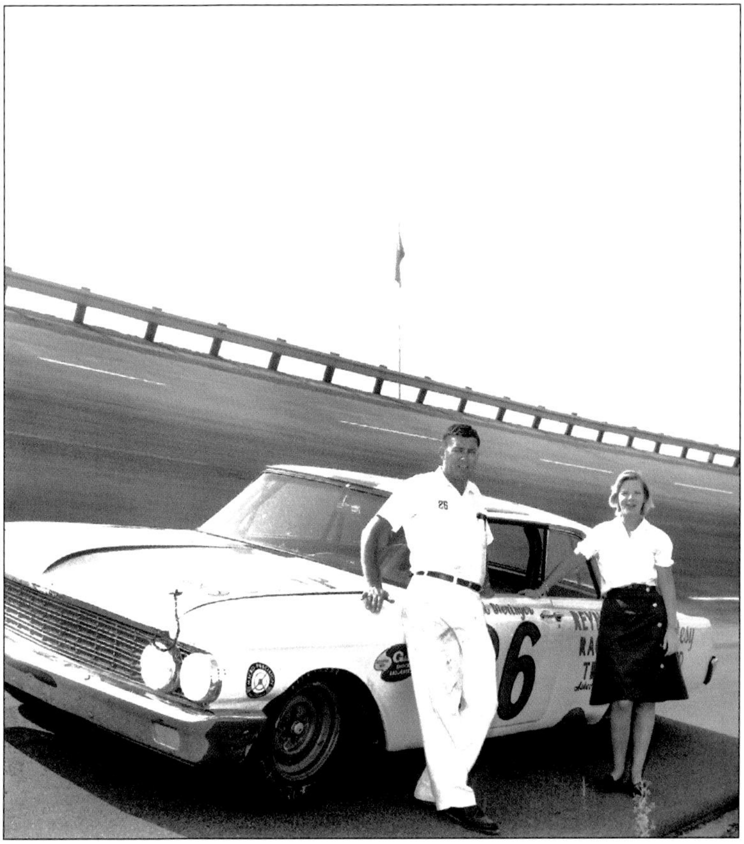

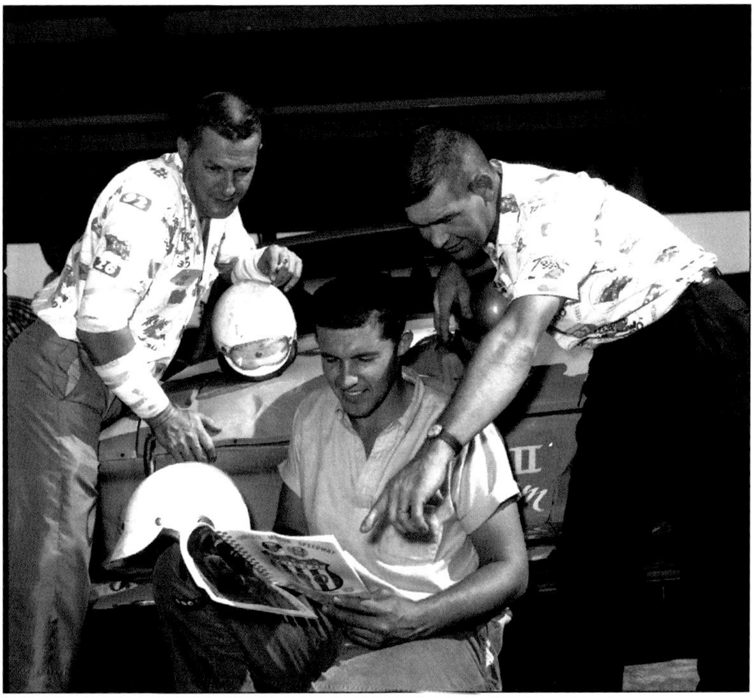

Petty Enterprises often entered two or three cars in NASCAR events in the 1960s. For the 1962 National 400, Petty Enterprises entered three Plymouths. They were driven by, from left to right, Jim Paschal, Richard Petty, and Speedy Thompson. Paschal finished sixth, Thompson ninth, and Petty 16th in the October event. Paschal drove his Petty Enterprises Plymouth to victory in the 1964 World 600.

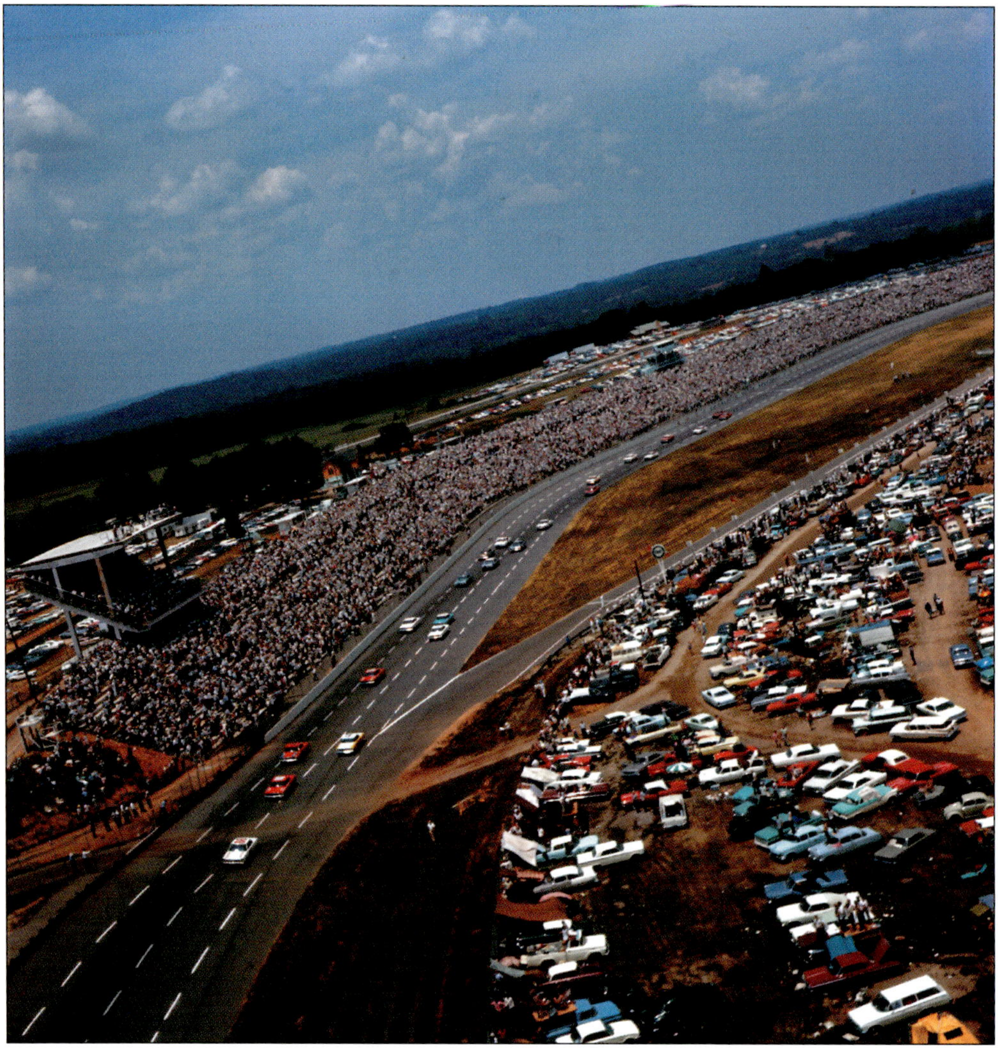

The bankruptcy and debt that plagued Charlotte Motor Speedway during the 1960s prevented track head Richard Howard from making many, if any, improvements. Four months after the mortgage burning in June 1967, very little had changed at the track since it opened in 1960. The old yellow, two-story farmhouse still housed the track's offices and walk-up ticket windows. Small cemeteries created by the original property owner remained beneath large shade trees. Parking was in dirt lots and fields. The steep concrete steps leading from the parking lot to the grandstands were crumbling. Still, Howard managed to construct the Ford Tower above the Ford Grandstand during that decade. The concrete structure provided fans with a more aerial view of the pit road exit and first-turn entrance. Attendance figures during the speedway's first 10 years ranged from a low of 29,166 for the inaugural National 400 in October 1960 to 75,000 for the 1969 World 600.

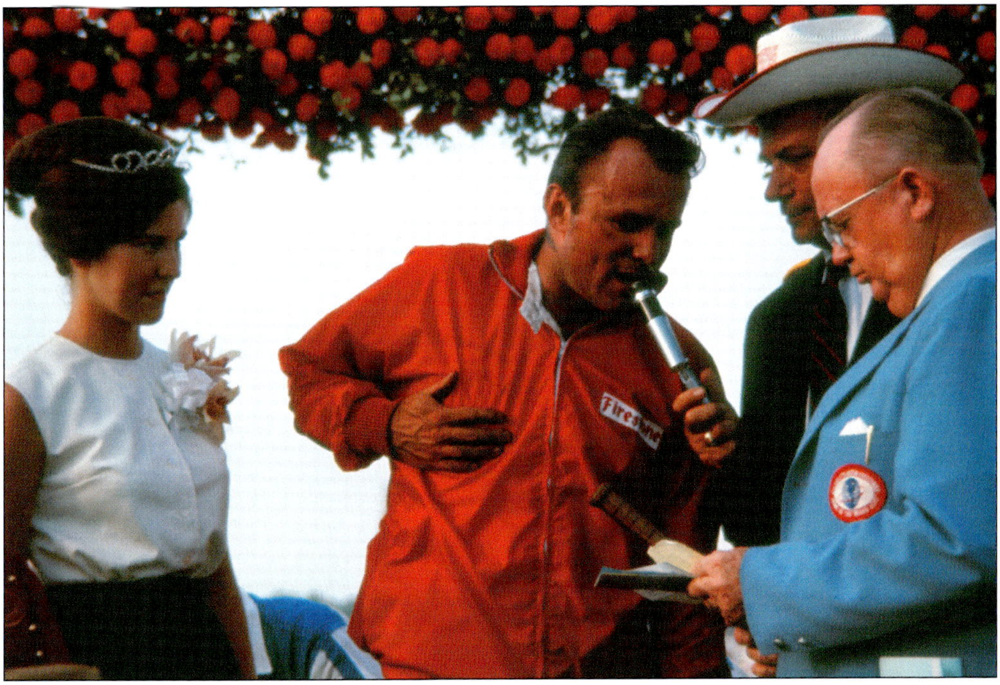

Fred Lorenzen (center) acquired the nickname "Golden Boy" in 1963 when he became the first stock car driver to surpass $100,000 in winnings in a single season. He claimed his first Charlotte pole in 1961 and visited victory lane for the first time at the track in 1963. It was from 1964 to 1966, however, when he became the driver to beat at Charlotte, winning three consecutive races and three poles.

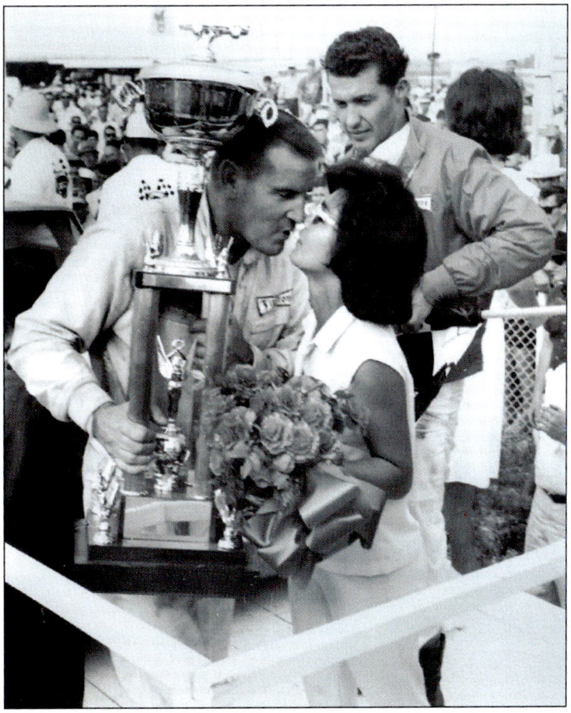

Marvin Panch shares a kiss with his wife, Betty, in victory lane following the 1966 World 600. Watching the celebration is Richard Petty, who was a relief driver for the 41-year-old Panch during the race. A member of the Ford factory team since 1962, Panch accepted Lee Petty's offer to drive his Plymouth since Ford was boycotting NASCAR over a rules dispute. The World 600 victory was the last of Panch's NASCAR career.

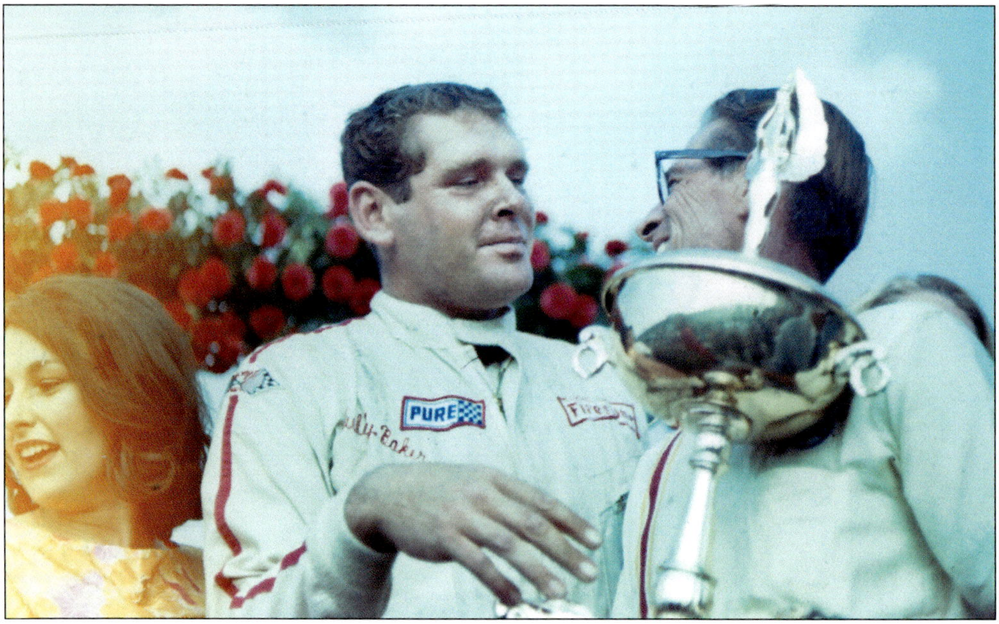

Buddy Baker (center) captured his first NASCAR premier series victory in 215 starts in the 1967 National 500 driving a Dodge owned and prepared by Ray Fox (right). After finishing one lap ahead of runner-up Bobby Isaac, the emotional Baker wept in victory lane. His victory ended Richard Petty's 10-race win streak.

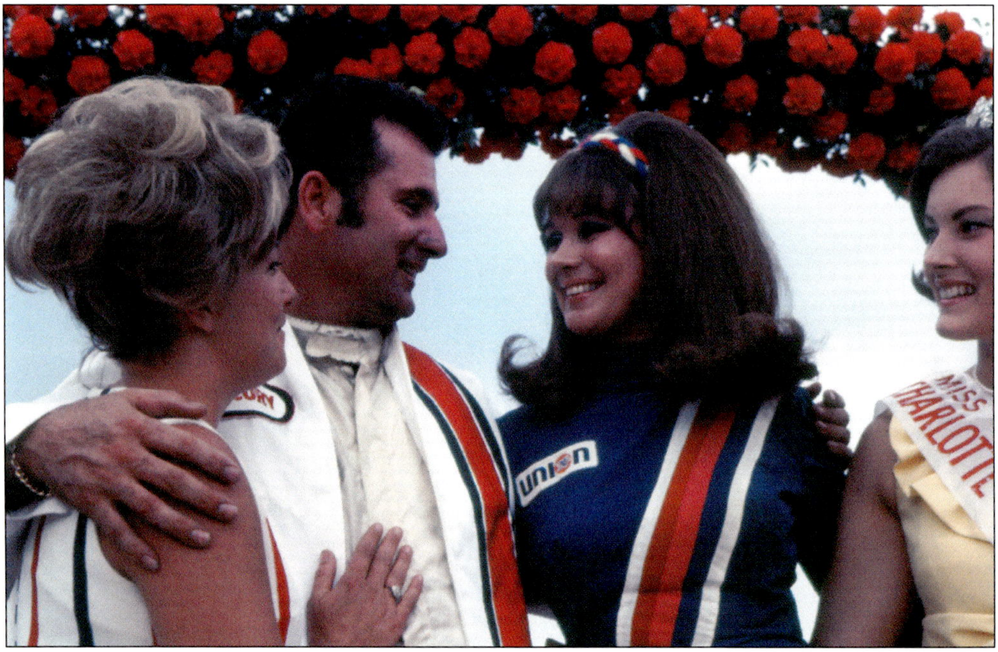

LeeRoy Yarbrough's victory in the 1969 World 600, his second at Charlotte, poised the Florida native to capture NASCAR's triple crown. Earlier that year, he won the Daytona 500, driving a Junior Johnson–owned Ford. By winning Darlington's Southern 500 in September, Yarbrough became the first driver to claim NASCAR's triple crown. He shared the Charlotte victory lane with his wife, Gloria (left), and Union 76 RaceStopper Sharon Brown.

Two

History is Made

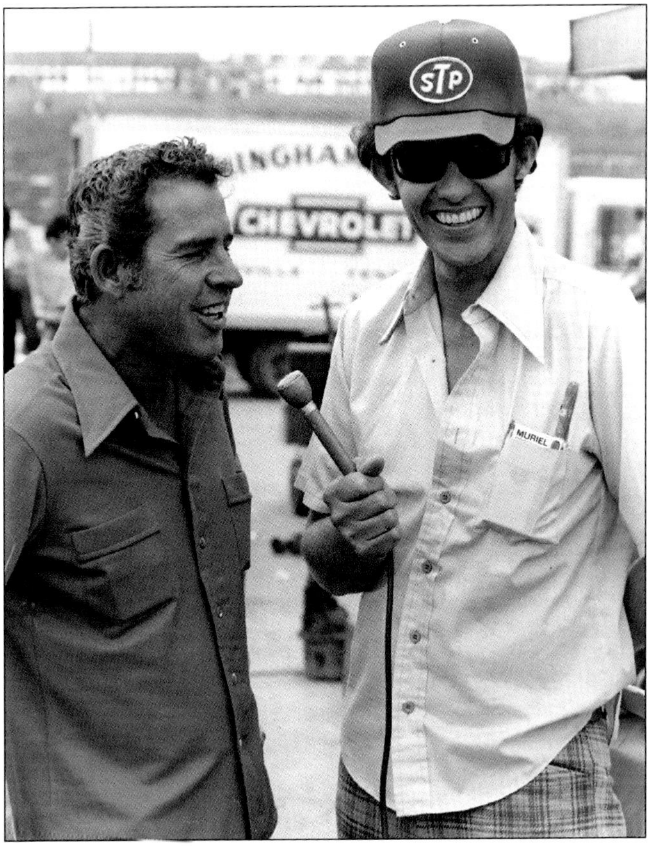

David Pearson (left) and Richard Petty (right) dominated the 1970s, often racing each other for the victory. Pearson collected 47 victories in the decade, while Petty totaled 89. Petty also won five of his seven championships during those 10 years. At Charlotte, Pearson was the qualifying king, earning a dozen poles. He also claimed three victories. Petty swept the Charlotte races in 1975 and captured his second World 600 in 1977.

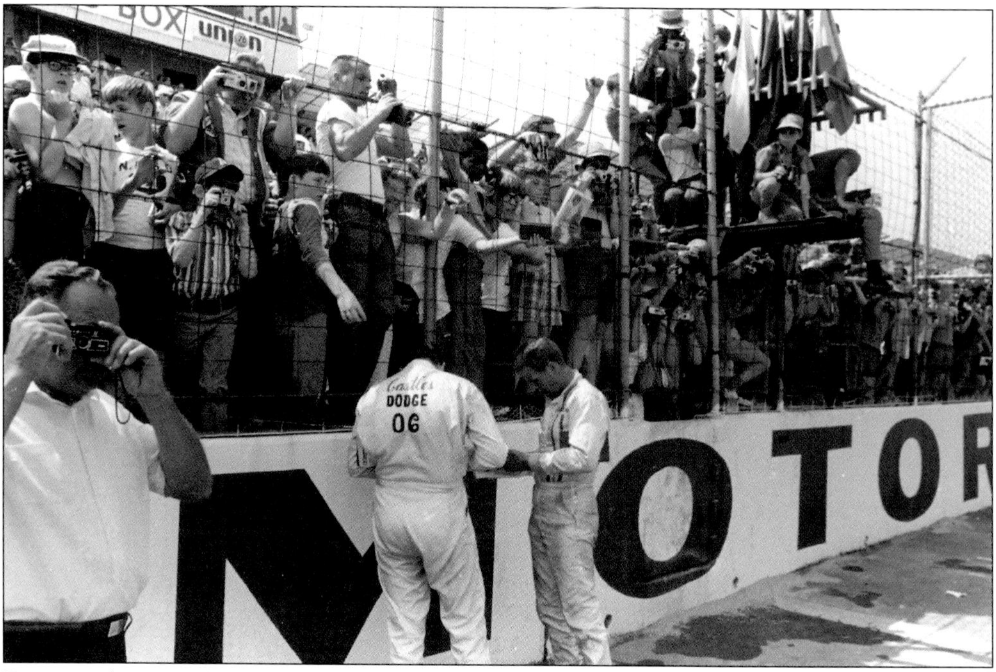

Fans crowd against the frontstretch fence at Charlotte Motor Speedway to obtain photographs and autographs of drivers prior to the 1970 World 600. In addition to often scheduling the autograph sessions, speedway officials would open the frontstretch gate and allow fans to come onto the track and the grassy frontstretch apron after an event.

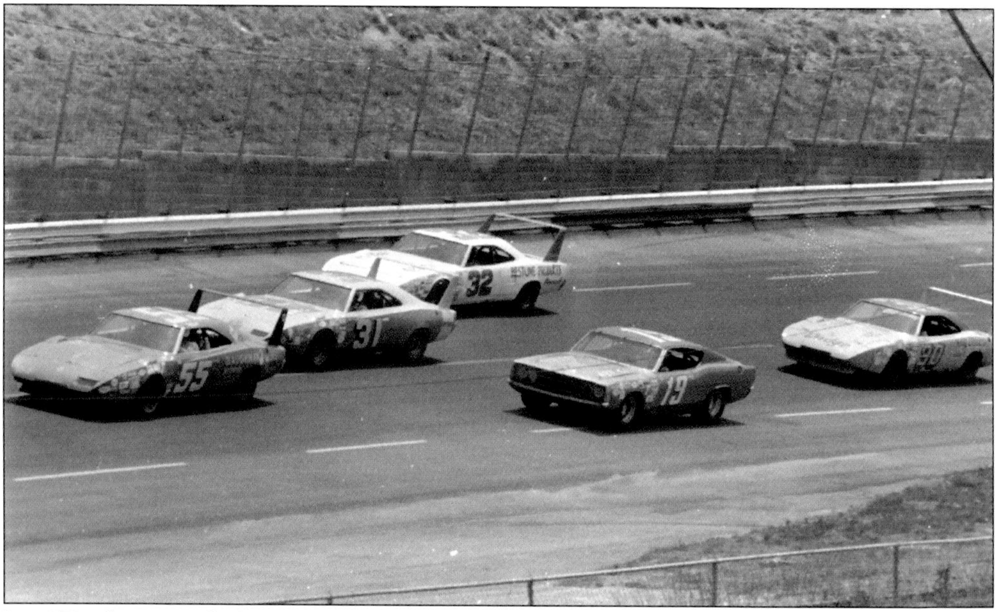

In 1970, the winged Plymouth Superbirds and Dodge Daytonas and the sloped-back Mercury Cyclones and Ford Torino Talladegas battled for supremacy on the superspeedways. Those driving a Dodge Daytona in the 1970 World 600 included Tiny Lund (No. 55), Jim Vandiver (No. 31), and Dave Marcis (No. 30). Dick Brooks (No. 32) drove a Plymouth Superbird, and Henley Gray (No. 19) piloted a Ford Torino.

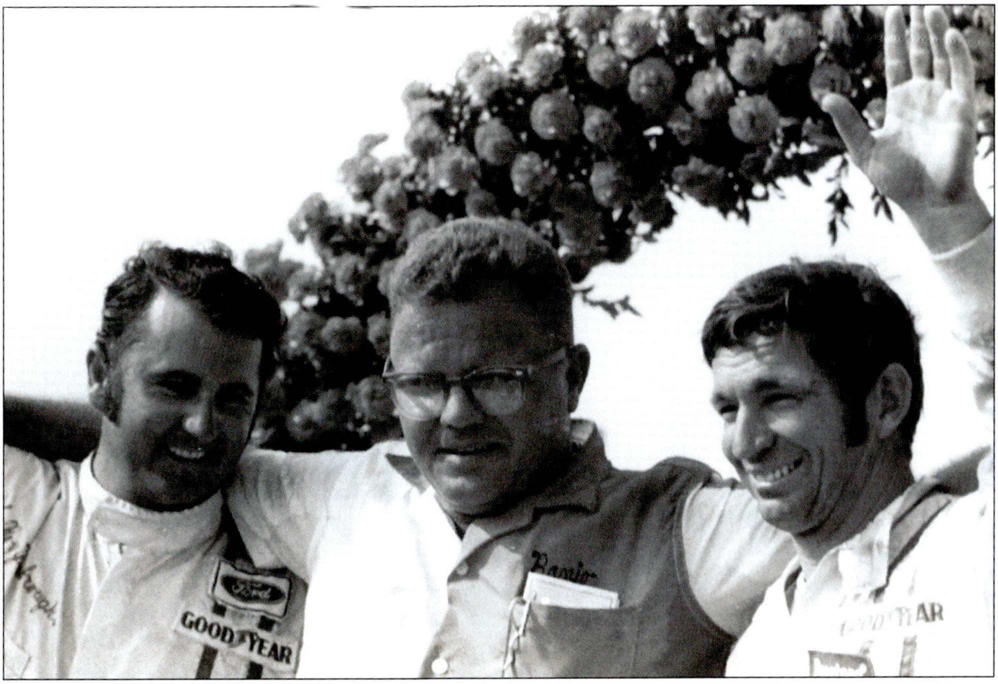

Donnie Allison (right) won the 1970 World 600 driving a Ford owned by Banjo Matthews (center). LeeRoy Yarbrough relieved Allison on lap 355 of the 400-lap race. The floorboard's insulation in Allison's car came apart, and his feet blistered. Six days later, Allison finished fourth in the Indianapolis 500 to claim rookie honors. Yarbrough placed 19th in the same race.

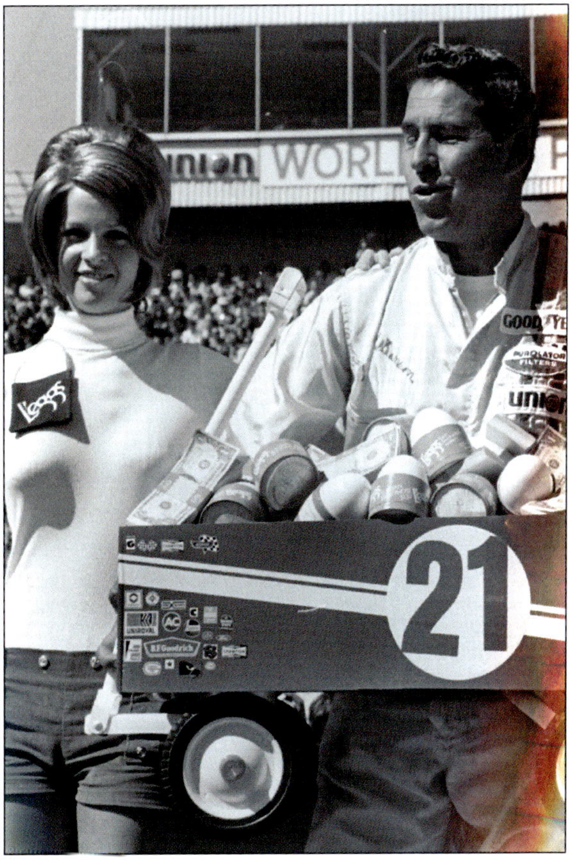

When David Pearson and his Wood Brothers–prepared car dominated qualifying at Charlotte Motor Speedway, he was given various awards. At this particular race, L'eggs sponsored pole day, and Pearson was given a wagon load of the pantyhose. However, it was the domination Pearson enjoyed the most. Beginning with the 1972 National 500, Pearson won 12 of the next 13 poles, including 11 straight.

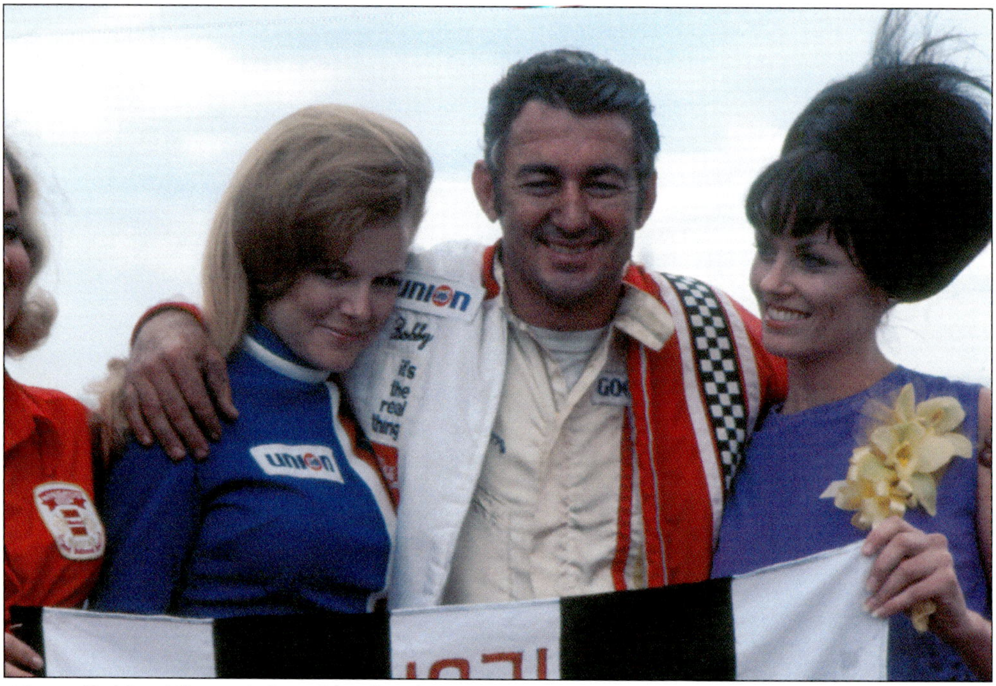

Above, Bobby Allison defeated his brother Donnie by 33.9 seconds to claim his first Charlotte Motor Speedway victory in the 1971 World 600. Bobby led 263 of the 400 laps in recording the victory. Both men drove a 1969 Mercury that day (below). Bobby's Mercury (No. 12) was fielded by Holman-Moody, while Donnie piloted a Wood Brothers Mercury (No. 21). Bobby had joined Holman-Moody just two weeks earlier. His victory came in his second start for the race team. Donnie Allison's second-place finish to his older brother came a day after he placed sixth in the Indianapolis 500. It was the second straight year that Donnie had competed in the World 600 and the Indianapolis 500, which were held on different days.

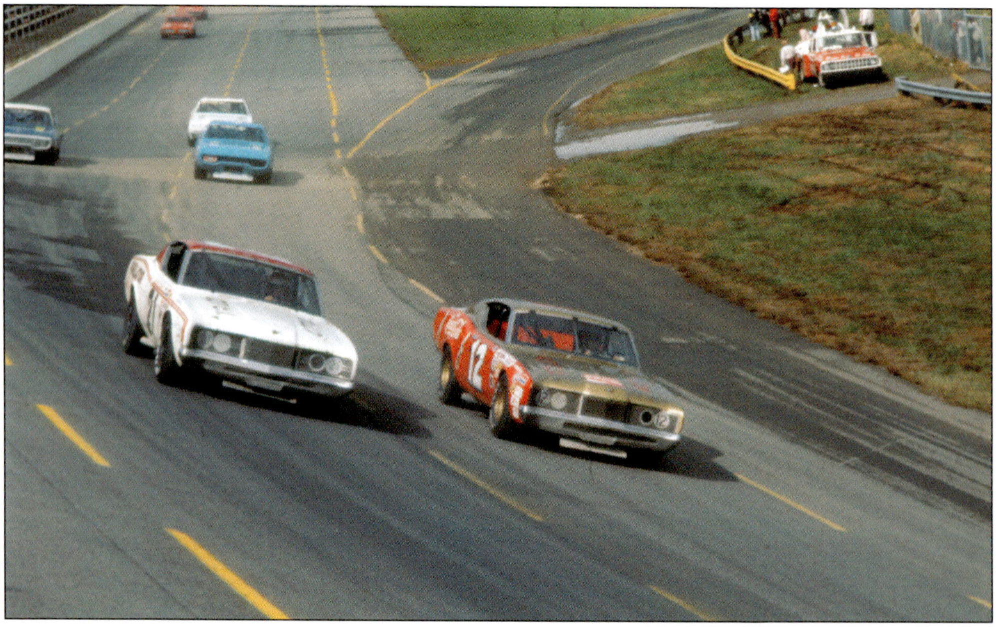

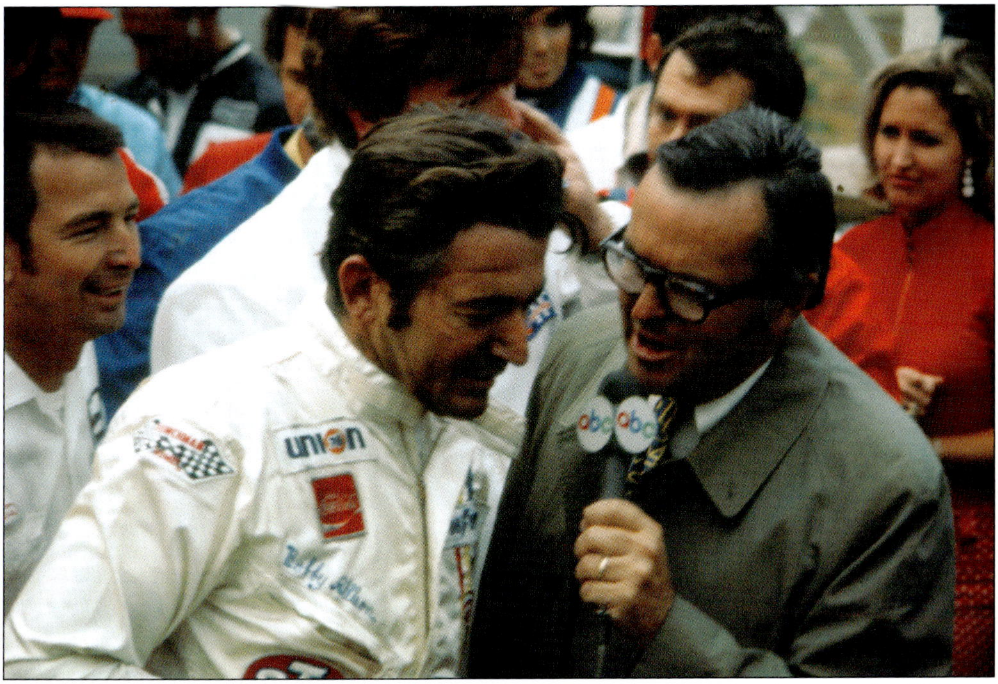

Above, Bobby Allison (left) is interviewed in victory lane by ABC's Chris Economaki following his win in the 1971 National 500. The win was Allison's fourth straight superspeedway victory and his seventh of the season. Bobby Isaac finished second in the rain-shortened race, five seconds behind Allison. It was a joyous occasion for Allison, who was joined in victory lane by his wife, Judy (below, second from left); his parents, Edmond Jacob "Pop" Allison (left) and Katherine "Mom" Allison (right); and team owner Ralph Moody (behind Allison's mother). The Charlotte victory was Allison's last superspeedway win of the 1971 season. His final victory that year came at the half-mile Macon, Georgia, track. Allison ended the 1971 season with 11 victories, making it the most successful of his career in the win department.

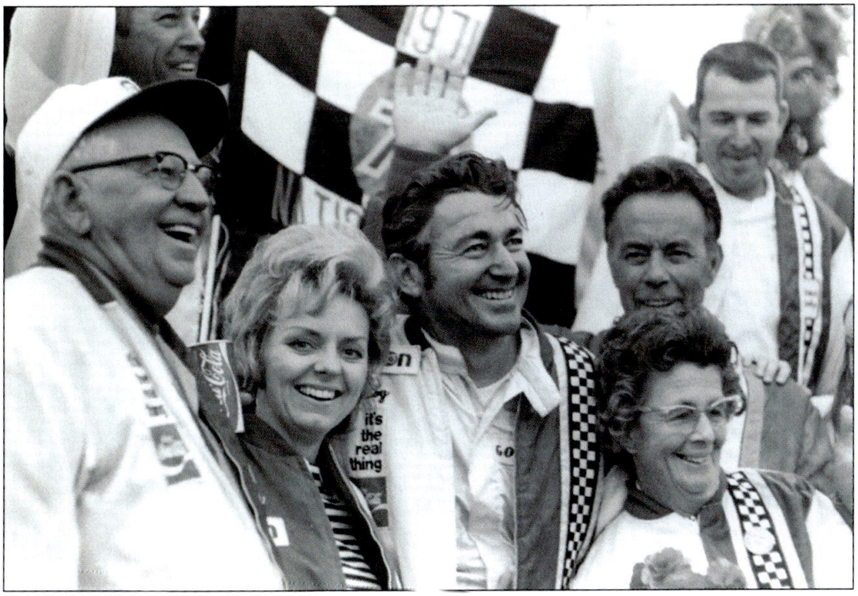

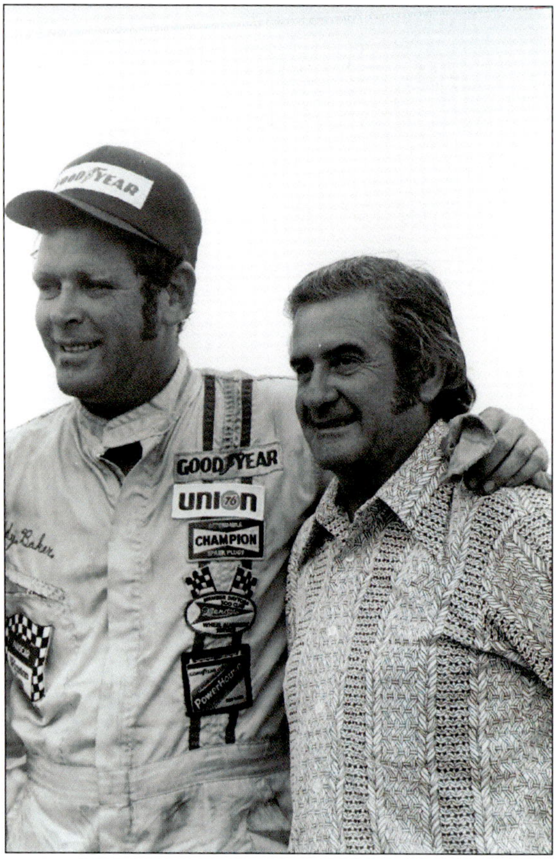

At left, Buddy Baker (left) and his father, Buck, were involved in NASCAR from its beginning. Buck competed in NASCAR's premier division from 1949 through 1976, but he never won at Charlotte in 17 starts. Buddy celebrated four victories at the 1.5-mile track. Below, Buddy Baker's second World 600 victory came in May 1972 in a Petty Enterprises Dodge (No. 11). Baker inherited the lead from Bobby Allison (No. 12) when Allison cut both right-side tires on lap 370 of the 400-lap race. Allison possessed a 4.2-second lead at the time. He still finished second but was 23.7 seconds behind Baker. They were the only two competitors to finish on the lead lap. Baker's last Charlotte victory came in the 1973 World 600. He drove a Dodge to all four Charlotte wins.

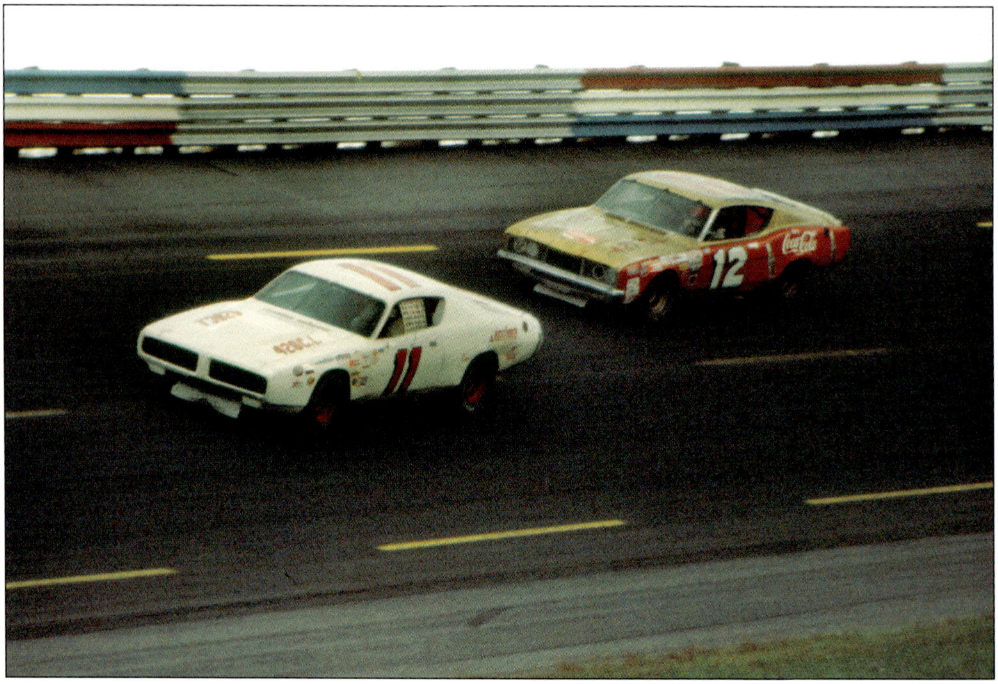

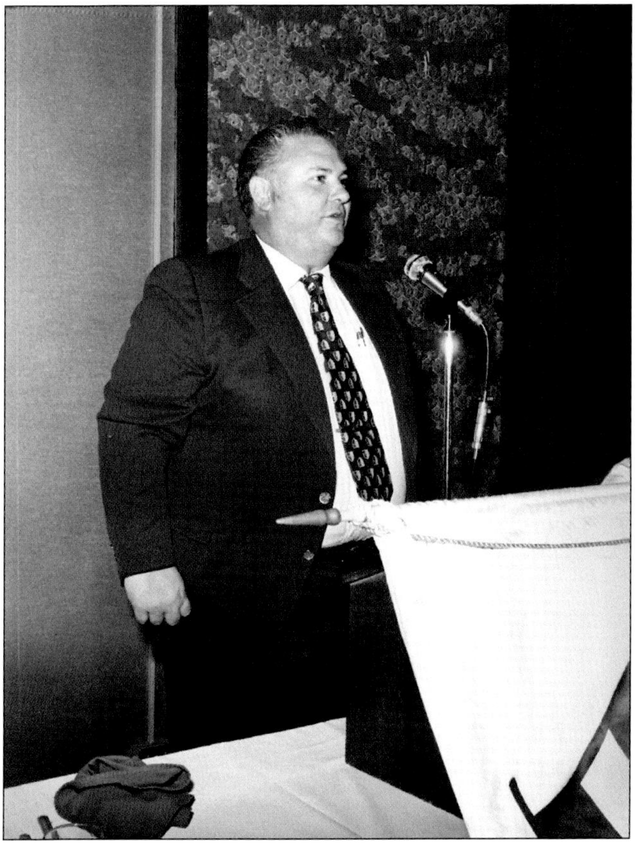

Even while serving as general manager of Charlotte Motor Speedway, Richard Howard (right) often entered a car in one of the track's events. In October 1973, Howard fielded a Chevrolet for Cale Yarborough with Herb Nab as the crew chief. Yarborough defeated Richard Petty by 1.4 seconds, but it was a controversial National 500 due to third-place finisher Bobby Allison's protest of the first two cars. For six hours after the race, NASCAR officials poured over the engines from the top three cars. Eventually, NASCAR decided the results would stand, and no penalties would be issued. The Charlotte victory was Cale Yarborough's final win of the 1973 season. Joining Yarborough (below, left) in victory lane are his wife, Betty Jo (center), and his crew chief Herb Nab (right).

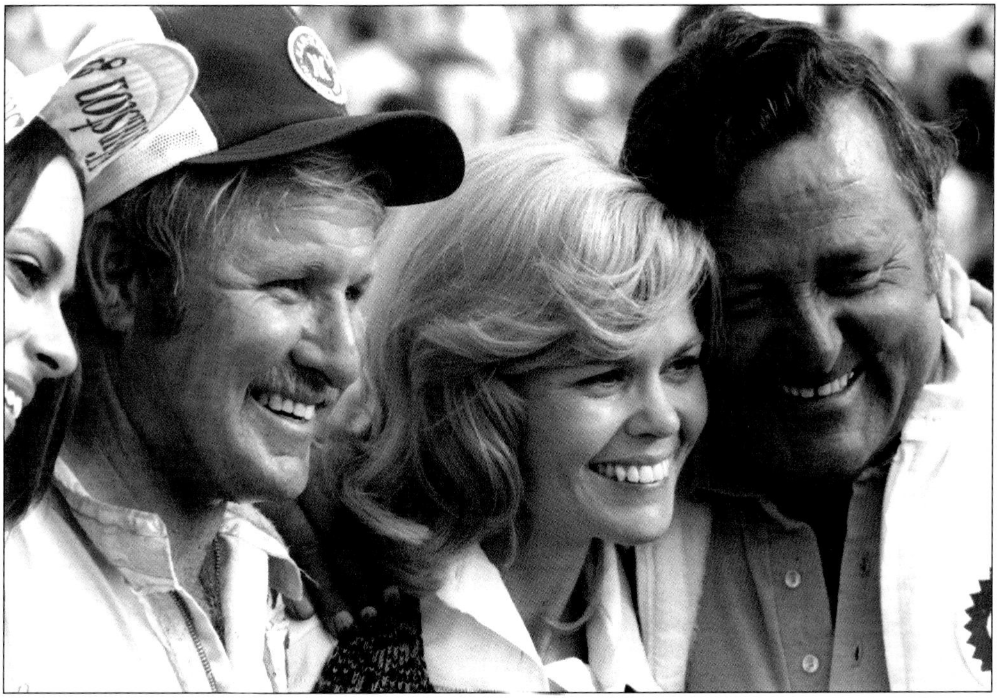

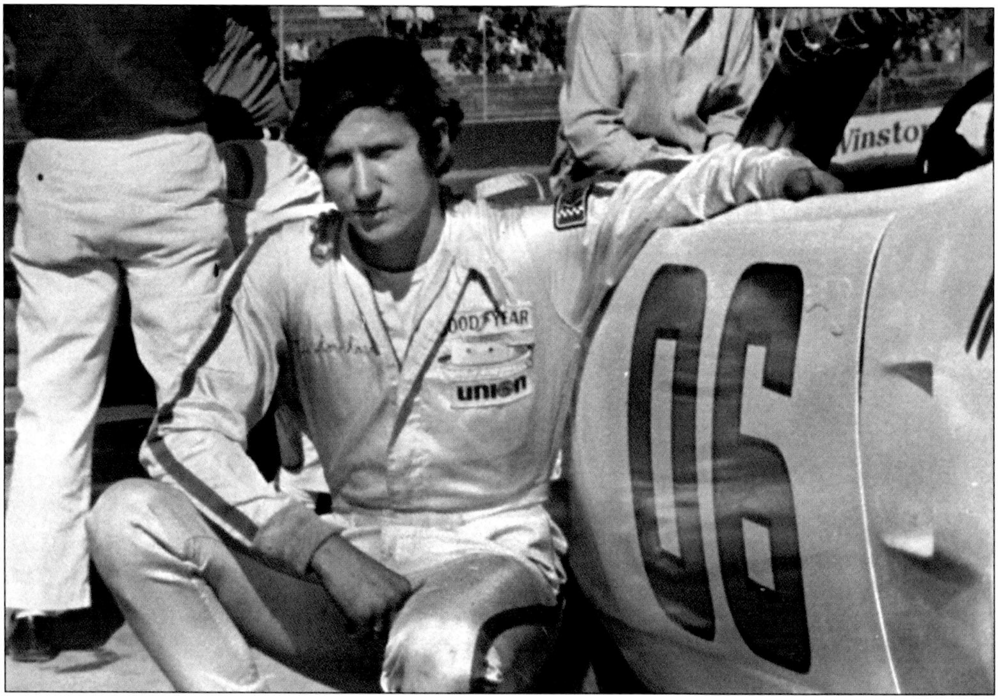

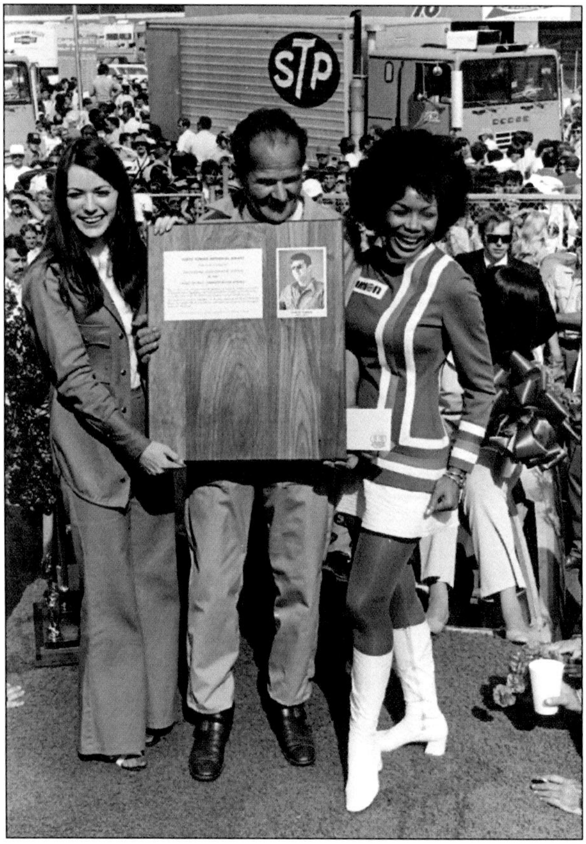

Dale Earnhardt tested at Charlotte Motor Speedway in 1974, but he did not make his debut at the track in NASCAR's premier series until the 1975 World 600. Driving a 1974 Dodge for Ed Negre, Earnhardt qualified 33rd and then drove to a 22nd-place finish, 45 laps behind winner Richard Petty.

Wendell Scott was honored with the Curtis Turner Memorial Award following the 1972 World 600 for his outstanding achievement in that race. Scott qualified 11th for the event and was running ninth when the engine expired in his 1971 Chevrolet. He finished 22nd. The award was decided by the media covering the race. It was given to the competitor exhibiting the "driving abilities and other characteristics that distinguish him in the World 600."

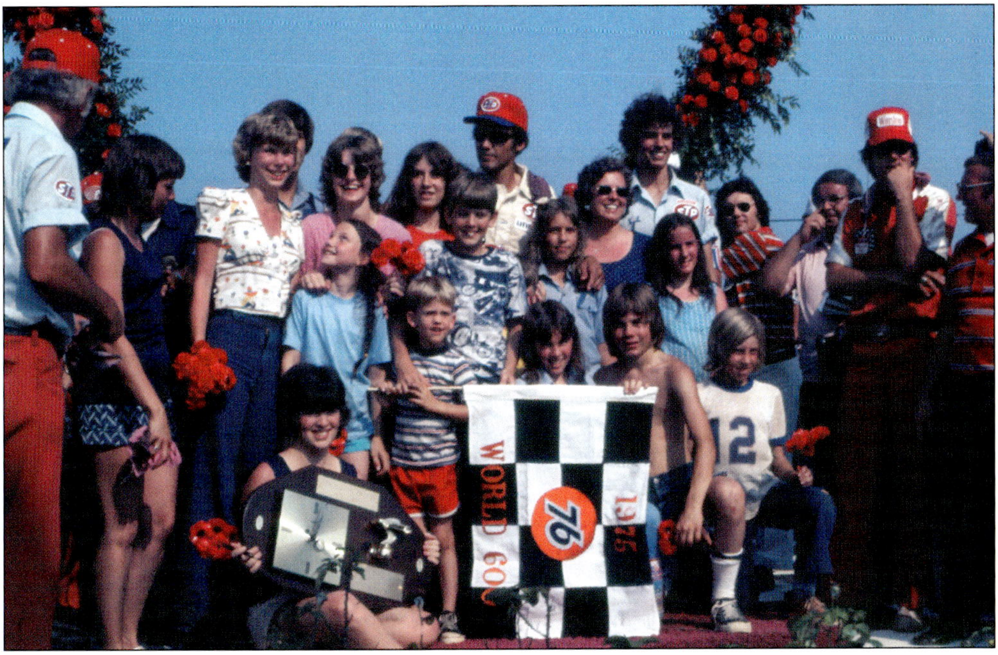

Richard Petty (center) visited victory lane at Charlotte Motor Speedway for the first time in a long-distance event in 1975. That year, he defeated Cale Yarborough by a lap in the World 600. Then he narrowly edged David Pearson for his National 500 victory in October. Previously, Petty had won a 100-mile qualifying race for the 1961 World 600.

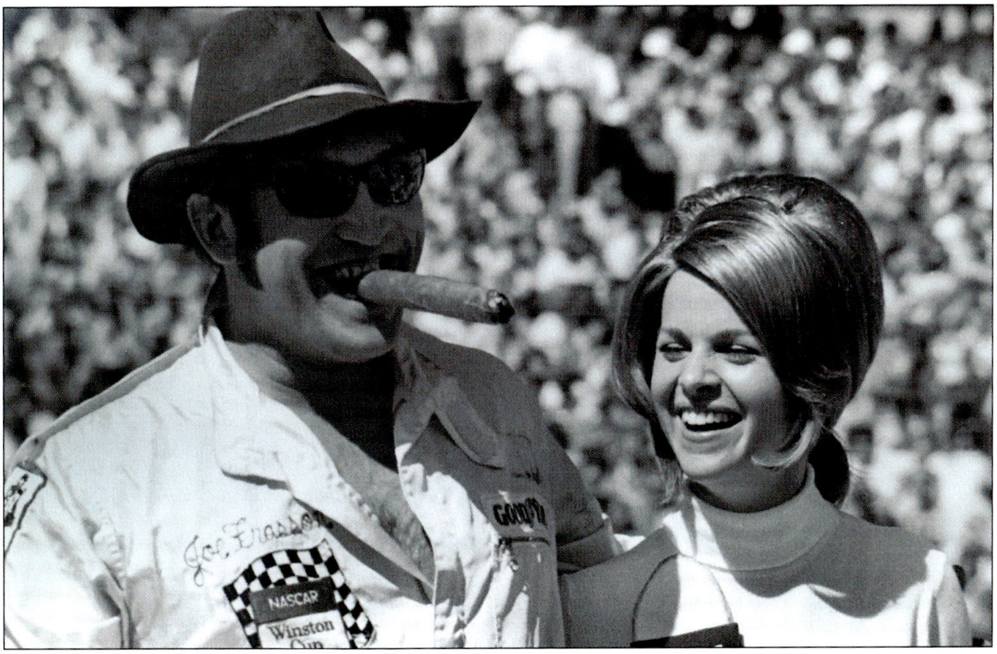

During the 1970s at Charlotte Motor Speedway, several drivers had disputes with NASCAR. One of those was Joe Frasson. When he failed to make the field for the 1975 World 600, he took a jack handle and pounded his Pontiac in front of photographers and reporters. NASCAR fined Frasson $100 and suspended him for 15 days for the public outburst.

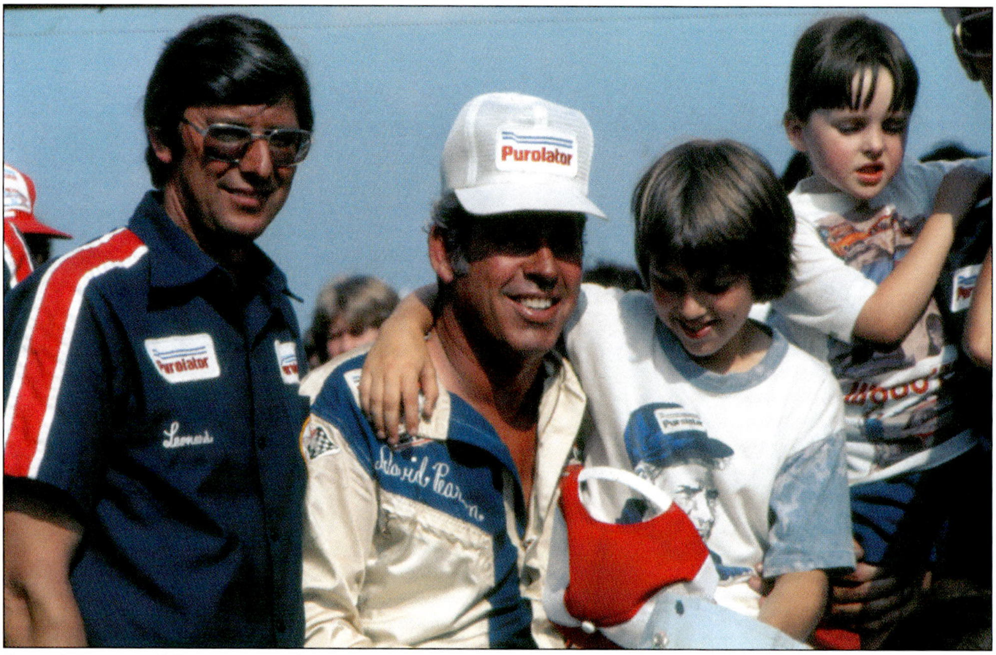

David Pearson (above, center) won his third World 600 in May 1976 and that put him in position to win NASCAR's triple crown. Pearson had defeated Richard Petty in a last-lap wreck between the two to win the Daytona 500 in February, and it was his rival that he beat once again to claim the second leg in NASCAR's triple crown. With Leonard Wood (left) as his crew chief, Pearson captured his sixth straight pole at Charlotte during preparations for the 1976 World 600. He then led 230 laps in the potent Wood Brothers Mercury en route to victory (below). A few months later, Pearson became only the second driver to earn NASCAR's triple crown when he defeated Petty in the Southern 500 at Darlington.

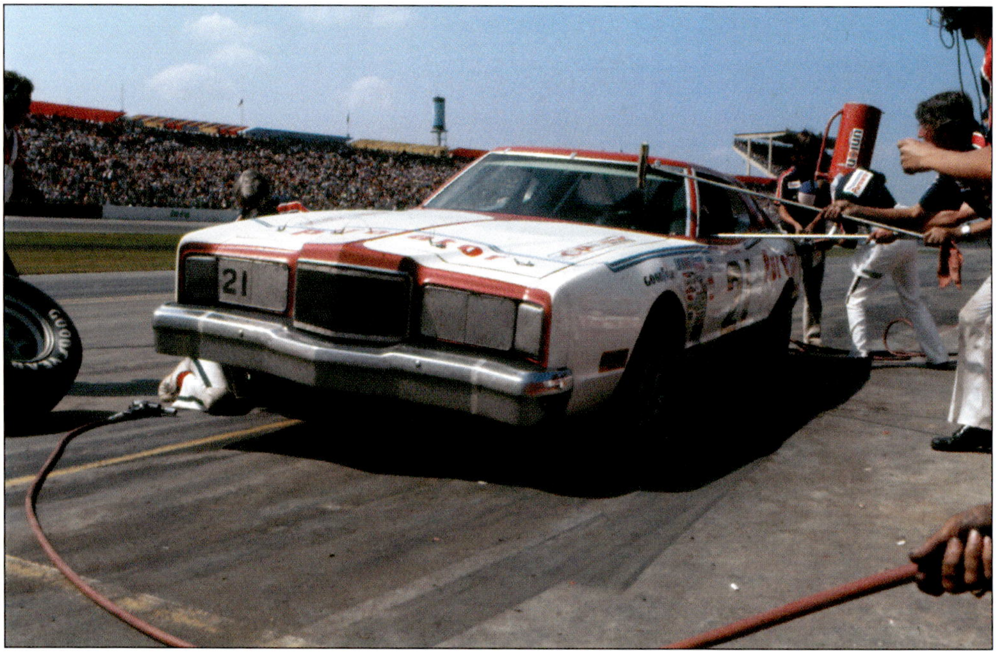

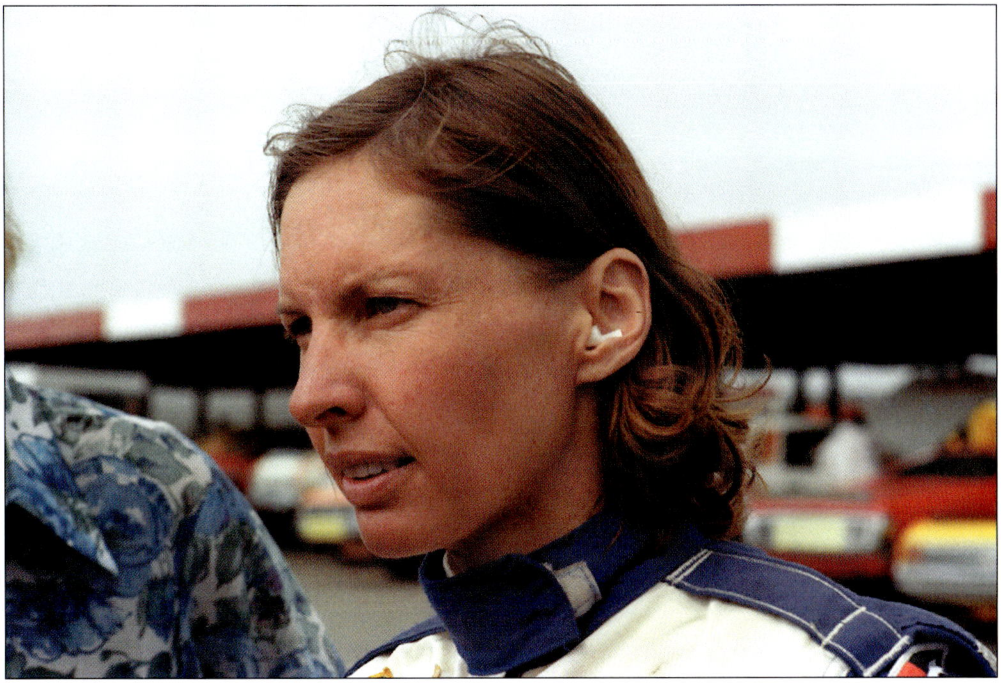

When Janet Guthrie (above) was left without a ride for the 1976 Indianapolis 500 due to A.J. Foyt withdrawing her car, she headed to Charlotte Motor Speedway for the World 600. At the time, women were not allowed in the NASCAR garage, but that did not stop speedway executives Bruton Smith and H.A. "Humpy" Wheeler from recruiting her and 32-year-old Lynda Ferreri, vice president of First Union National Bank, to be Guthrie's car owner. Ralph Moody, a former driver and co-owner of Holman-Moody, had become a renowned crew chief. He was retained to serve in that position for Guthrie. Below, with Kelly Girl as the sponsor, Guthrie qualified her Chevrolet 27th and became the first woman to compete in the World 600. She drove the 4,100-pound stock car, which had no power steering, to a 15th-place finish.

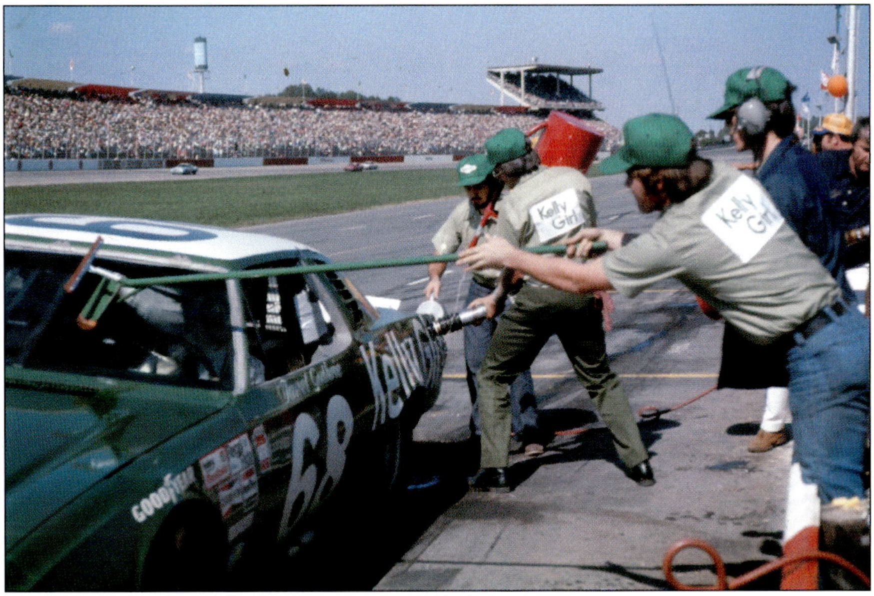

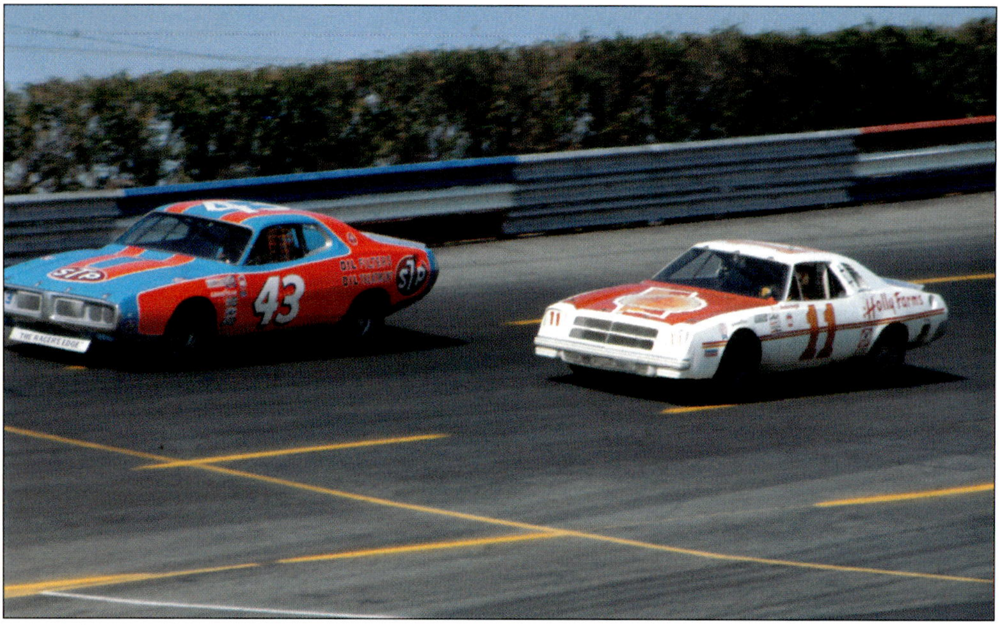

Richard Petty (No. 43) and Cale Yarborough (No. 11) dominated the driver standings during the 1970s. Petty won five of his seven championships during that decade, claiming the title in 1971, 1972, 1974, 1975, and 1979. Driving for Junior Johnson, Yarborough became the first NASCAR driver to earn three consecutive championships, accomplishing the feat from 1976 through 1978. He also won Charlotte's 1973 National 500 and the 1979 NAPA National 500.

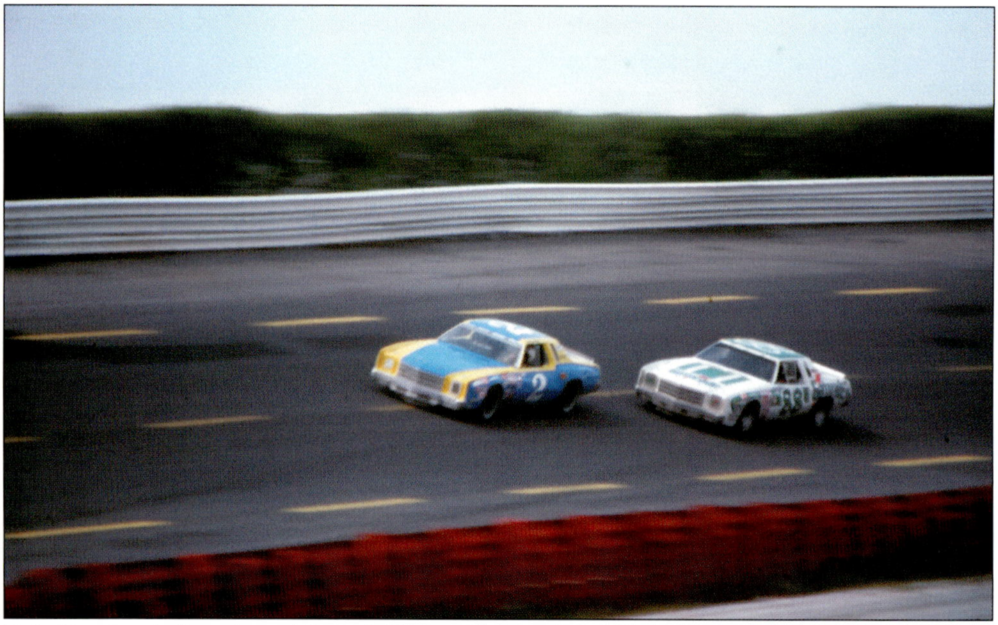

Dale Earnhardt (No. 2) and Darrell Waltrip (No. 88) established themselves as the leaders of NASCAR's next generation with their performances in the 1979 season. That year, Waltrip won his second consecutive World 600 and challenged Richard Petty for the championship. Earnhardt posted top-10 finishes in both Charlotte races, a third and a 10th, and was the top rookie of the series.

Three

A New Era Begins

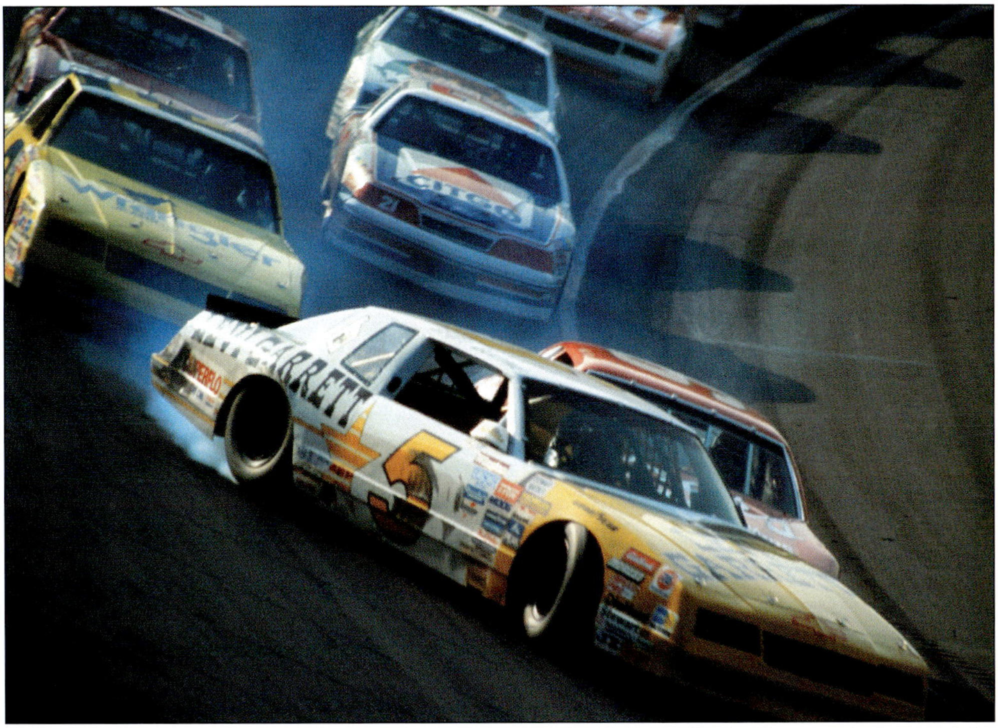

An incident involving Geoff Bodine (No. 5), Dale Earnhardt, and Bill Elliott at the start of the final 10 laps in the 1987 NASCAR All-Star Race at Charlotte Motor Speedway transformed the event into an intensely emotional, often controversial race. Earnhardt tagged Bodine and sent him spinning. Elliott avoided being collected by Bodine, but the intense racing that followed between Elliott and Earnhardt led to Earnhardt's "pass in the grass" and his first all-star race victory.

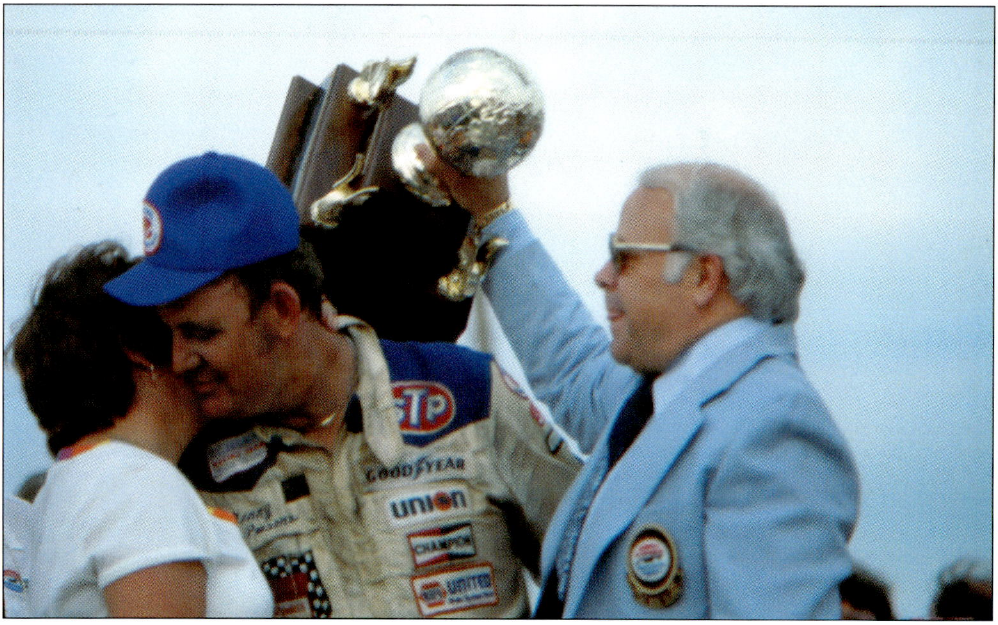

Benny Parsons (center) kicked off the 1980s by defeating Darrell Waltrip in an intense battle in the 1980 World 600. The two men exchanged the lead eight times in the final 26 laps. Parsons took the lead for good two laps from the finish and then held off Waltrip's last-lap challenge to win by half a car length. Track owner Bruton Smith (right) presented Parsons with his only World 600 trophy.

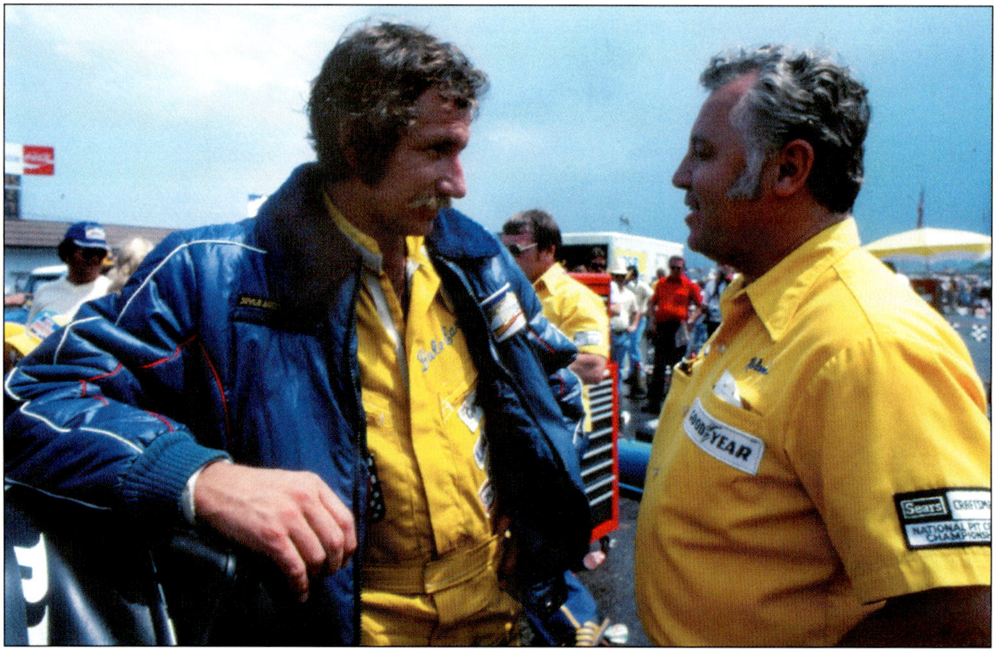

Dale Earnhardt (left) captured his first NASCAR premier series victory at Charlotte Motor Speedway in October 1980. The fifth win in his sophomore season gave him a 115-point lead in the driver standings and propelled him to his first series championship. Earnhardt remains the only driver to have won rookie honors and then a championship in successive seasons in the series.

At 39 years old, Harry Gant entered NASCAR's premier series full-time, when most drivers that age are planning for retirement. It was the decision to join Hollywood director Hal Needham and actor Burt Reynolds as the driver of their Skoal Bandit entry, however, that turned Gant into a household name. His first Charlotte victory came in the 1982 National 500 when he defeated Bill Elliott by 2.93 seconds.

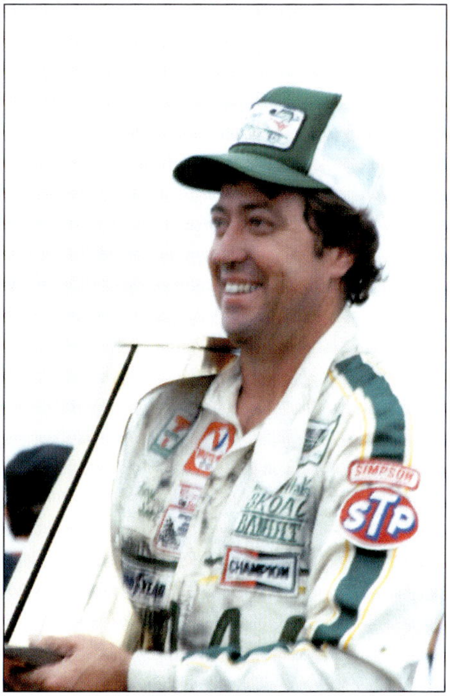

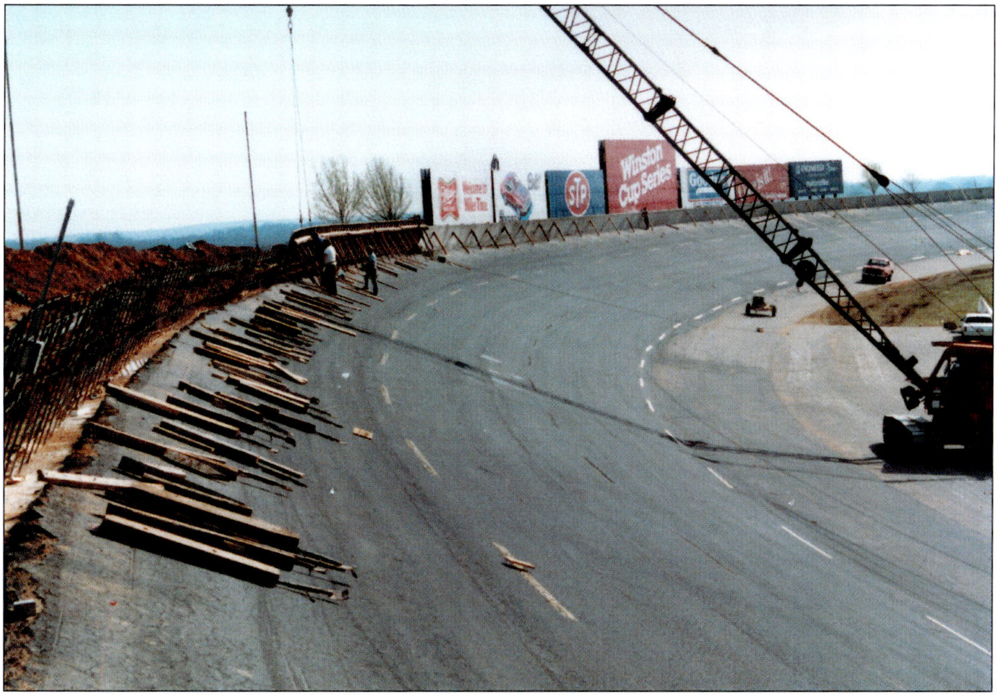

Bruton Smith regained ownership of Charlotte Motor Speedway in 1975, and in the 1980s, he and track president H.A. "Humpy" Wheeler embarked on a decade of massive improvements at the 1.5-mile track. That included replacing the guardrail barriers in the turns with concrete walls. In racing's early years, many drivers died or lost limbs from guardrails piercing their cars during an accident. It was believed a concrete wall was safer.

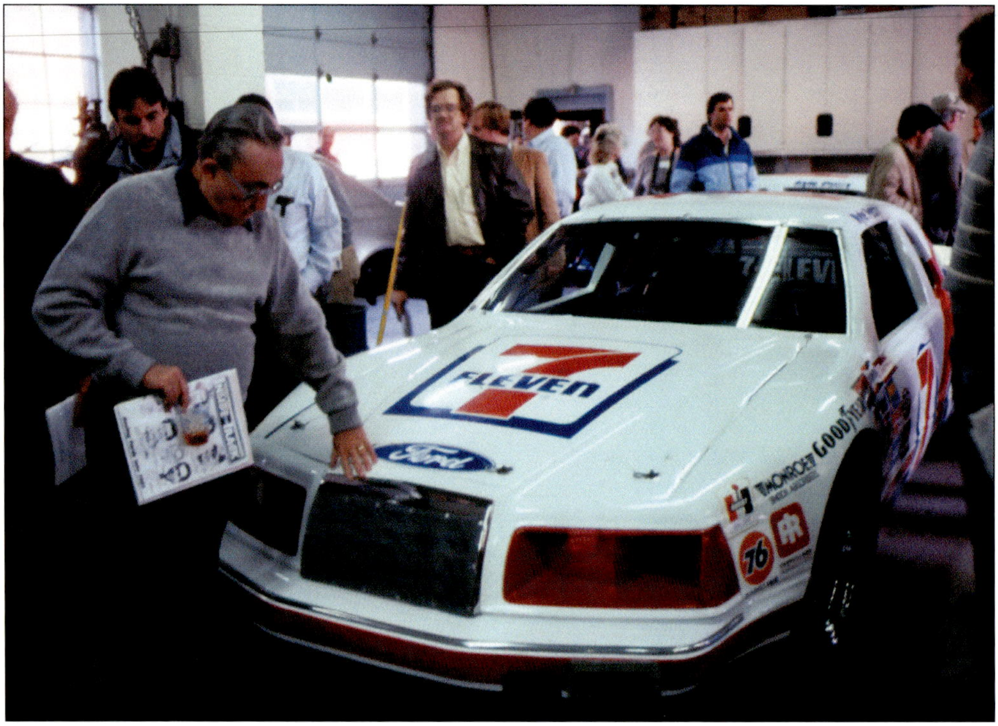

In the early 1980s, Charlotte Motor Speedway communications department heads Ed Clark and Bob Kelly created the Media Tour. The idea was to foster interest in the sport in January by giving reporters the opportunity to preview the upcoming season by talking with drivers, crew chiefs, team owners, and engine builders. The tour's first year was 1983 and only one touring-style bus was needed to transport reporters to the various race shops each day. It was the first time NASCAR teams had ever experienced such an event, and they wanted to make a good impression. With the sport's growth, the tour became extremely popular, and at least three buses were eventually required to transport the media to the race shops. Today, the Media Tour no longer travels to the race shops. Instead, it interviews the drivers at the Charlotte Convention Center.

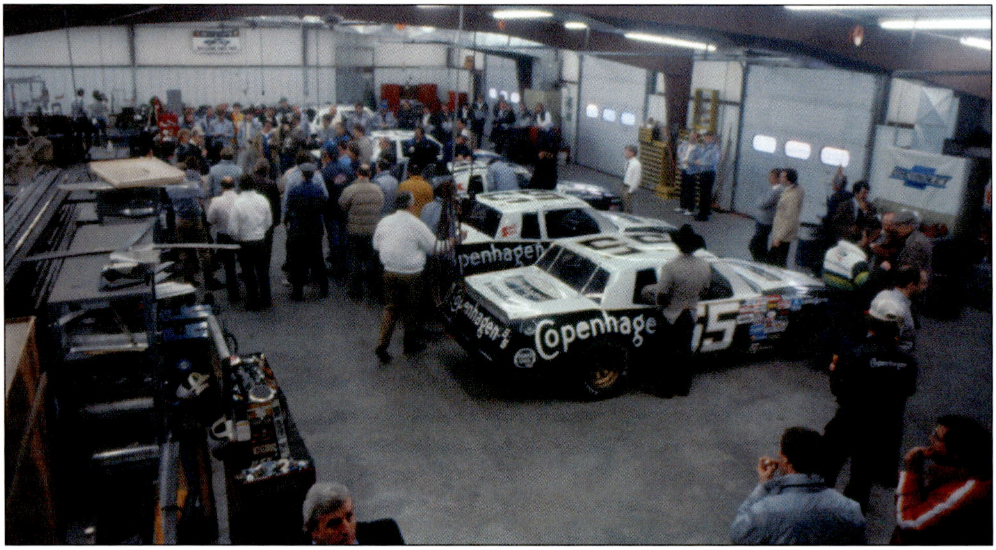

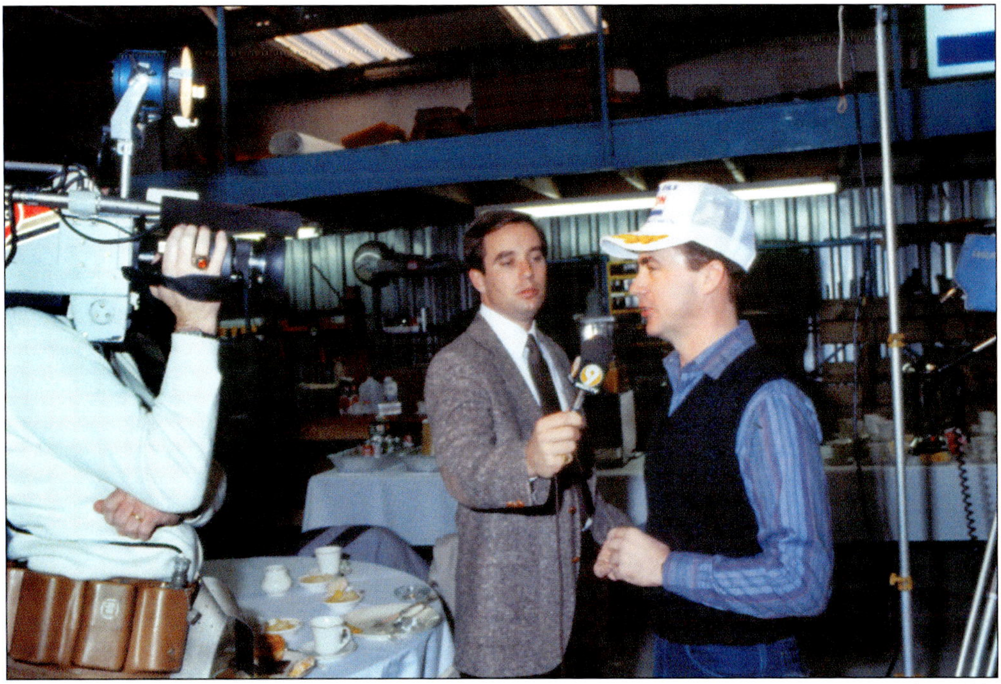

In the early days of Charlotte Motor Speedway's Media Tour, television stations were often able to obtain one-on-one interviews with the drivers. The above interview with Geoff Bodine (right) occurred in the shop where crew chief Harry Hyde oversaw the preparation of Bodine's Hendrick Motorsports Chevrolets. Hendrick Motorsports is located on property once owned by Hyde, and team owner Rick Hendrick has preserved Hyde's facility. Below, in gratitude to Charlotte Motor Speedway for its establishment of the Media Tour, the National Motorsports Press Association (NMPA) gave its prestigious Myers Brothers Award to the facility in 1984. Speedway owner Bruton Smith (center) and track president H.A. "Humpy" Wheeler (left) accepted the award from NMPA president Harold Pearson (right) during a breakfast at the Waldorf-Astoria Hotel in New York City.

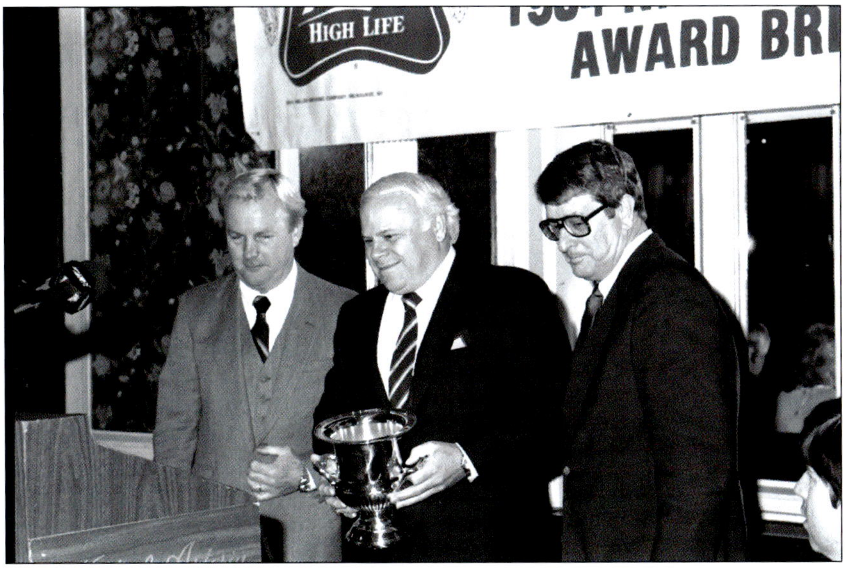

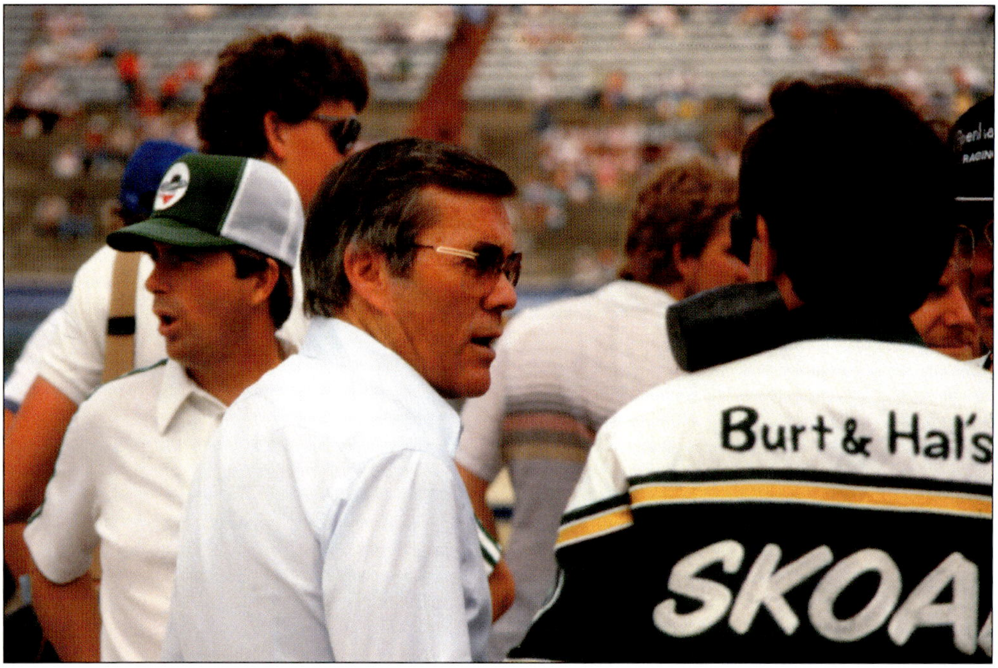

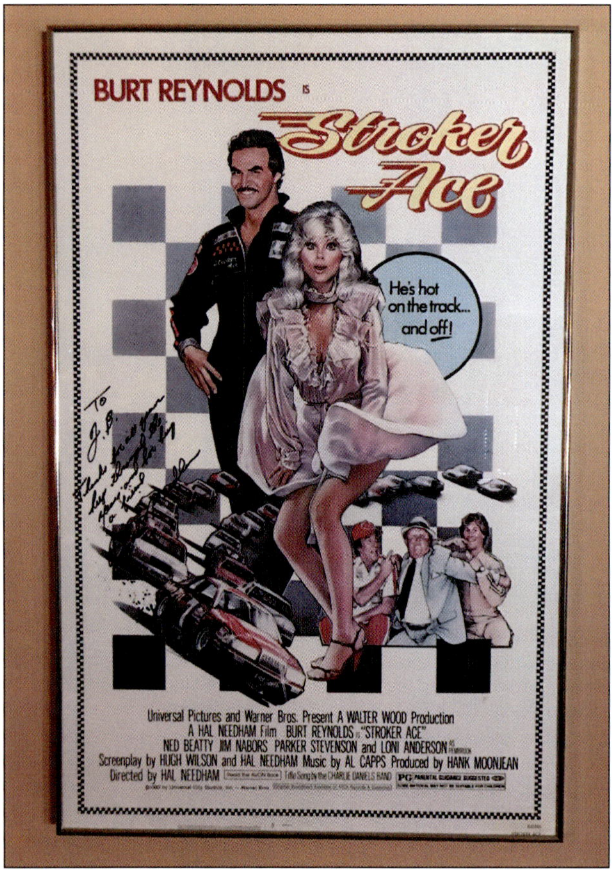

Hollywood director and stuntman Hal Needham (above center) became a regular at NASCAR events from 1981 through 1989, when he was a team owner. He began the venture with longtime friend and actor Burt Reynolds and remained in the sport after Reynolds chose to depart. During the time that Harry Gant was his driver, he gave parts to Gant in his movies *Stroker Ace* and *Cannonball Run II*. While Hollywood first featured Charlotte Motor Speedway in Elvis Presley's movie *Speedway*, it was not until the 1980s that it once again became a popular movie locale. Several scenes for *Stroker Ace* were filmed at the track, and the world premier was held at Charlotte's Ovens Auditorium. All of the movie's stars attended the premier, including Reynolds, Loni Anderson, and Parker Stevenson. (Left, courtesy of Johnny Bruce.)

Charlotte Motor Speedway's first condominium building (right) opened in 1984. Located above the first-turn Grand National Tower seats, the two-bedroom condos initially cost $120,000. Today, some have sold for more than $250,000. A few drivers or former drivers have either lived in or are now living in the building. Each condo's living area faces the track and provides a kitchen and dining section (below). There also is a step down to seats located in front of the large window that faces the track, thus providing a spectacular view to those who want to focus on the race. The bedrooms are located on the back side of the condo with windows facing the building's walkway.

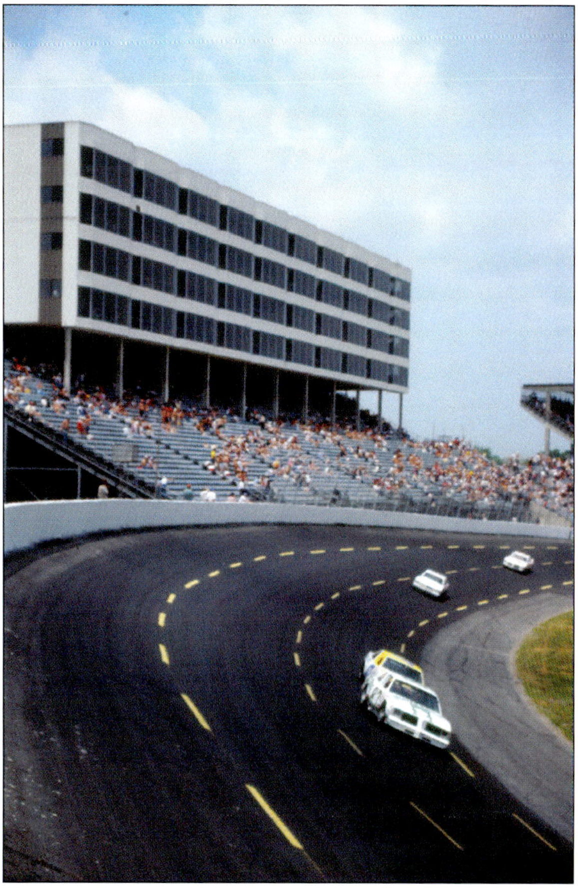

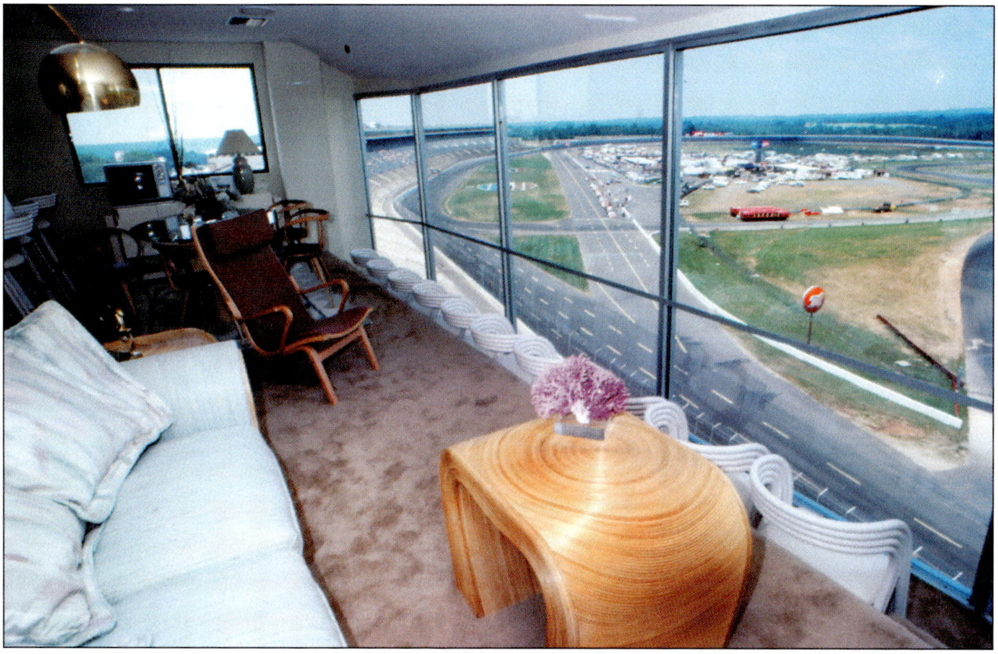

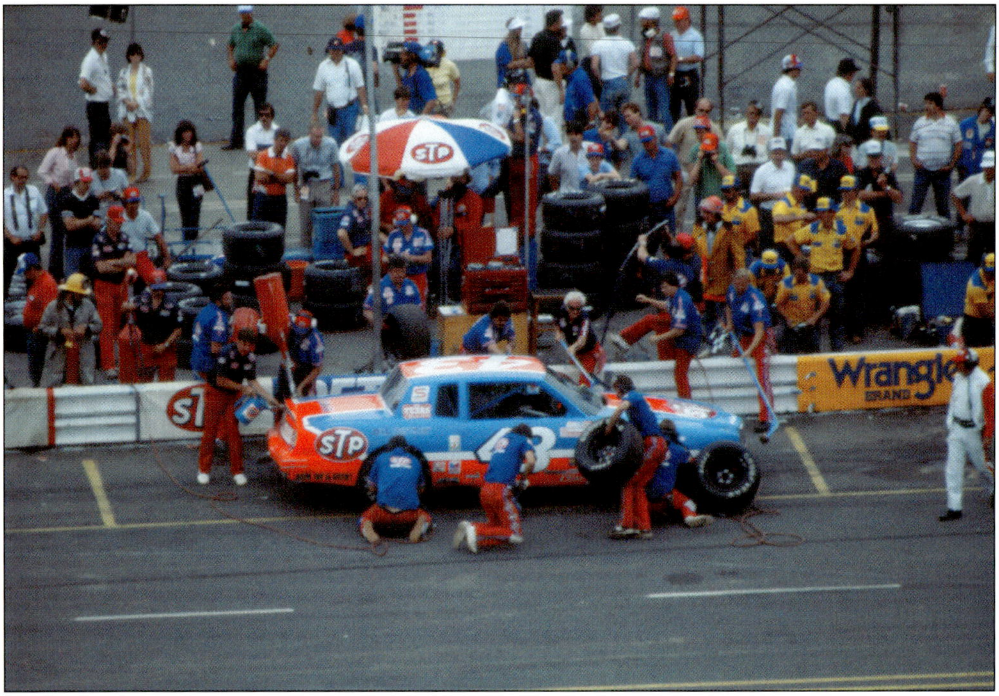

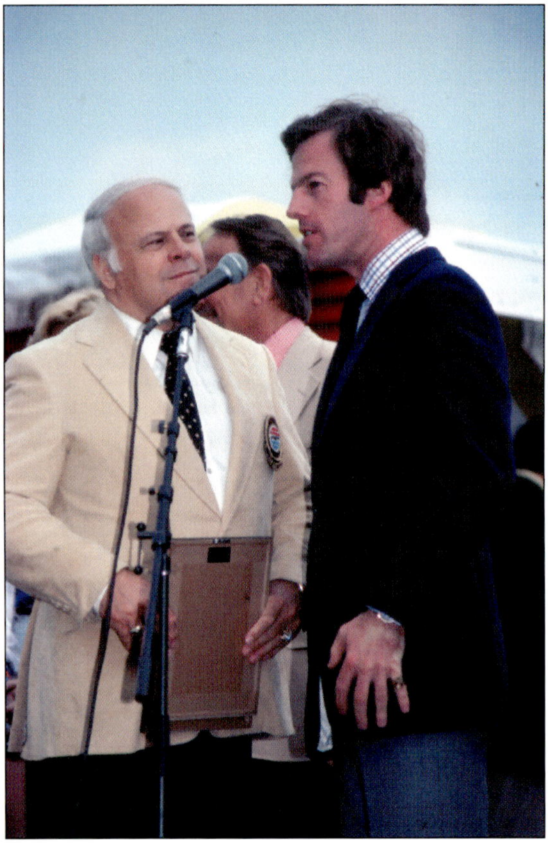

Richard Petty's 198th career victory came in Charlotte's 1983 Miller High Life 500, but it was not without controversy. After Petty claimed a 3.1-second victory over Darrell Waltrip, it was discovered that left-side tires had been placed on the car's right side to achieve better traction. The car also was powered by an oversized engine. NASCAR allowed Petty to keep the victory, but he was fined $35,000 and stripped of 104 driver points.

A bevy of celebrities, politicians, and world-class athletes attended Charlotte Motor Speedway races during the 1980s. At the 1983 World 600, speedway owner Bruton Smith (left) hosted Mark Thatcher (right), son of then British prime minister Margaret Thatcher. Another who attended the Charlotte races during the 1980s was television show host Dick Clark.

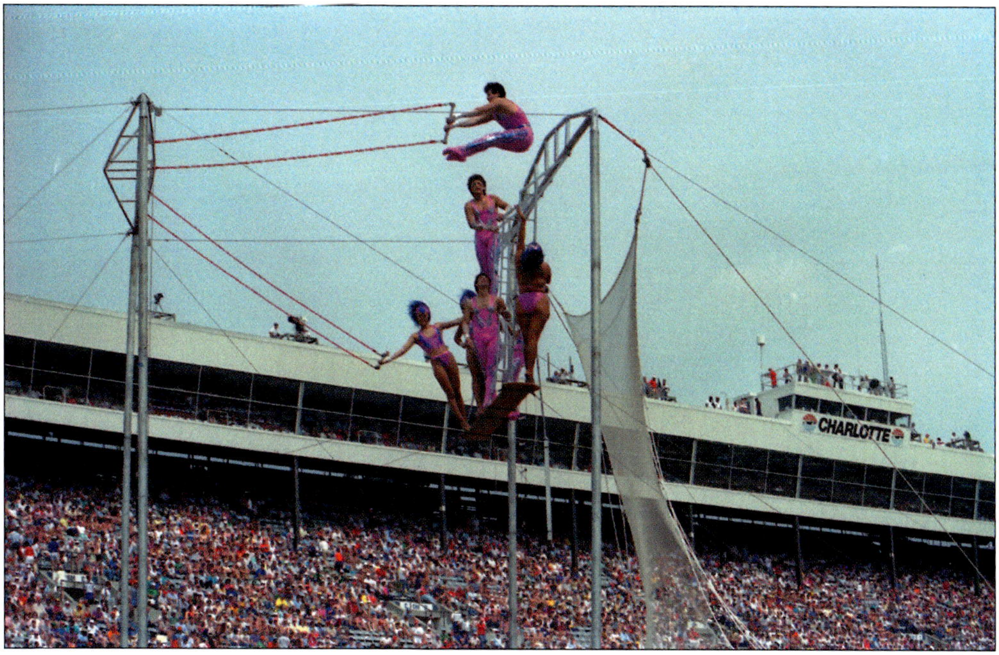

In an effort to get fans to come early to the speedway in the hopes of helping facilitate traffic flow, Charlotte Motor Speedway executives worked diligently to create spectacular prerace shows. One prerace show focused on the circus, and three rings were set up on the frontstretch's grassy apron (above). It included trapeze and high-wire acts. The high-wire act originated above the press box and progressed down to the frontstretch. At right, another high-wire act during a prerace show involved a motorcycle. Innovation was the key, and H.A. "Humpy" Wheeler said he learned during his tenure at the track that no idea was stupid because while someone might not be creative, it did not mean they could not recognize creativity.

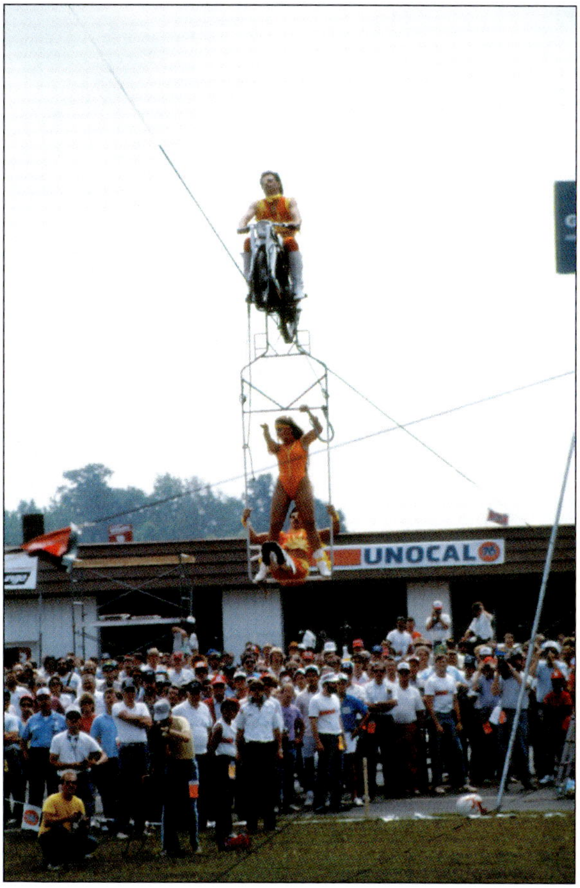

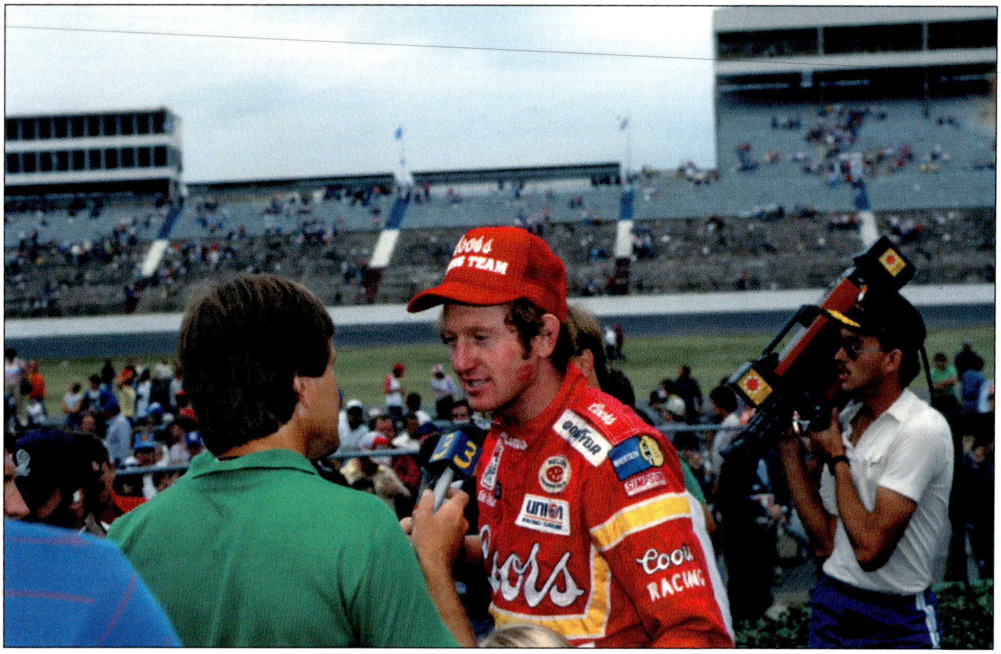

Bill Elliott acquired his first Charlotte Motor Speedway victory in the 1984 Miller High Life 500. He led the final 60 laps in obtaining his third career victory. Benny Parsons, who started from the pole and secured most of the lap-leader awards, finished 14.5 seconds behind Elliott in second place. Only two other drivers finished on the lead lap, Cale Yarborough in third and Harry Gant in fourth.

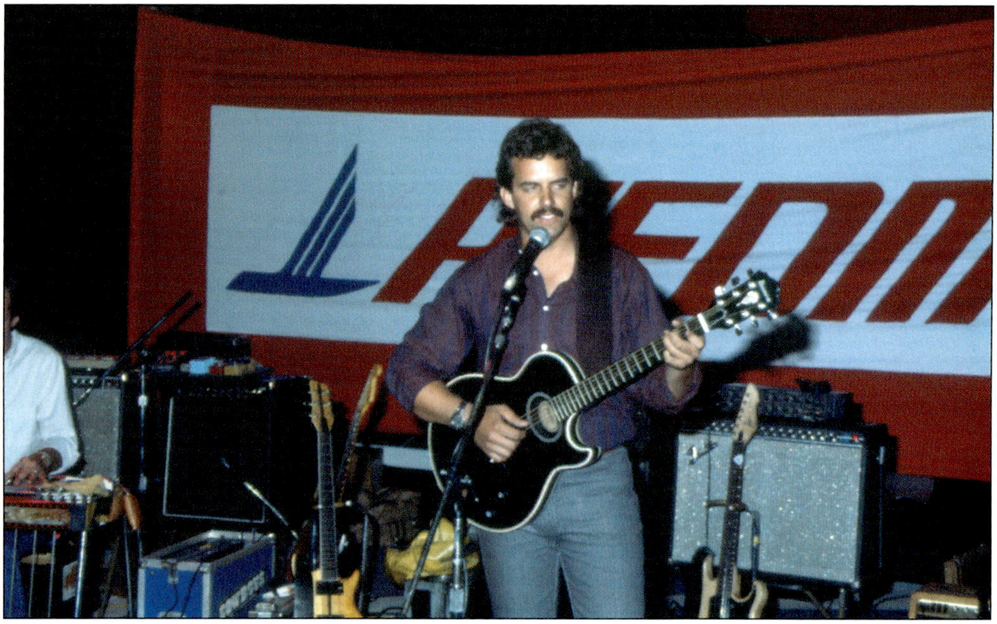

Since the races occurred during the day in the 1980s, evening social events were plentiful. Kyle Petty, who enjoyed writing songs, would sometimes pick up a guitar and perform. Mike Powell, a truck driver for one of the teams, also would perform, often singing the national anthem during prerace ceremonies.

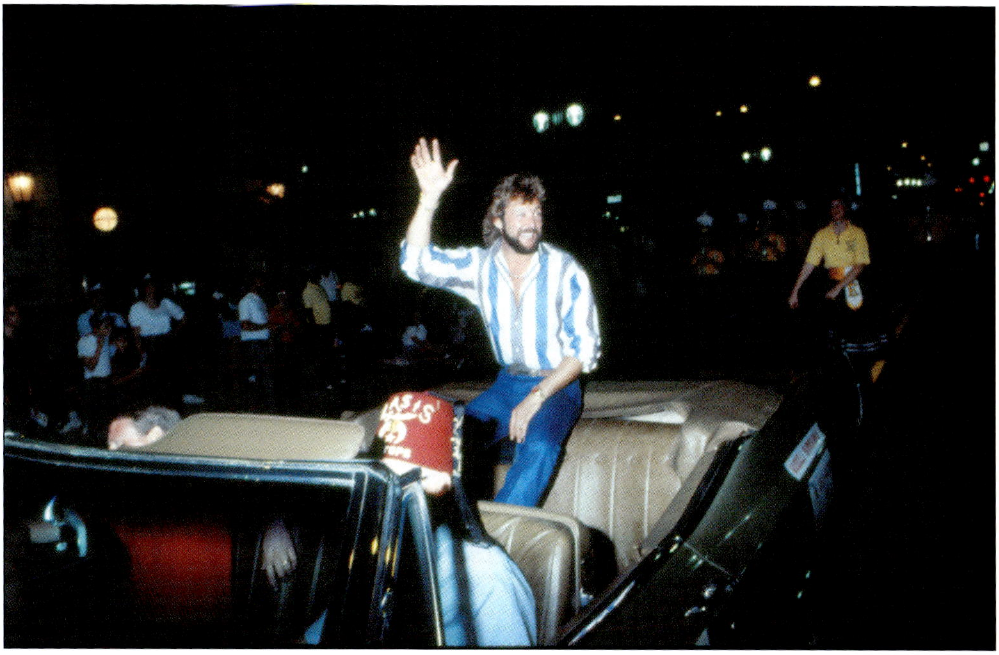

During the 1980s, speedway officials coordinated with the City of Charlotte to host the 600 Festival of Lights Parade. Conducted the week of the May race, all of the drivers participated when it began, either riding in convertibles or on floats. In this photograph, Tim Richmond enjoys waving at the fans lining Tryon Street in Charlotte.

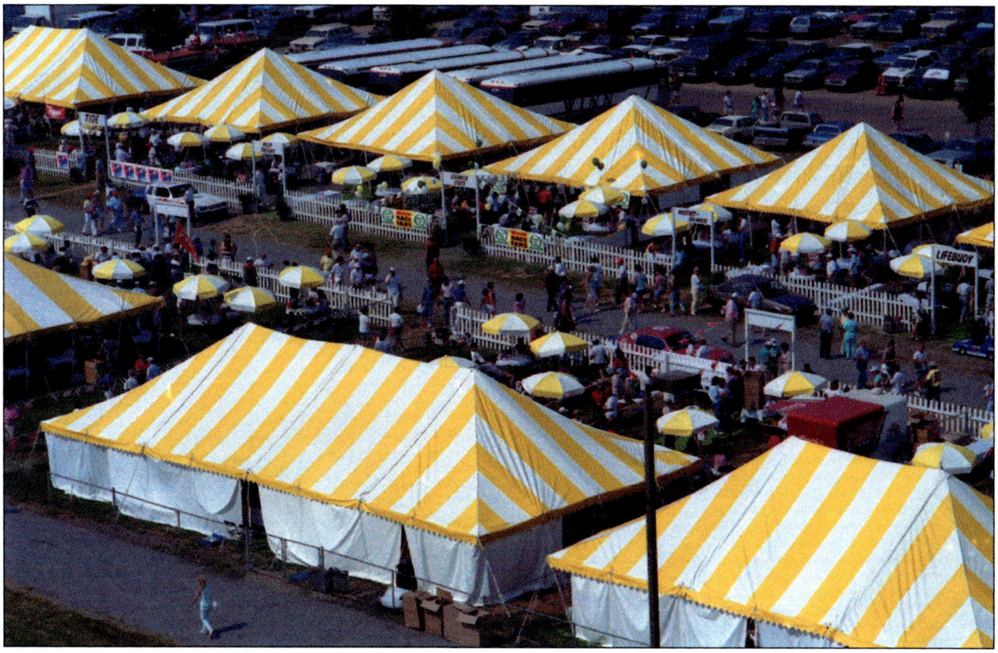

The sport's popularity explosion with corporate America in the 1980s resulted in Charlotte Motor Speedway creating a large Hospitality Village behind the frontstretch grandstands. Corporations would entertain potential clients or employees in the tents, which included a catered meal on race day and usually a driver appearance. A sponsor also might have a show car on display.

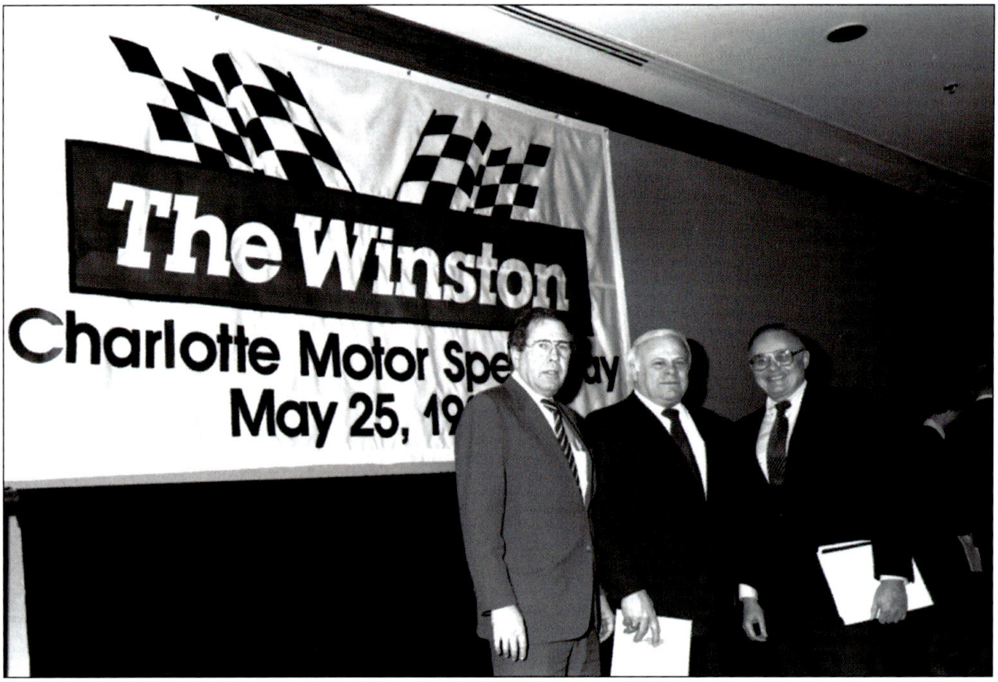

At the 1984 NASCAR Awards Banquet in New York City, R.J. Reynolds Tobacco Company (RJR) announced the sport would have an all-star race in 1985. Charlotte Motor Speedway emerged as the front-runner to host the special event. In January 1985, RJR president Jerry Long announced the race would indeed be at Charlotte. Those speaking at the press conference are, from left to right, NASCAR president Bill France Jr., speedway owner Bruton Smith, and Long.

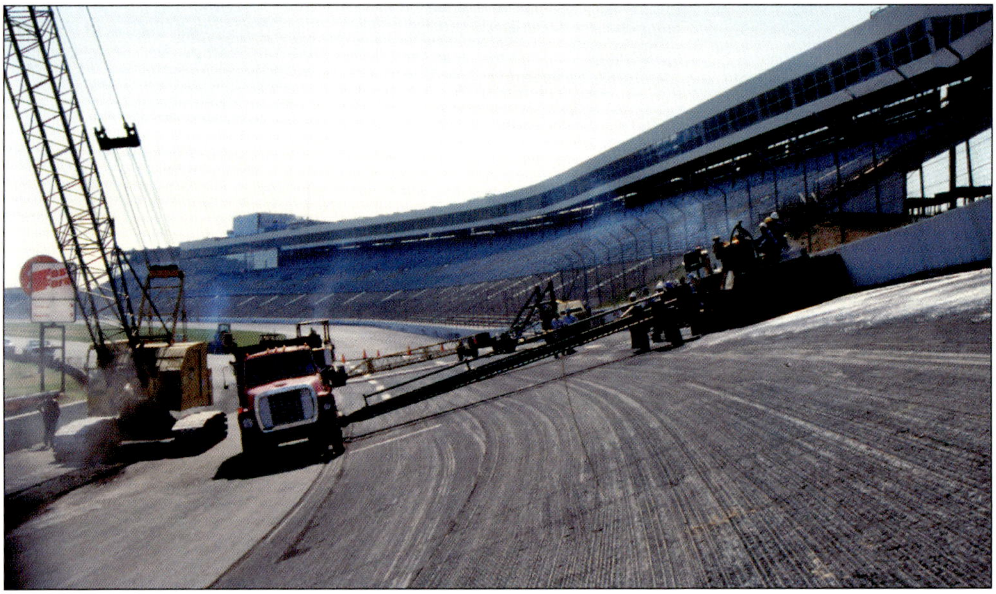

While buildings and grandstands were being constructed at the speedway, officials decided it was time to repave the track. The track's surface has always been temperature sensitive, and getting the correct mixture for it can sometimes be tricky. Also, any time a track repaves, it means additional work for Goodyear's tire engineers and testing by the teams.

Bill Elliott and his team entered the 1985 Coca-Cola World 600 under a great deal of pressure. In the first year of R.J. Reynolds Tobacco Company's Winston Million bonus program, Elliott won two of the events comprising it before the Charlotte race. He needed only to win one more race to collect the $1 million bonus, but it did not occur at Charlotte. Elliott earned the pole but had several problems during the race that relegated him to an 18th-place finish.

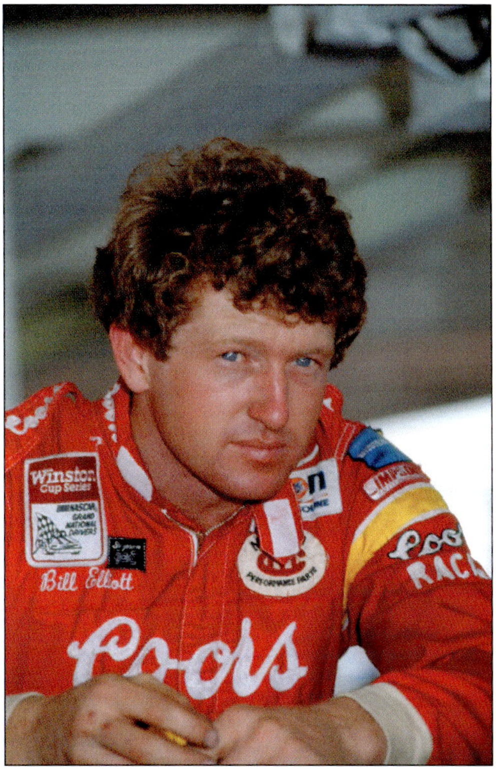

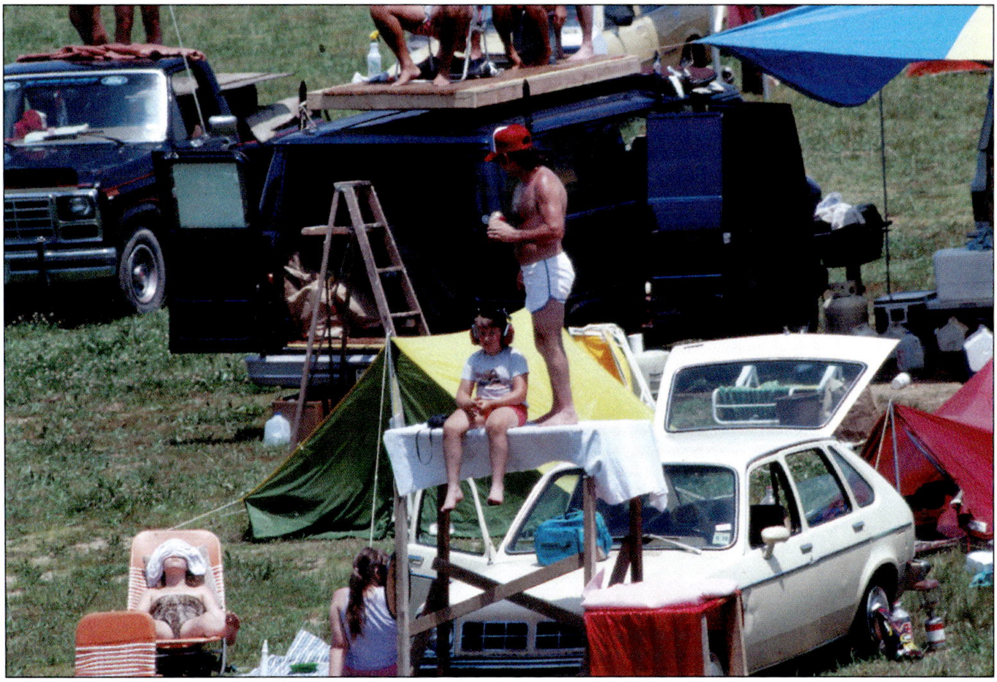

Even though the names of the stars in the sport were changing and VIP suites were being constructed, many fans still opted to cheer on their favorite driver from the infield. For those who liked to camp and bring their own food, this was a more conducive environment.

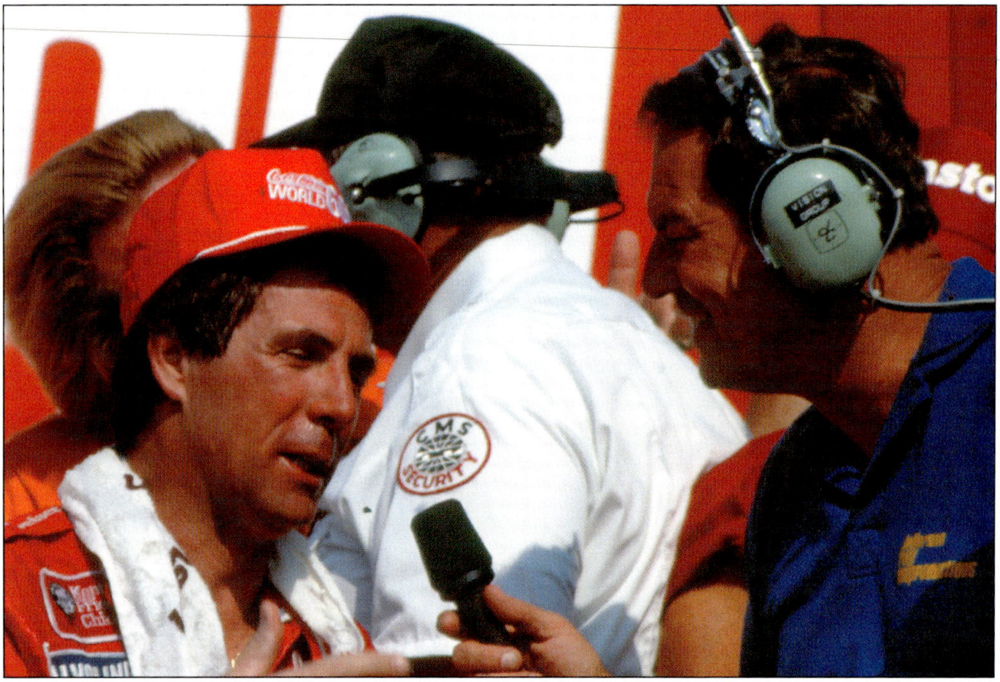

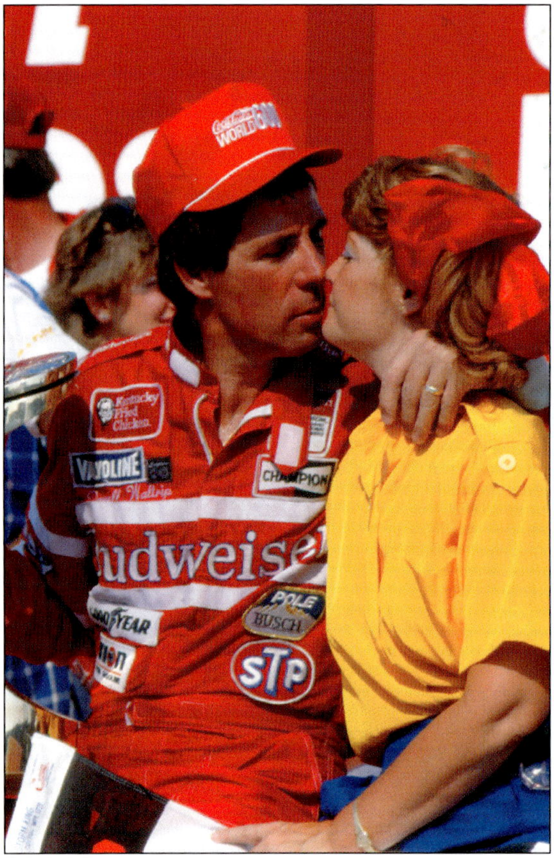

For Darrell Waltrip (above, left), the 1985 May weekend that had the all-star race and the Coca-Cola World 600 on back-to-back days was a memorable one, as well as lucrative for the Franklin, Tennessee, driver. On Saturday at Charlotte Motor Speedway, Waltrip won the inaugural all-star race, passing Harry Gant with just a lap and a half remaining in the 105-mile event. The engine in his Junior Johnson Chevrolet expired as he took the checkered flag, and there was speculation he had blown the engine on purpose to prevent a close inspection from NASCAR. The next day, Waltrip won his third Coca-Cola World 600, taking a 14.64-second victory over Gant. Waltrip's two-day payday totaled $290,733. At left, Waltrip and his wife, Stevie, celebrate in victory lane following his Coca-Cola World 600 victory.

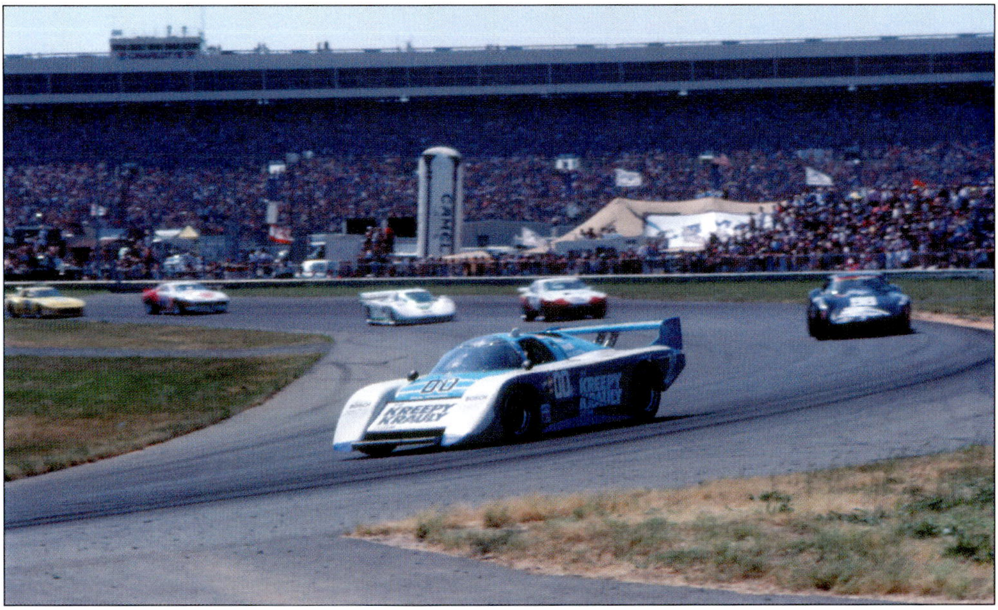

In the mid-1980s, Charlotte Motor Speedway executives incorporated professional road racing into the track's schedule. IMSA's Camel GT circuit brought prototype and GTO and GTU cars to the facility's road course. Also competing on the road course on the same weekend were the Kelly American Challenge Series, which was devoted to stock cars, and the small sedan Champion Spark Plug Series.

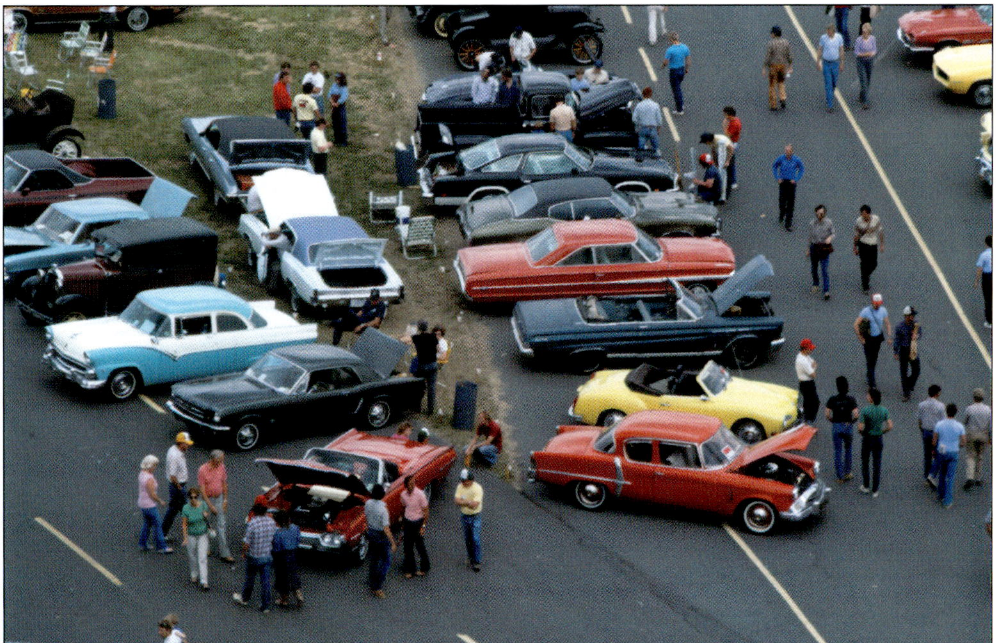

With Charlotte Motor Speedway executives constantly looking for ways to use the facility, the antique auto fair became a popular event. Initially, the auto fair was held only in the spring, but it eventually grew into two events annually. The Spring AutoFair occupies an April slot on the calendar, while the one in the fall has a September date.

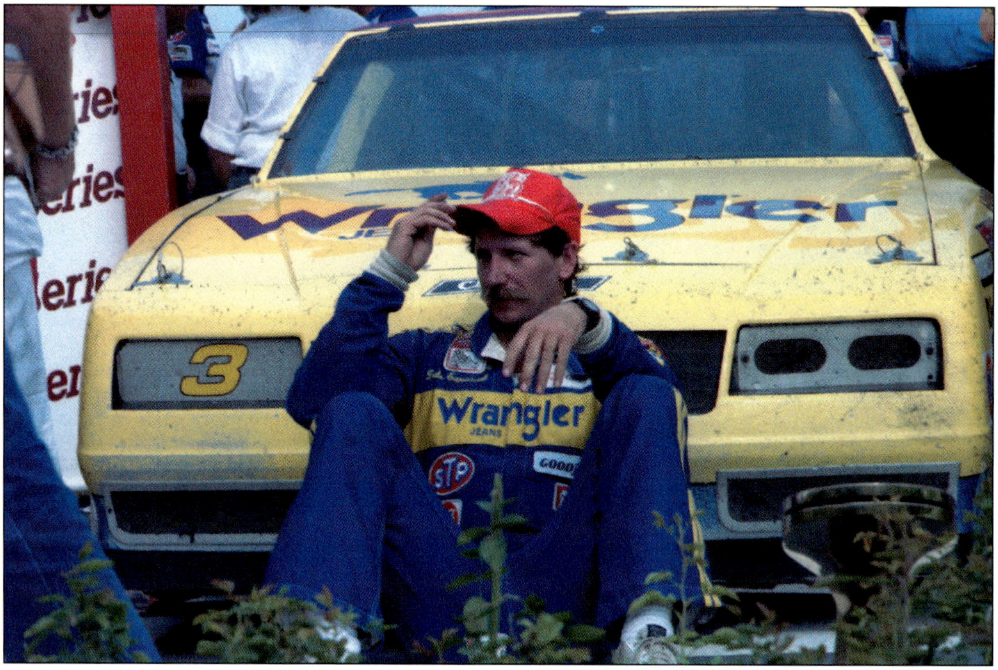

Dale Earnhardt (above) dominated Charlotte Motor Speedway in 1986. He swept the NASCAR premier series races, winning the Coca-Cola 600 and the Oakwood Homes 500. He also won the All Pro 300 Busch Series race in October. The Charlotte victories provided Earnhardt with the boost he needed to claim his second series championship and his first with Richard Childress. Below, Earnhardt recorded his third victory of the season in the Coca-Cola 600 after outrunning Tim Richmond (left) to the checkered flag. The Kannapolis, North Carolina, native led the final 16 laps and finished 1.96 seconds ahead of Richmond, who joined Earnhardt in victory lane to congratulate him. The stellar season the two drivers posted in 1986 resulted in them tying for National Motorsports Press Association Driver of the Year honors.

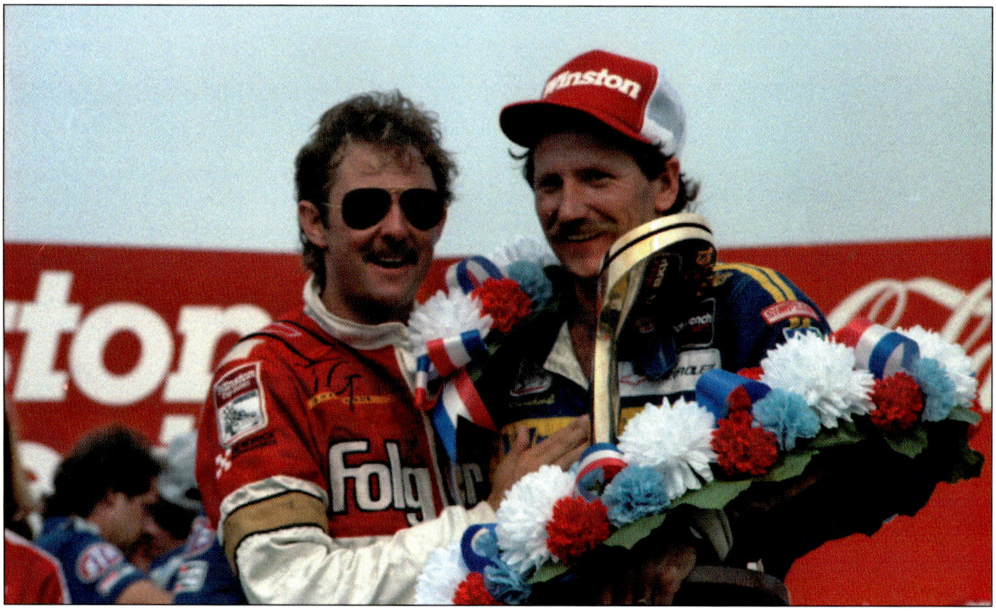

Kyle Petty's lone Charlotte Motor Speedway victory came in the 1987 Coca-Cola 600. Driving a Wood Brothers Ford, Petty finished a lap ahead of runner-up Morgan Shepherd. The 27-year-old Petty's second career victory was the 70th win for Wood Brothers on a superspeedway. The race had a heavy attrition rate, with only 17 of the 42 starters running at the finish.

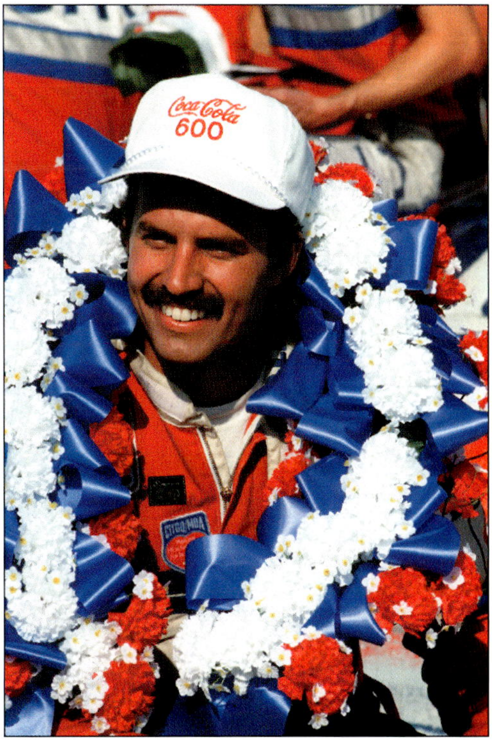

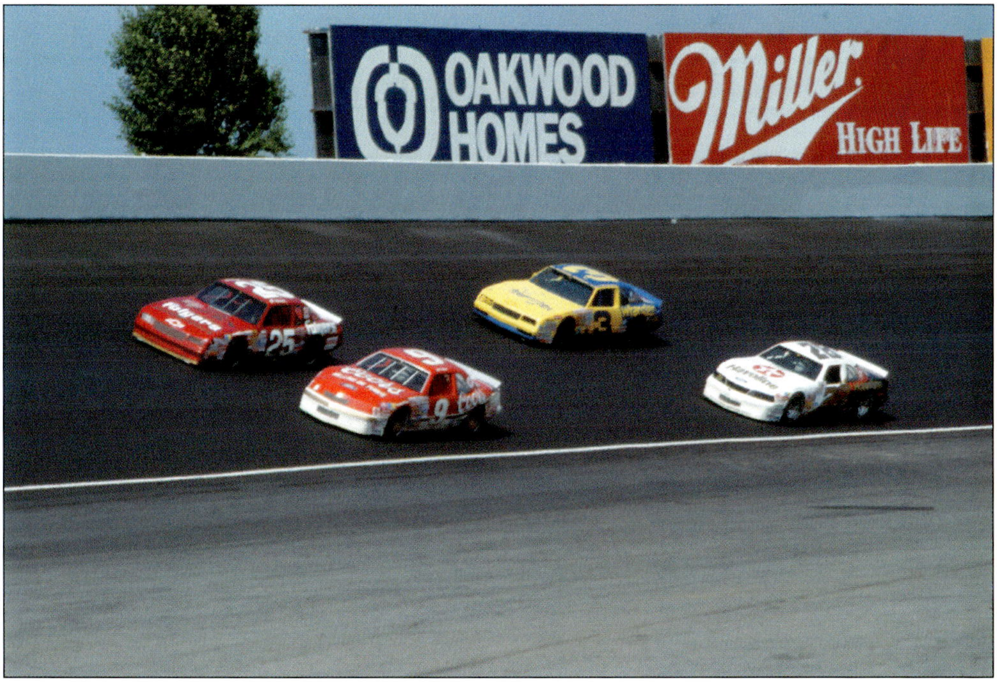

In the mid- to late 1980s, Bill Elliott (No. 9), Tim Richmond (No. 25), Davey Allison (No. 28), and Dale Earnhardt (No. 3) emerged as four of NASCAR's new superstars. In that decade, Elliott won 32 races and a series championship. Richmond was victorious in 13 events, and Allison took six in three years. Earnhardt posted 38 victories and three championships.

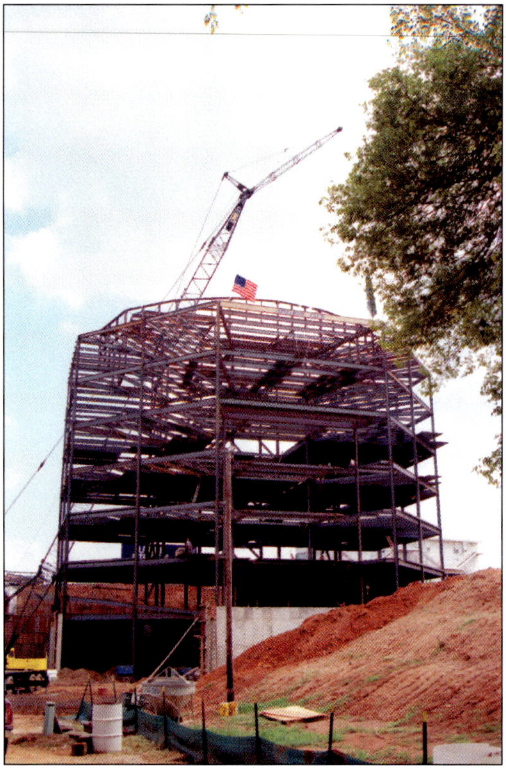

Shortly after Charlotte Motor Speedway owner Bruton Smith shocked the motorsports community in the 1980s with the condominium announcement, he held another press conference. This one announced a new seven-story office tower that would include a membership club where people could dine, dance, and watch races. The club has a beautiful oak bar area and marble accents. The Speedway Club is located on the tower's sixth floor. The seventh floor is devoted to the speedway's offices while the third and fourth floors contain offices that may be rented. Located on the second floor is the speedway's ticket office and souvenir store. There is a workout room on the first floor and Performance Racing Network's state-of-the-art facility is attached to the Smith Tower.

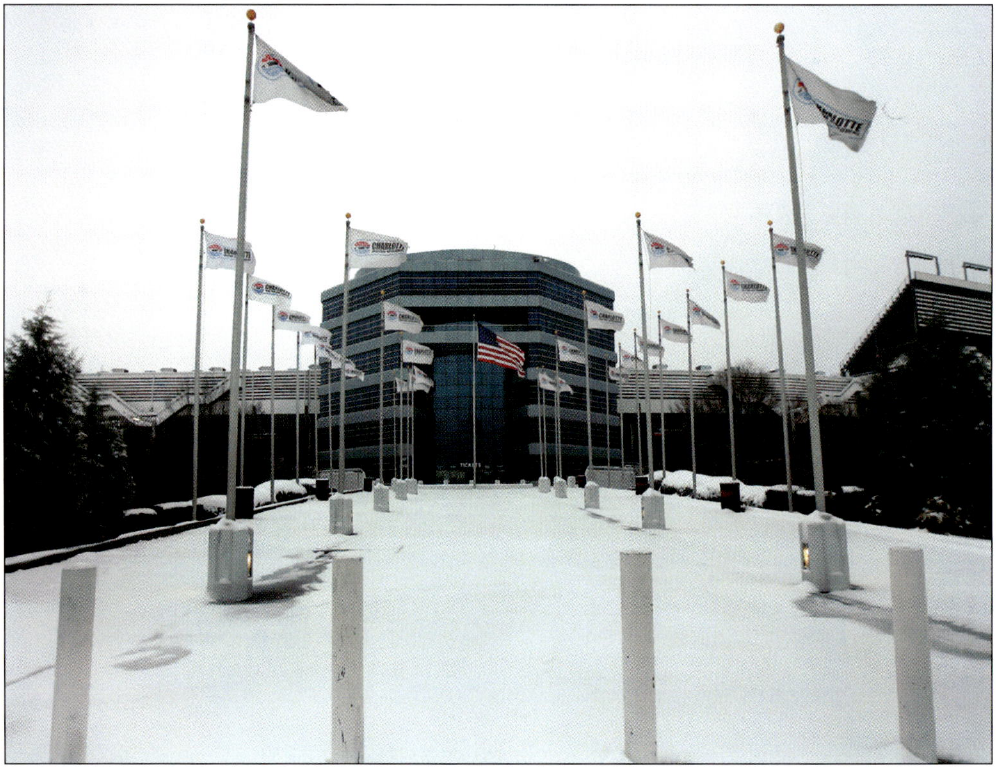

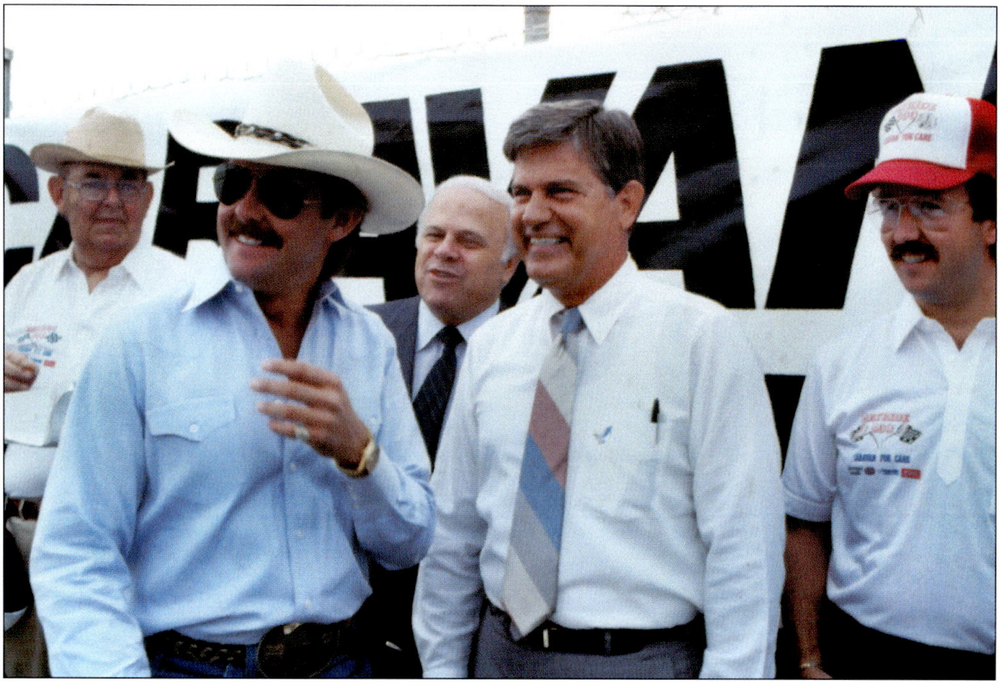

A severe drought in the summer of 1986 left many North Carolina farmers on the verge of losing their herds. Several in the NASCAR community wanted to do something to help them, so on an off-weekend, a group of the race team truck drivers came together to form the Hayride 500. Charlotte Motor Speedway served as the staging area for the tractor-trailers, which went to Ohio to pick up hundreds of bales of hay for the starving livestock. Tim Richmond (second from left) was the only NASCAR driver to make the round-trip. Those attending the sendoff included, from left to right, North Carolina agriculture commissioner Jim Graham, Richmond, Bruton Smith, North Carolina governor James G. Martin, and RJR employee Steve Tucker. Below, the tractor-trailers make a lap around the speedway before heading to Ohio.

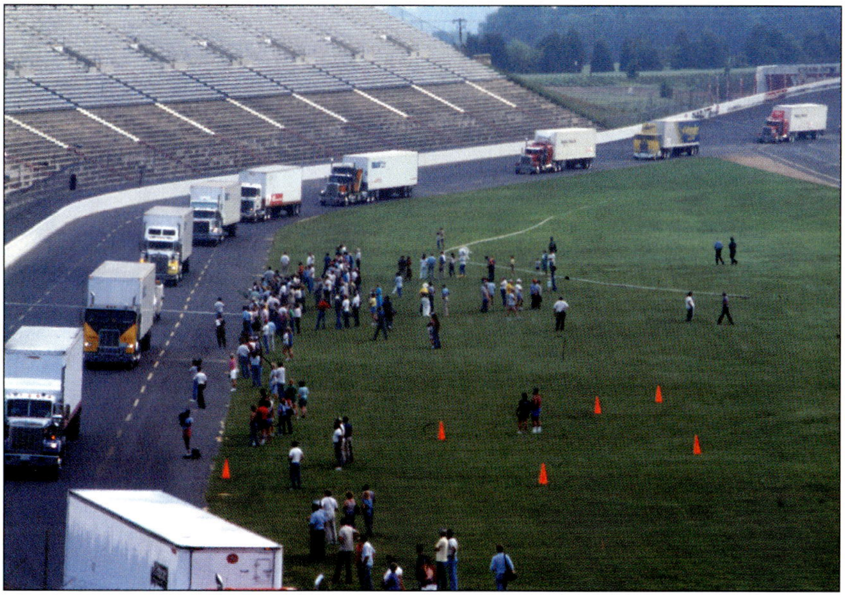

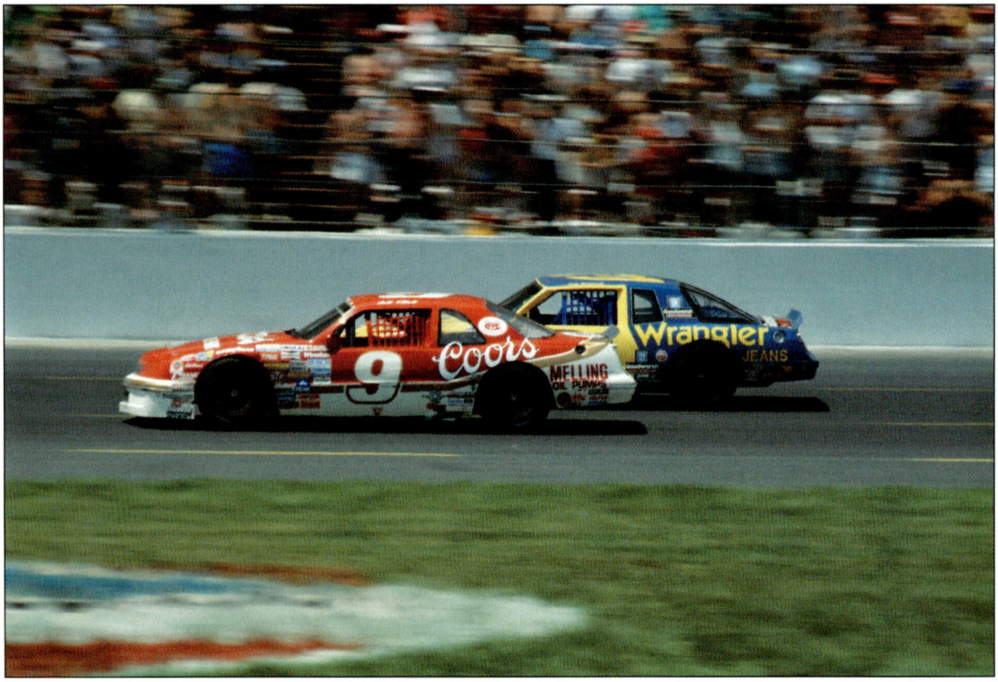

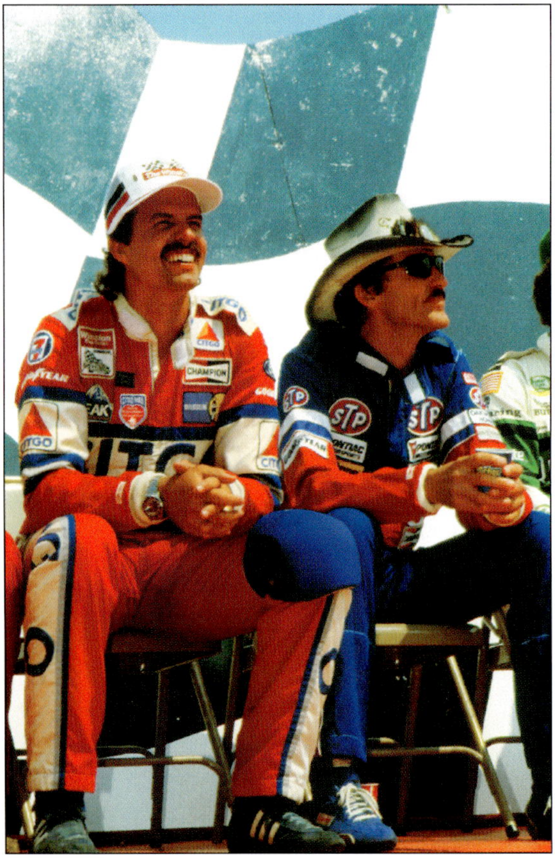

The battle between Bill Elliott (No. 9) and Dale Earnhardt in the final 10 laps of the 1987 all-star race is one of the event's most memorable moments. It was a sheet metal banging affair that left tempers flaring. Earnhardt maintained Elliott ran him into the frontstretch grass. Elliott claimed Earnhardt nearly put him into the wall. Earnhardt won, but Elliott ran into Earnhardt's car on the cool-down lap. NASCAR fined both of them.

When Kyle Petty (left) earned his way into the 1987 all-star race with a victory at Richmond, Virginia, it meant he and his father, Richard Petty (right), would be the first father-son duo to compete in the all-star event. Kyle, driving a Wood Brothers Ford, finished sixth. Richard placed 19th in his Petty Enterprises Pontiac.

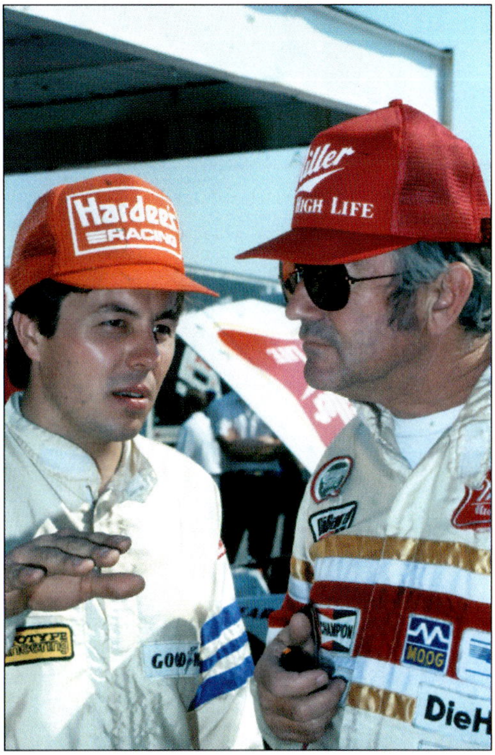

Alan Kulwicki (left) made his Charlotte Motor Speedway debut in the 1985 Miller High Life 500. He qualified 24th and finished 13th in a Ford fielded by Bill Terry. One of the people from whom Kulwicki sought advice was Bobby Allison (right). Ironically, Allison finished one position behind Kulwicki in 14th place after qualifying 21st.

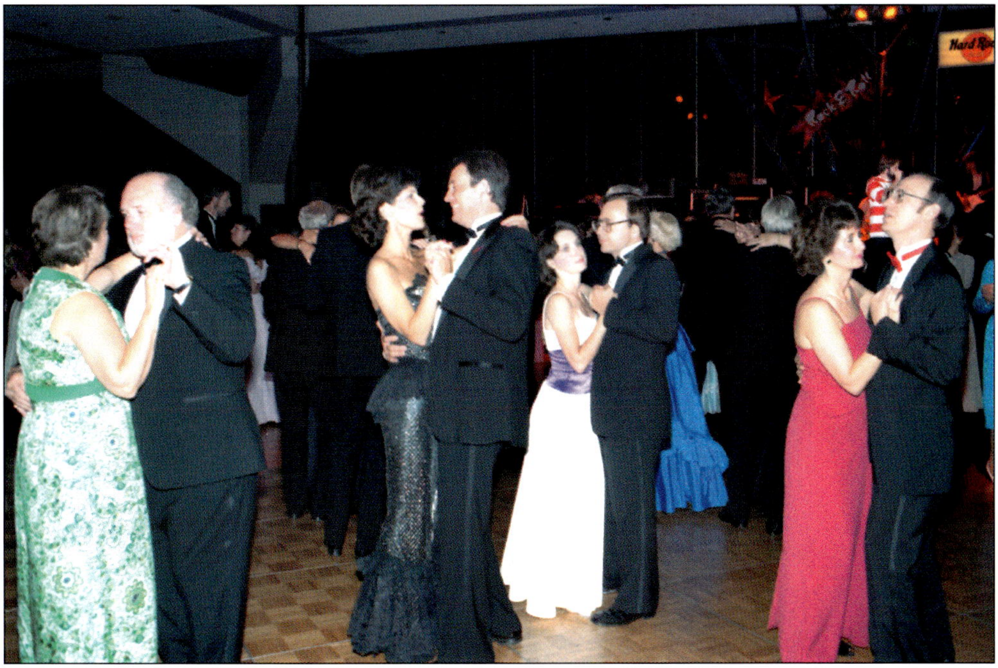

When Speedway Children's Charities was established in the 1980s, an annual ball held during Coca-Cola 600 week was created as one of its fundraisers. In 2016, the Charlotte Motor Speedway chapter distributed $815,000 to 93 local nonprofits. Each track owned by Speedway Motorsports Incorporated (SMI) now has a Speedway Children's Charities chapter.

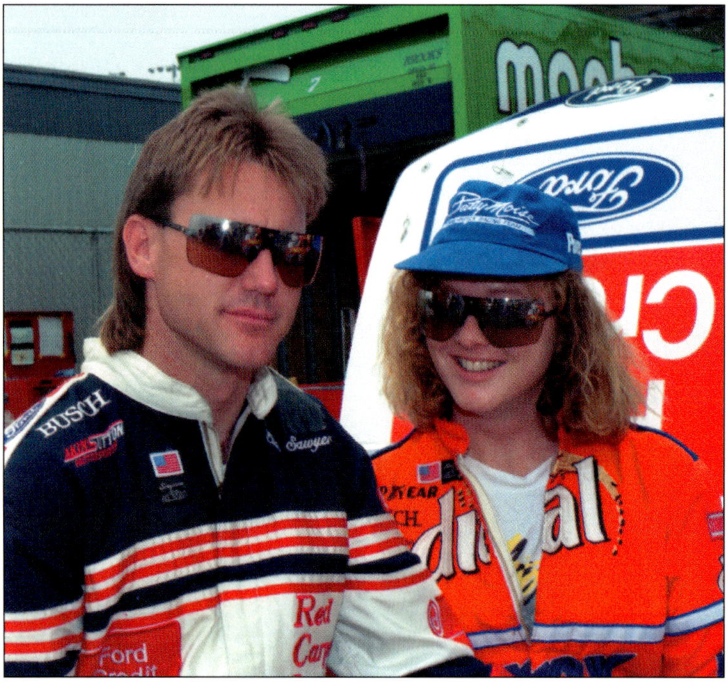

Patty Moise (right) first competed at Charlotte Motor Speedway in IMSA's Kelly American Challenge Series in the mid-1980s. However, she did not make her NASCAR debut at the track until the 1987 Winn-Dixie 300. She finished 22nd in that event. She was competing in NASCAR's Busch Series against Elton Sawyer (left) when the two began dating. They continued to race against each other for a short time after they were married.

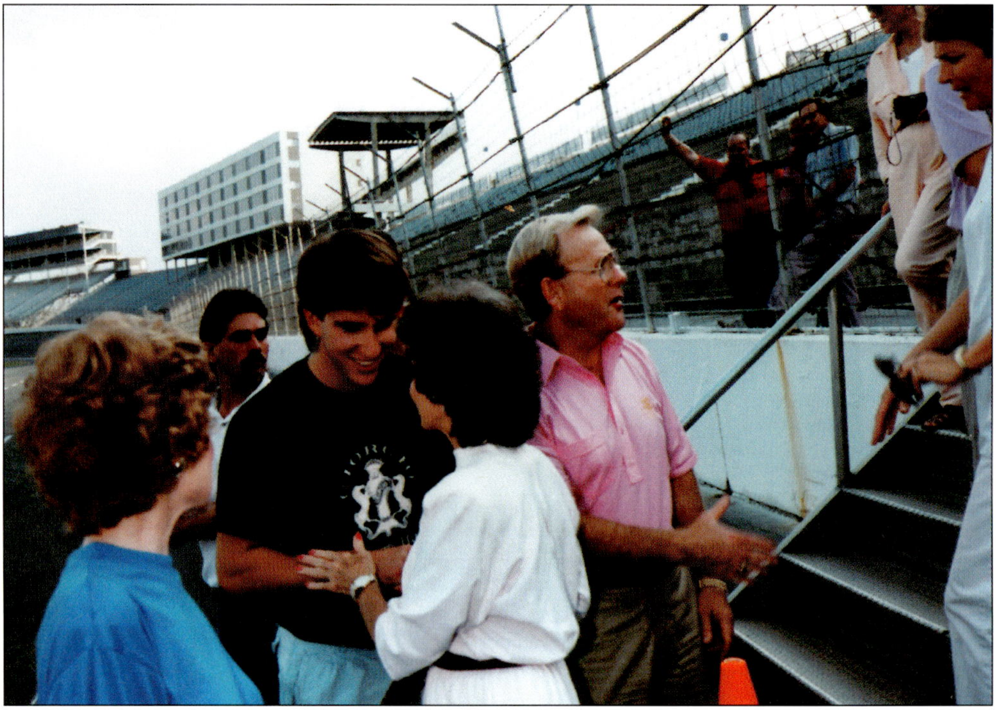

Rob Moroso (center) was 18 years old when he made his Charlotte Motor Speedway debut in NASCAR's Busch Series. He qualified 33rd and finished 28th in the 1987 Winn-Dixie 300. It was a different story, however, the following year. Beginning with the 1988 October All Pro 300, Moroso won three consecutive Busch Series races at the track before moving to NASCAR's premier series full-time in 1990.

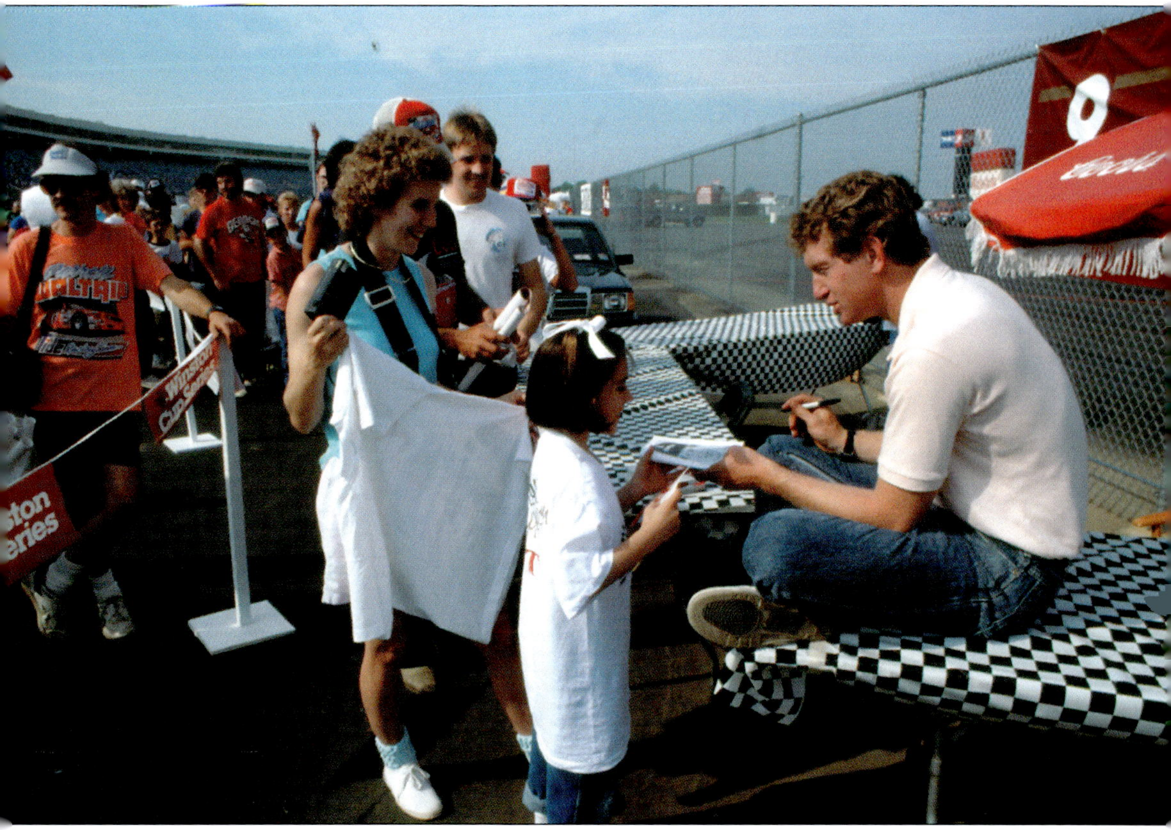

Prior to one of the all-star races, RJR scheduled a driver autograph session for the fans. Bill Elliott (right), who won the National Motorsports Press Association's Most Popular Driver award a record 16 times, elected to sit on the table instead of behind it. He was popular with fans of all ages during his driving career.

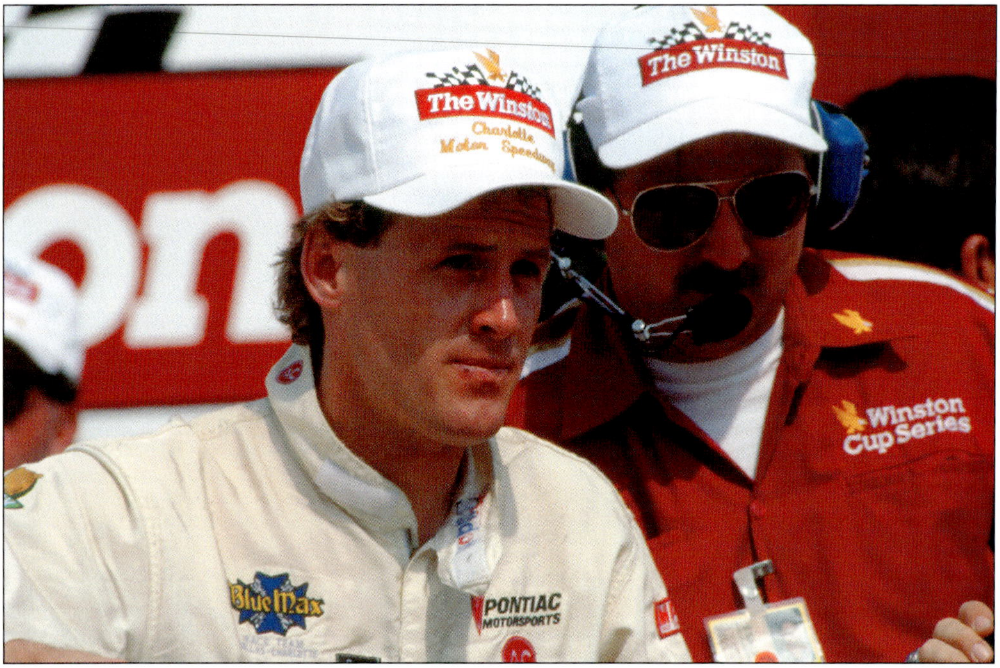

Rusty Wallace (above) claimed his all-star race victory in 1989, but it was his duel with Darrell Waltrip that remains in fans' memories. Below, the two men were racing for the lead with a little more than two miles remaining when contact between them sent Waltrip spinning off turn four and through the frontstretch's grassy apron. NASCAR put Waltrip at the rear of the field for the restart, and Wallace led the final two laps to defeat Ken Schrader. After the race, the men's crews scuffled briefly as Wallace drove to victory lane. It was Waltrip's remark after the race that became famous: "I hope he chokes on that $200,000." The incident removed the black hat persona from Waltrip. Years later, Waltrip, who was sponsored by Tide, said: "He put me in the spin cycle and I came out squeaky clean."

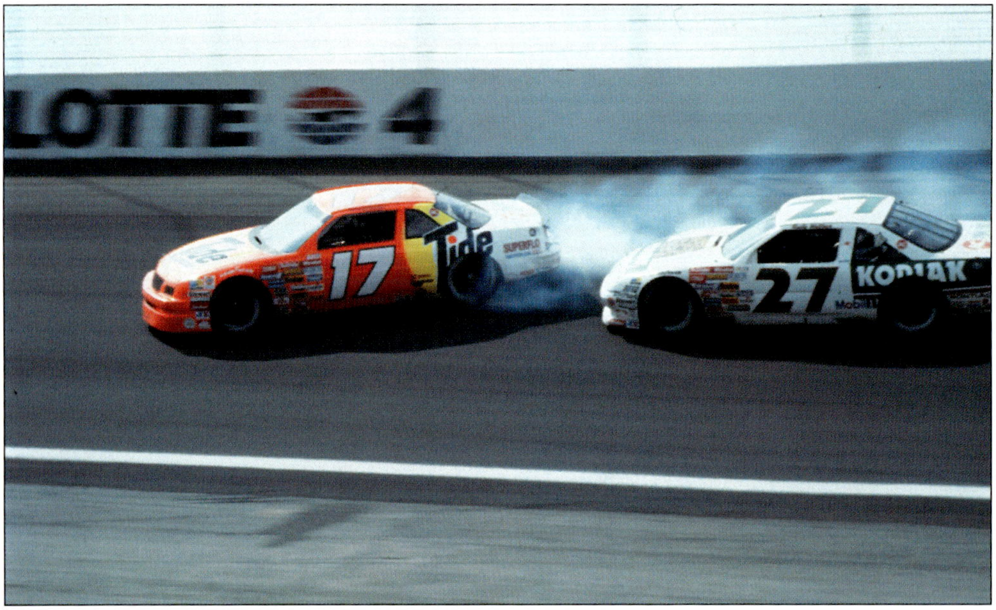

Four

Lights Change Everything

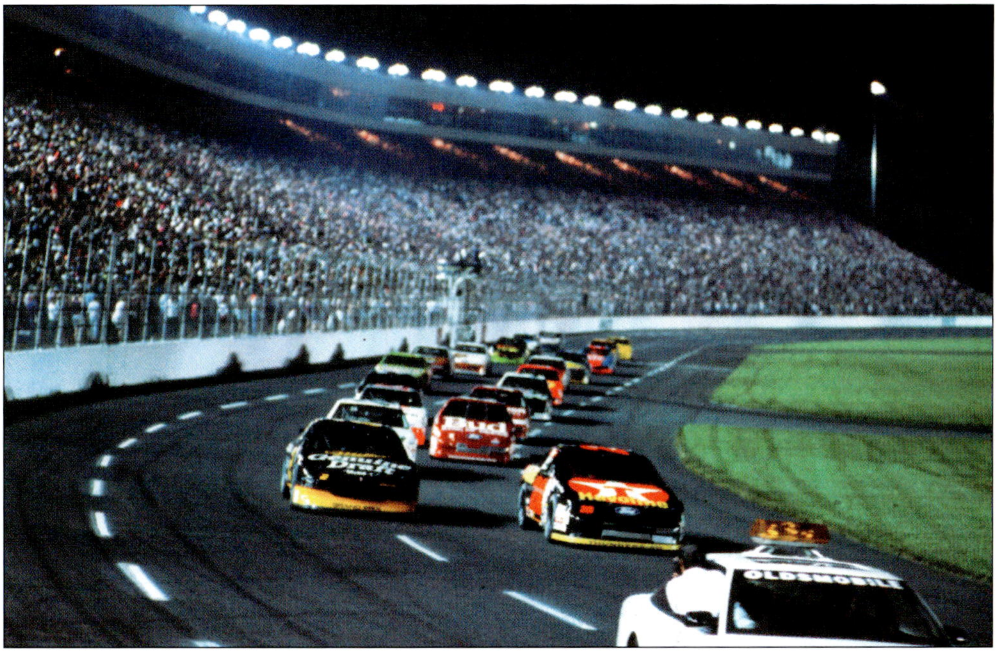

Charlotte Motor Speedway ushered in a new era in NASCAR when it installed lights, thus allowing night racing on superspeedways. Musco Lighting was given the task of developing and installing the lights—a $1.7 million project. The 1992 all-star race was the first one under the lights, and it was electrifying.

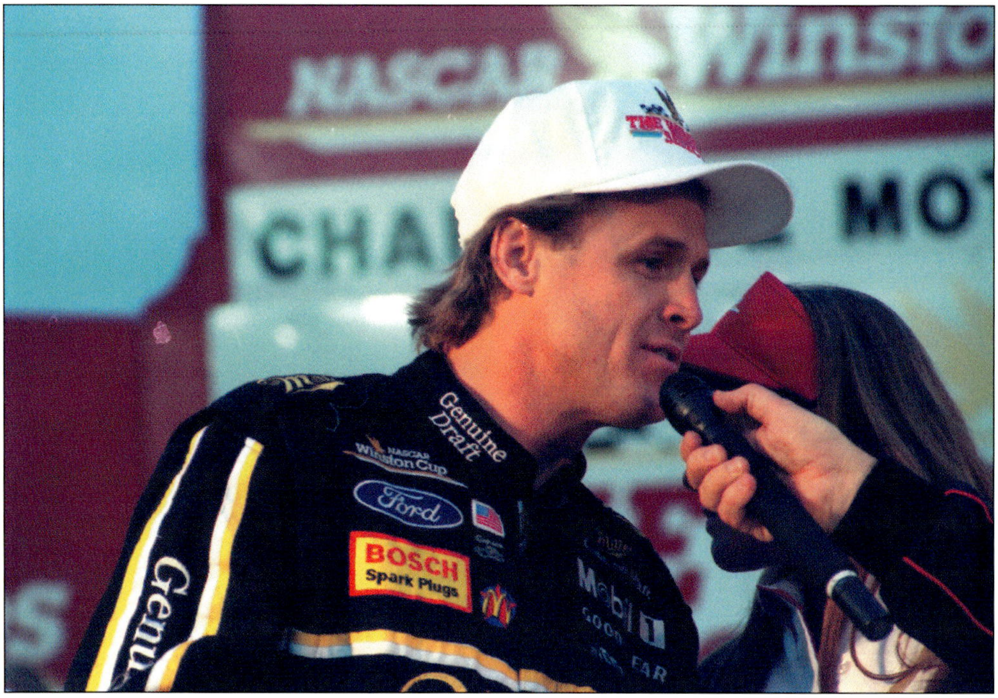

Rusty Wallace visited a familiar place at Charlotte Motor Speedway in May 1990—victory lane. The 1989 NASCAR premier series champion defeated Bill Elliott by less than a second in that edition of the Coca-Cola 600. The win was Wallace's final victory at the 1.5-mile speedway, where he recorded two wins in addition to the all-star race during his career.

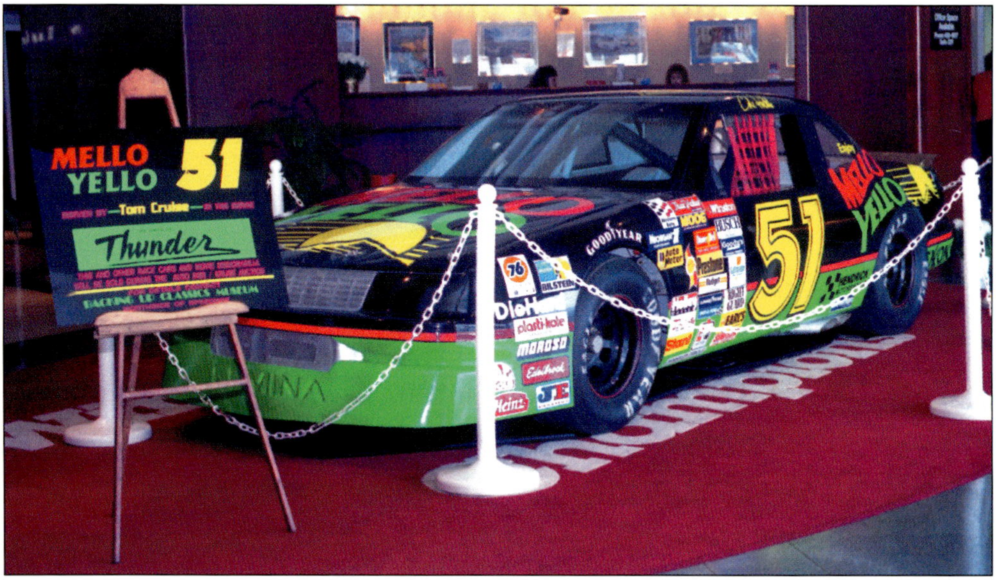

When Jerry Bruckheimer and Don Simpson decided to make the movie *Days of Thunder*, Charlotte Motor Speedway once again became a key filming locale. In fact, the scene where Harry Hogge (Robert Duvall) meets Cole Trickle (Tom Cruise) occurs at Charlotte. A private movie premier for the racing community was held at a South Charlotte theater. Cole Trickle's car was temporarily displayed at the track, near the ticket office and the souvenir shop.

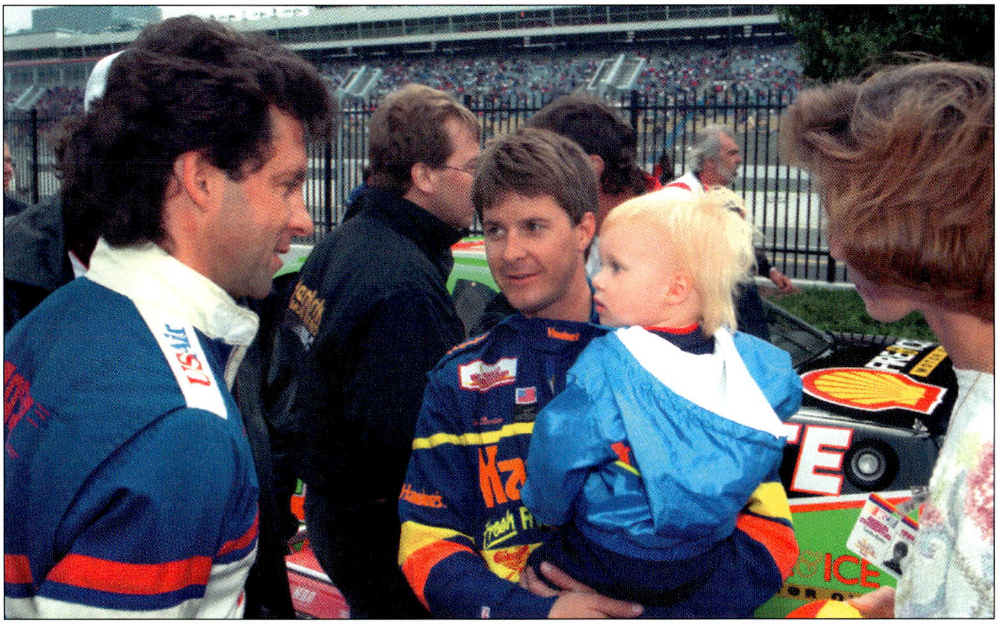

Jeb Burton was two years old when his father, Ward Burton (center), earned his first pole at Charlotte Motor Speedway. Burton secured the top starting position for the Mello Yello 500 with a lap of 185.759 miles per hour in just his second NASCAR premier series start at the 1.5-mile track. He accomplished the feat in a Chevrolet owned by Alan Dillard Jr. Greg Sacks (left) qualified 14th.

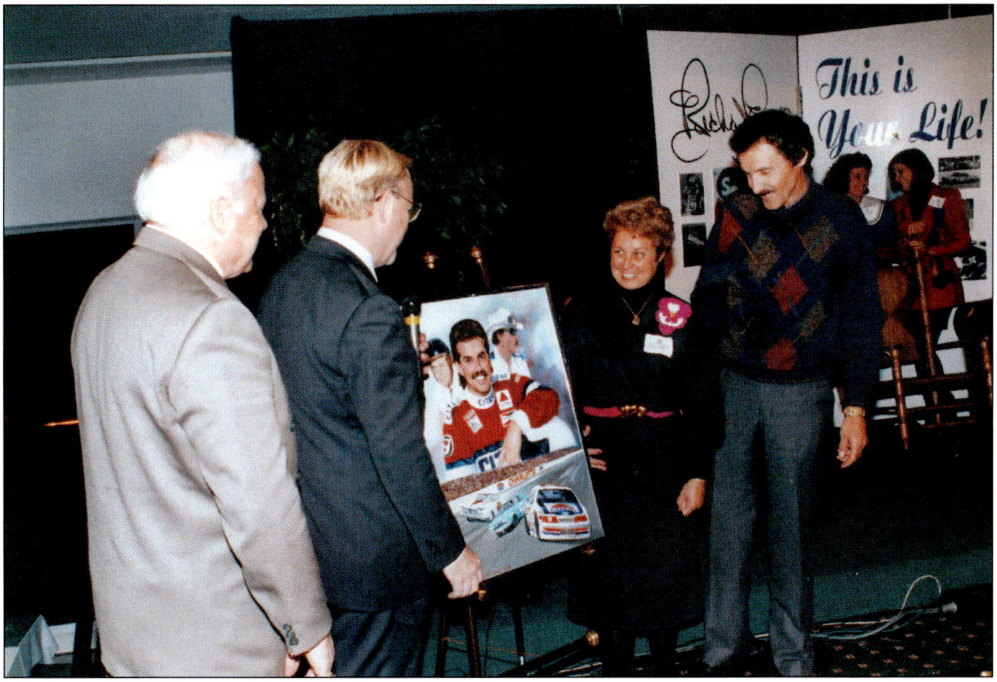

During Richard Petty's 1992 "Farewell Tour," the Speedway Club hosted a "This Is Your Life" evening for the seven-time NASCAR champion. A painting of three generations of drivers from the Petty family was presented to Richard Petty (right) and his wife, Lynda, by speedway executives Bruton Smith (left) and H.A. "Humpy" Wheeler.

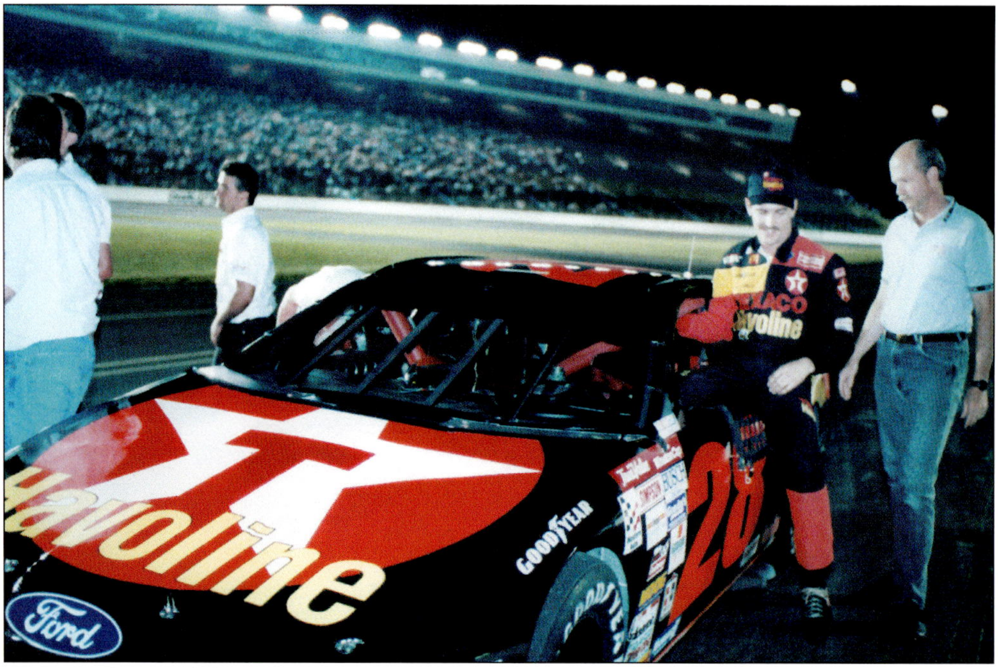

A two-night test of the speedway's new lighting system resulted in Davey Allison walking off with a $1,000 bonus. Musco Lighting, which designed and installed the system, provided the money to the driver producing the quickest lap in the bonus money run. Of the drivers who participated in the second night of practice, Darrell Waltrip was the only other one who made an attempt at the bonus money.

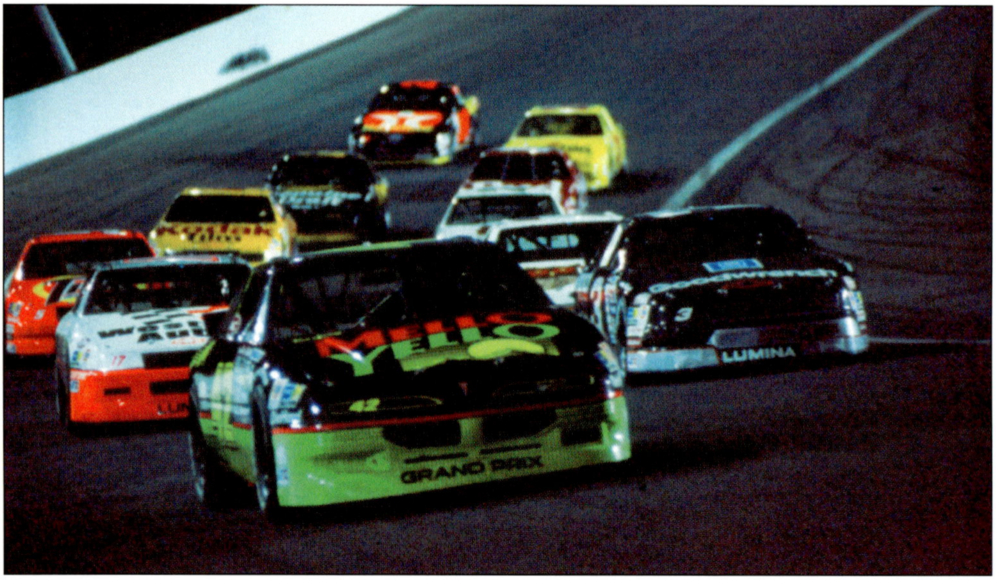

Charlotte Motor Speedway promoted the 1992 all-star race as "One Hot Night," and it lived up to its billing. On the final lap, it appeared Dale Earnhardt (No. 3) was headed for another all-star victory. That changed, however, in turn three when he spun and handed the lead to Kyle Petty (No. 42). It changed again as Petty and Davey Allison banged sheet metal in their charge to the checkered flag. Allison emerged the winner.

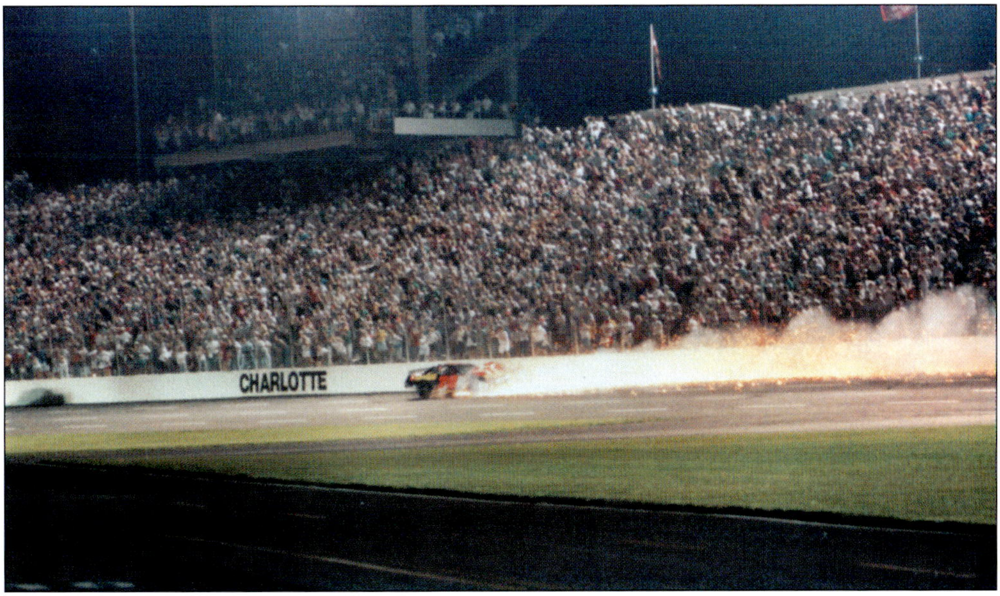

Davey Allison never got to celebrate his 1992 all-star victory. Just as he edged Kyle Petty at the checkered flag, the two cars banged together, and Allison's Ford spun, slamming into the concrete wall on the driver's side. Allison was knocked unconscious and did not know he had won until team owner Robert Yates and crew chief Larry McReynolds told him. He suffered a concussion, bruised lung, and bruised legs.

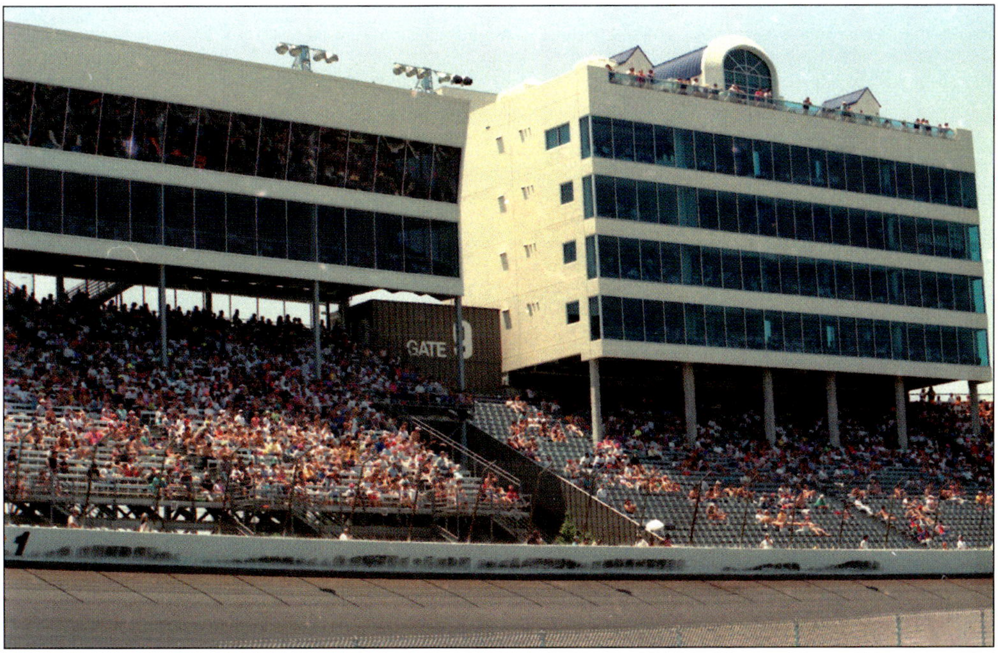

A second condominium building was added between the speedway's first and second turns in the early 1990s. Named the First Turn Condominiums, their initial price ranged from $375,000 to $500,000. They were more luxurious and larger than those in the first 40-unit complex. Ranging in size from 1,300 to 1,500 square feet, each condominium featured two baths, two bedrooms, a kitchen, and a living area with a seating section for 18 people.

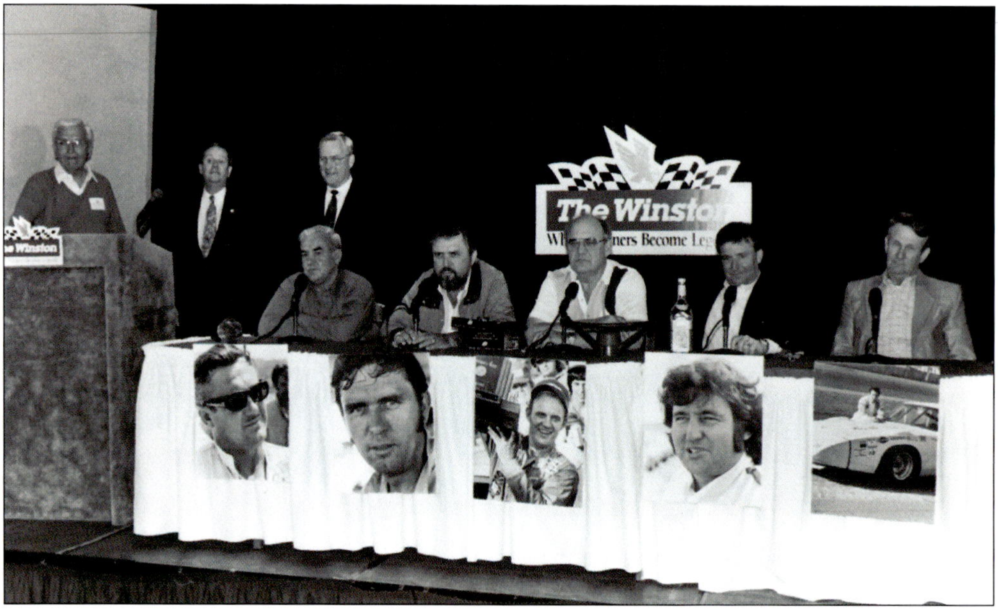

RJR celebrated its 20th anniversary in NASCAR by creating the Winston Legends race in 1991. The event, which honored the retired drivers who helped build the sport, was held on the speedway's quarter-mile track during all-star weekend. Twenty-two drivers from the sport's first three decades raced cars painted and decaled to resemble the ones in which they competed. The cars were supplied by NASCAR premier series teams. Elmo Langley won the 30-lap race. Above, attending the press conference announcing the event are, from left to right, Tim Flock, RJR's T. Wayne Robertson, H.A. "Humpy" Wheeler, Langley, Dick Brooks, Benny Parsons, Richard Childress, and Neil Castles. A few years after the event, Charlotte Motor Speedway executives created Legend cars (below), which raced on the quarter-mile track every Tuesday night from June to August.

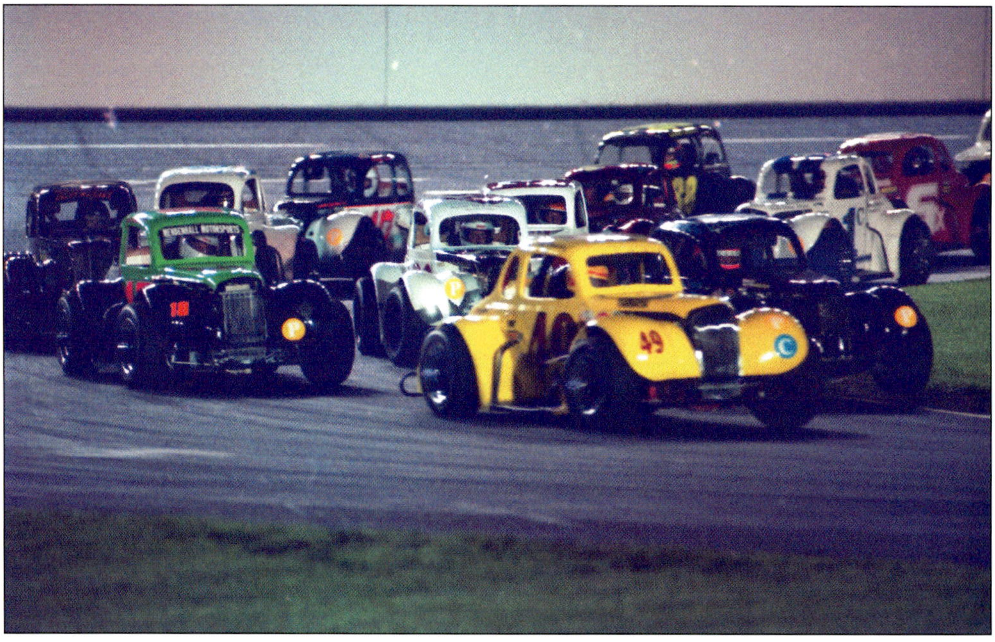

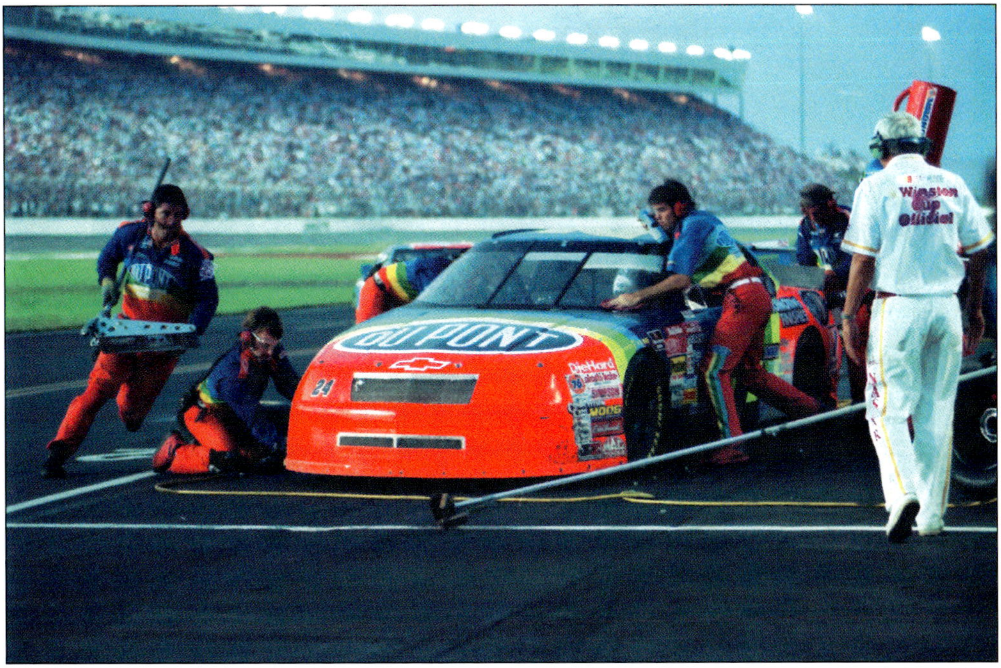

A 22-year-old Jeff Gordon stunned the motorsports community in May 1994 when he won his first NASCAR premier series race—the Coca-Cola 600—in just his second full-time season. When it came time for the final pit stops in the race, all of the drivers received four fresh tires except for Gordon. Crew chief Ray Evernham made the decision to change only two tires. That maneuver returned Gordon to the track in second behind Ricky Rudd, who was attempting to win on fuel mileage. With nine laps remaining, Rudd had to pit for fuel, and Gordon inherited the lead. Rusty Wallace attempted to catch him but fell 3.91 seconds short. Speedway owner Bruton Smith (below, left) joined the emotional Gordon in victory lane. Gordon wept as he received a congratulatory hug from his mother, Carol Bickford.

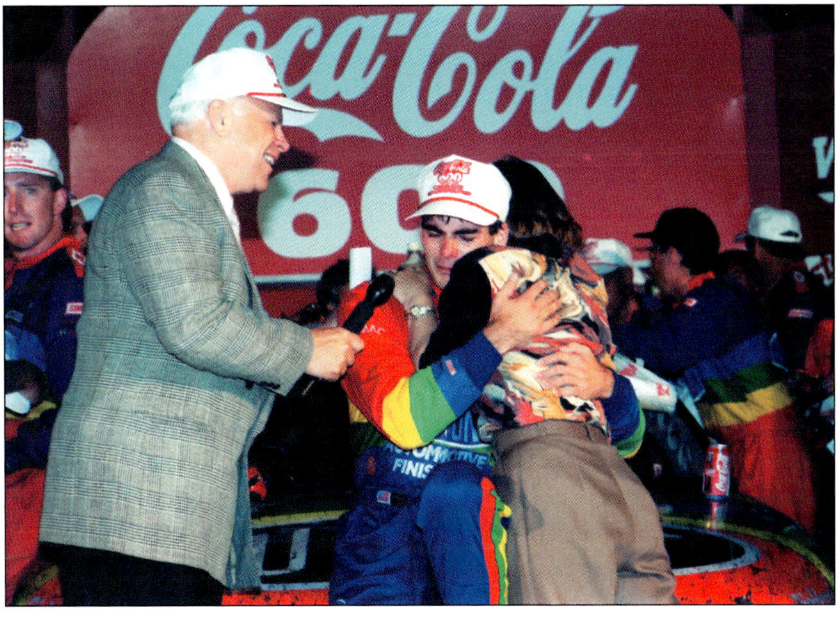

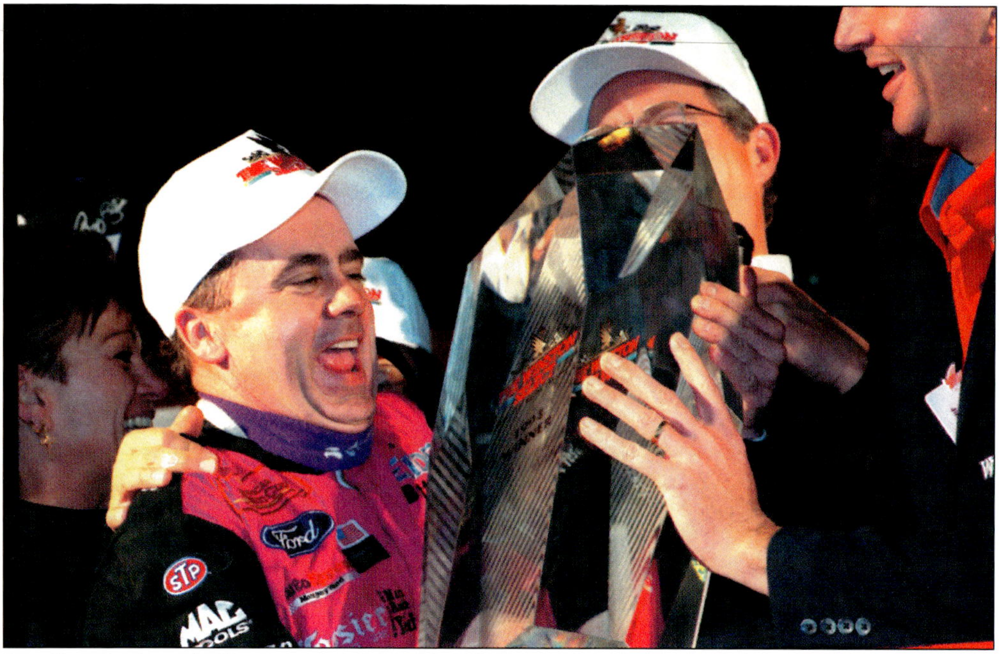

Geoffrey Bodine (left) was ecstatic after winning the 1994 all-star race with the team he had purchased from Alan Kulwicki's estate following the 1992 NASCAR champion's death in an April 1, 1993, plane crash. Bodine used Hoosier tires instead of Goodyear on the car, which was under development at the time of Kulwicki's death. The Chemung, New York, native edged Sterling Marlin for the win by less than half a second.

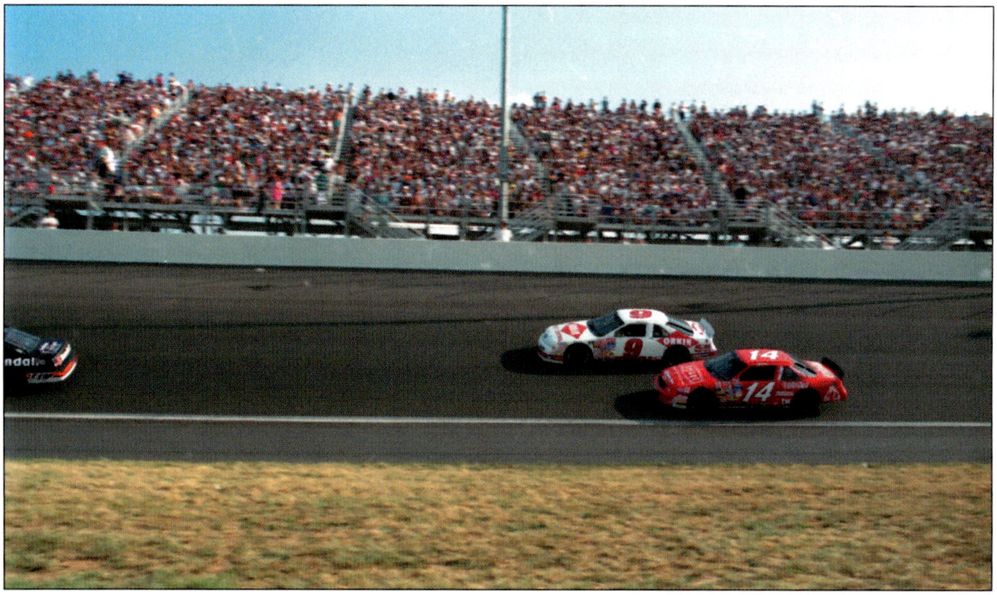

In 1994, John Andretti (No. 14) became the first NASCAR driver to attempt the Charlotte-Indianapolis double. In earlier decades, the two races were held on different days, but because of the federal government's restructuring of Memorial Day weekend, the Coca-Cola 600 and Indianapolis 500 were now on the same day. Andretti finished 10th in the Indianapolis 500 and 36th in the Coca-Cola 600. In this photograph, Andretti is racing Rich Bickle (No. 9).

On the walkway leading to the Smith Tower is the Walk of Legends. Similar to the Hollywood Walk of Fame, competitors who have excelled at the speedway place their handprints and footprints in cement for future generations. Joe Lee Johnson (kneeling), winner of the inaugural World 600, was one of the first to join the Walk of Legends.

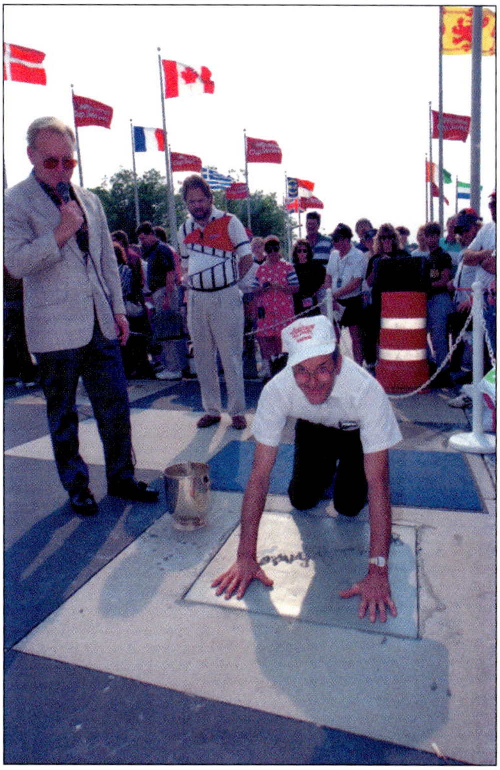

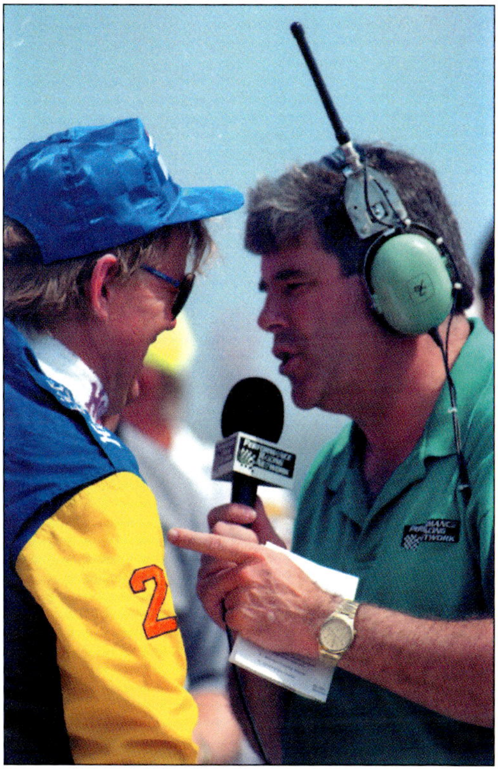

Speedway Motorsports Incorporated's Performance Racing Network (PRN) expanded in the 1990s as SMI built and acquired racetracks. With Doug Rice at the helm, PRN is one of two NASCAR licensed multi-broadcast radio networks that produce, market, and distribute programming year-round. PRN's state-of-the-art studio is attached to the Smith Tower and located to the left of the building's entrance.

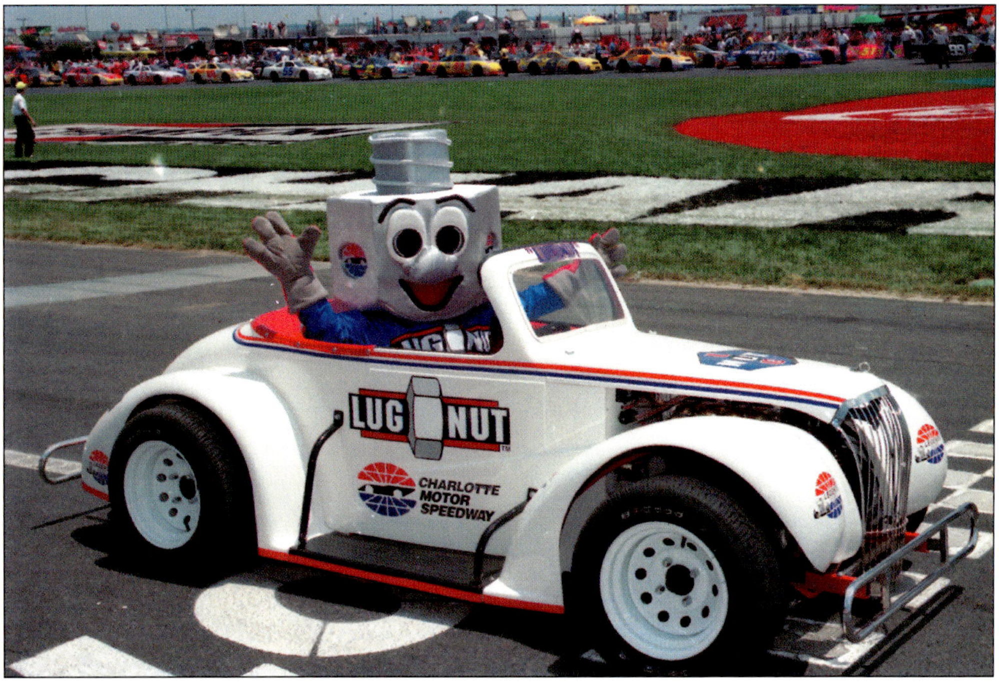

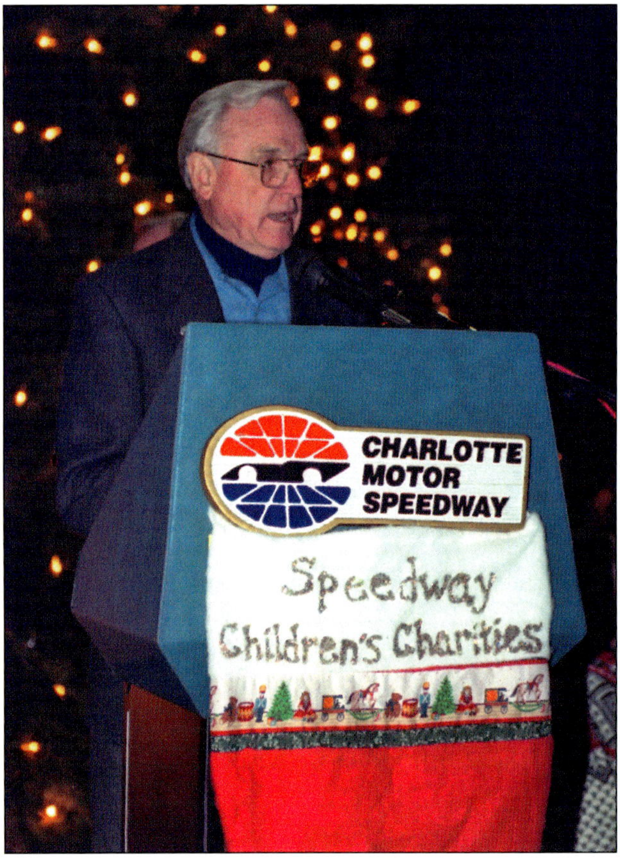

Charlotte Motor Speedway executives decided in the 1990s that the track needed a mascot, and Lug Nut was born. The mascot's popularity has grown through the years, especially with the children. He is always present on race weekends, appearing at the Play Zone and driving his personal vehicle. Since Lug Nut's creation, other Speedway Motorsports Incorporated tracks have created a mascot.

After Gen. Tom Sadler retired from the Air Force, Bruton Smith recruited him to oversee the Speedway Children's Charities. Each year in early December, a Christmas tree is lit at the Smith Tower entrance, and grants are distributed to local organizations on behalf of Speedway Children's Charities. The grants are designed to assist nonprofit charities, making a direct and significant impact on the lives of needy children.

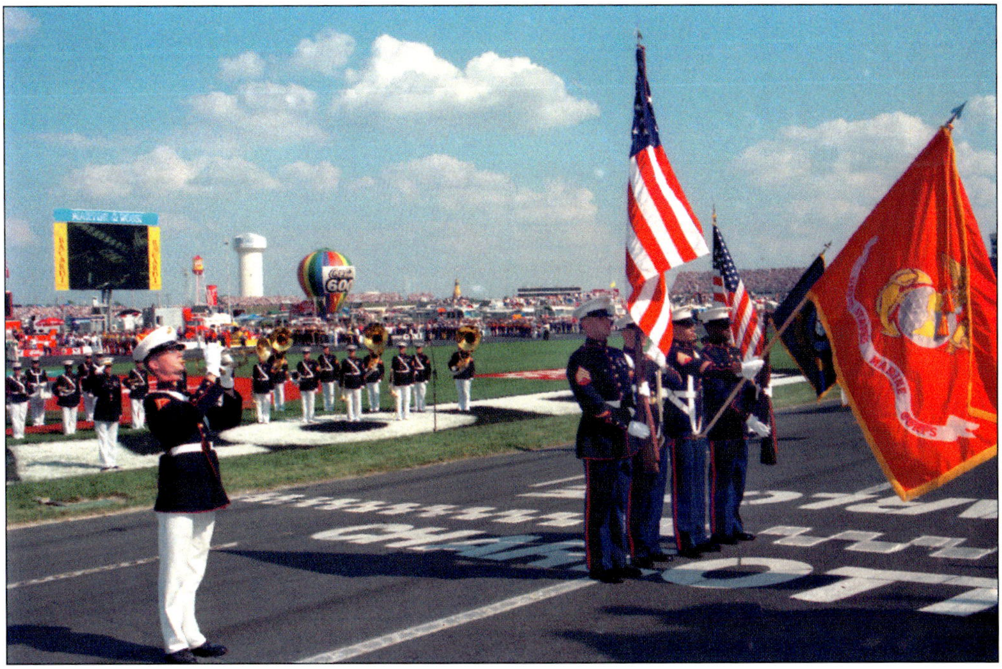

After the invasion of Grenada was reenacted for one of the speedway's prerace shows, the track began moving more towards honoring the military before each Coca-Cola 600. Today, a military prerace show is status quo for the Coca-Cola 600, and military personnel and their families are often hosted by organizations or the track. The speedway has also had a program where a race ticket could be purchased for someone in the military.

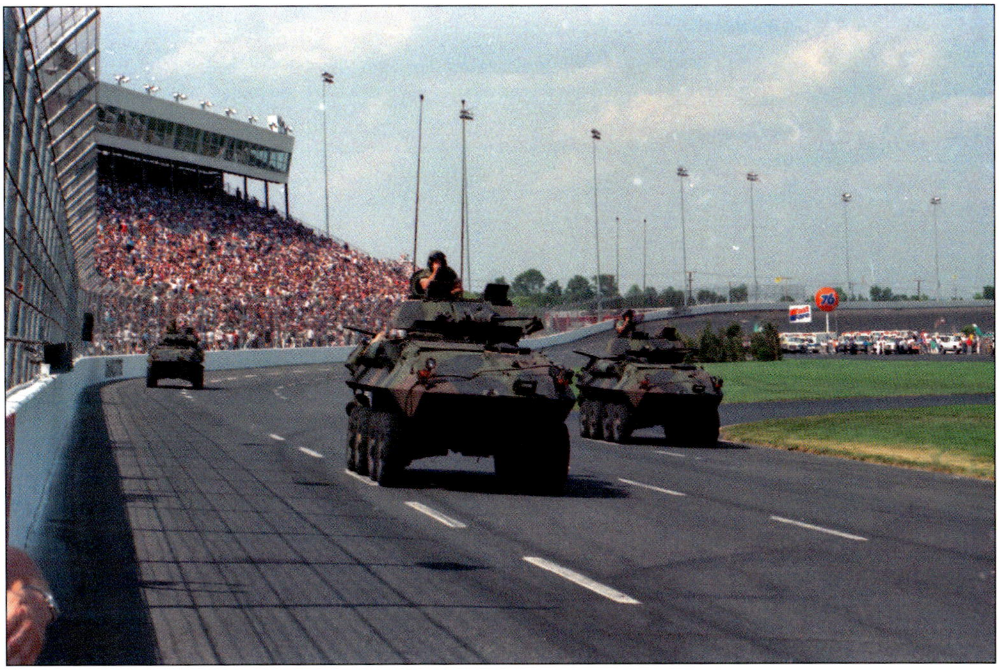

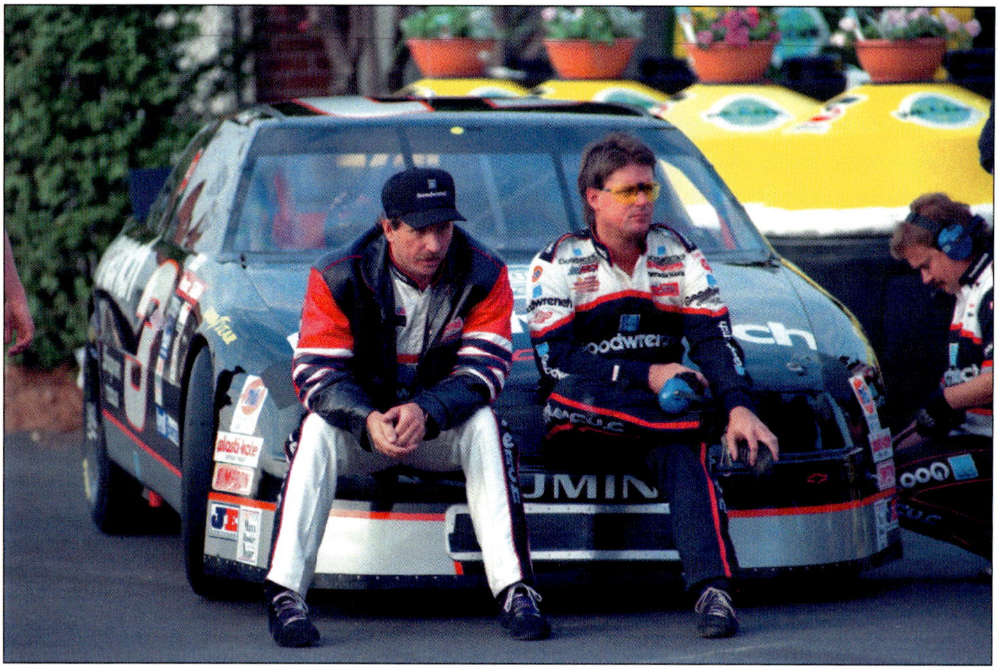

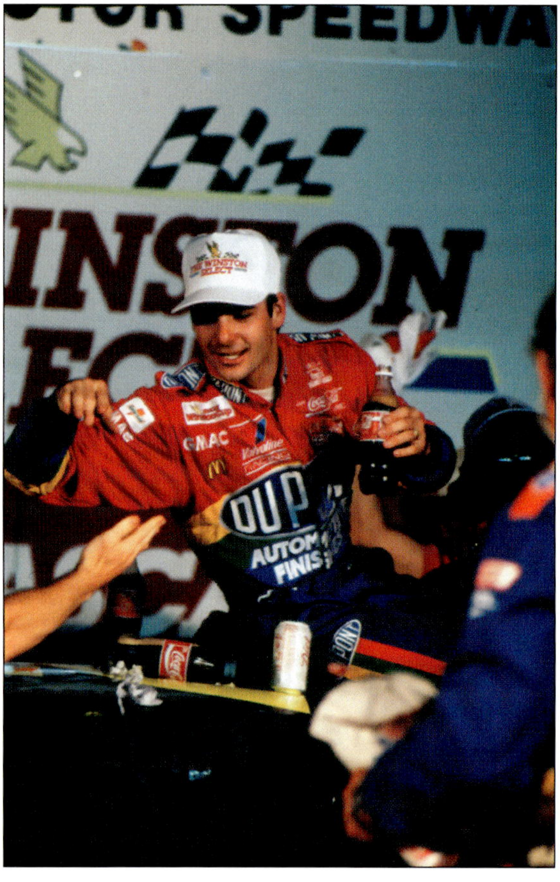

Dale Earnhardt (left) and crew chief Andy Petree (right) enjoyed only one Charlotte point race victory together—the 1993 Coca-Cola 600. In that race, Earnhardt finished 3.73 seconds ahead of Jeff Gordon, whom he nicknamed "The Kid." The victory was Earnhardt's fifth—and last—in 48 starts at Charlotte Motor Speedway.

Jeff Gordon's first victory in the NASCAR All-Star Race came in 1995. Gordon easily captured the win, cruising to a 1.07-second victory over Sterling Marlin. Darrell Waltrip and Dale Earnhardt knocked each other out of the race while battling for the lead with 10 laps remaining. They were exiting turn four when they got into each other and the wall. While they were crashing, Gordon shot to the inside and passed them.

Laptops became just as common as wrenches in the NASCAR garage during the 1990s. Terry Labonte (center) studies data along with his crew chief Gary DeHart (second from right) and head engine builder Randy Dorton (right). Labonte won the 1999 NASCAR All-Star Race in a Hendrick Motorsports Chevrolet, defeating Tony Stewart by 1.229 seconds. It was Labonte's second victory in the special event.

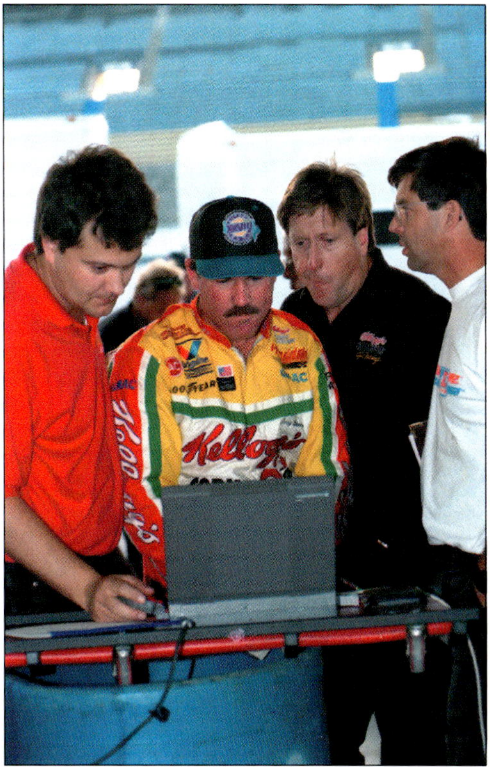

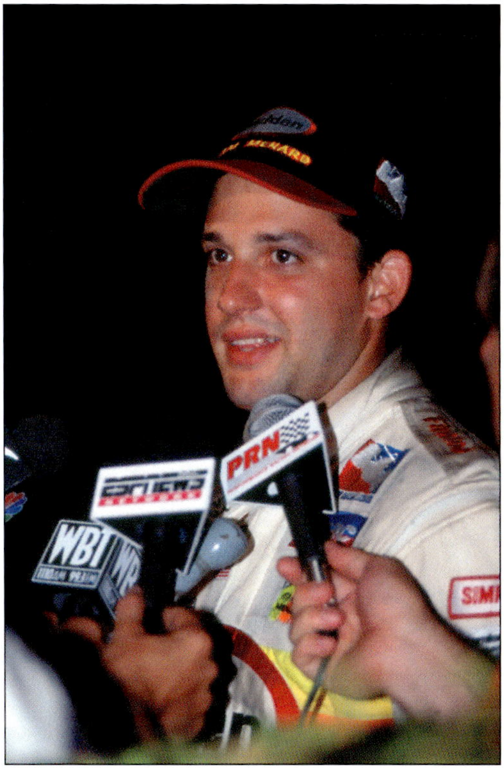

Tony Stewart won the pole for the first two IndyCar races held at Charlotte. When the Indy Racing League made its initial visit to the track in 1997, Stewart posted a 217.164-mile-per-hour lap to earn the pole for the Visionaire 500. He finished seventh in that race. The following year, he claimed the pole for the Visionaire 500K with a 220.498-mile-per-hour lap. Stewart placed 21st in that event.

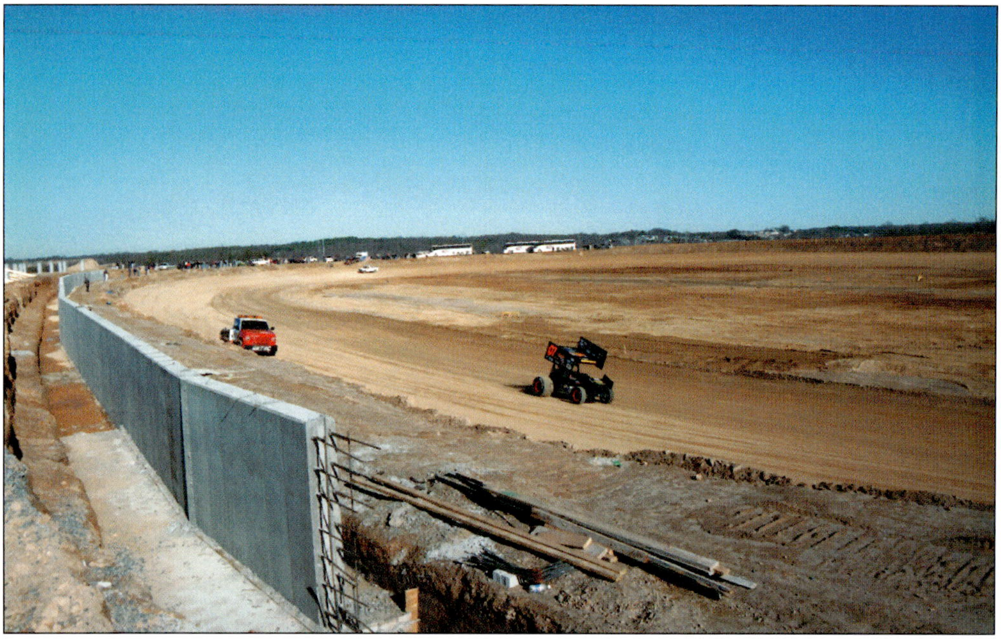

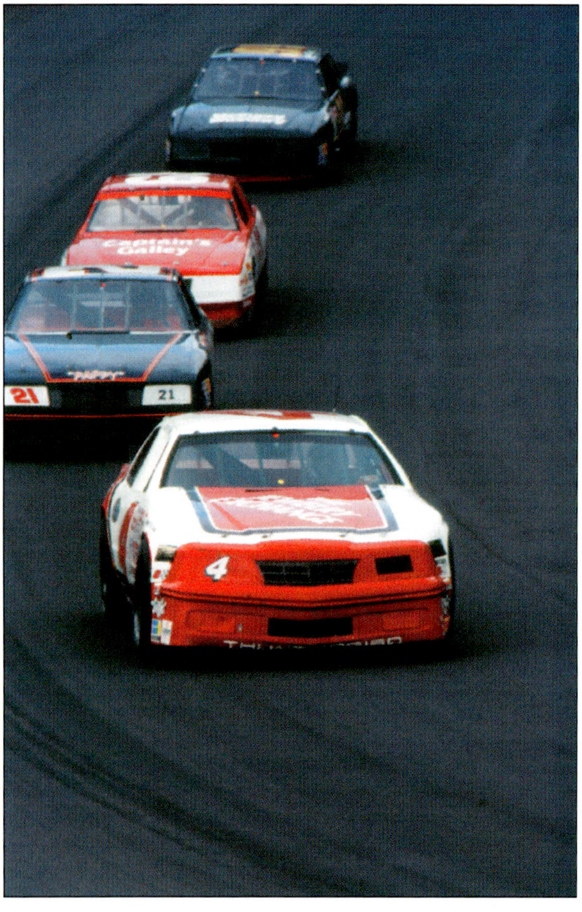

A half-mile dirt track was added to Charlotte Motor Speedway's inventory in the late 1990s. Since its construction, it has hosted various events. Some have been stand-alone, while others have been in conjunction with a NASCAR weekend. One of the most popular is the World of Outlaws World Championships, which is always held before a sold-out grandstand.

In an effort to help drivers get superspeedway experience and provide a place for discarded NASCAR Cup cars to find a home, Charlotte created the Sportsman division. Races for the series were usually scheduled on pole-qualifying day for NASCAR's premier series. However, several issues developed, and the series was discontinued.

Michael Waltrip, driving for Wood Brothers, pulled off the biggest upset in all-star history when he won the 1996 event. Prior to that night, his only two victories since entering NASCAR's premier series full-time in 1986 had been in the Winston Open, a preliminary to the all-star race. The night he won the all-star race he squeaked into the event by narrowly edging Johnny Benson for fifth, the last transfer position in the preliminary race.

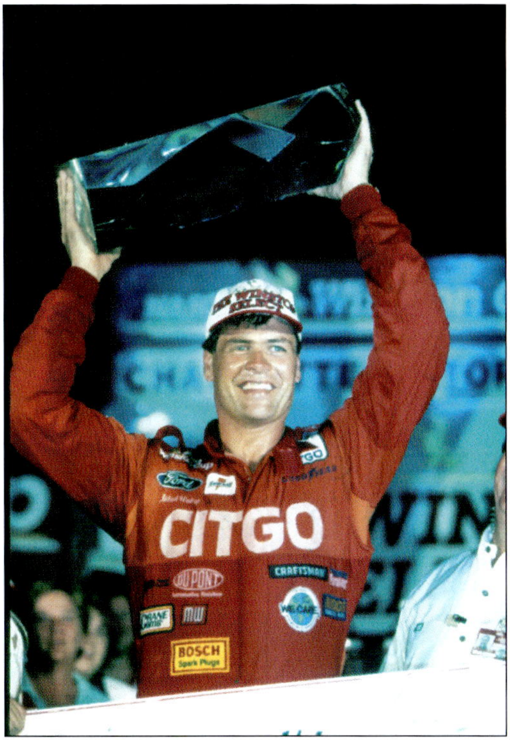

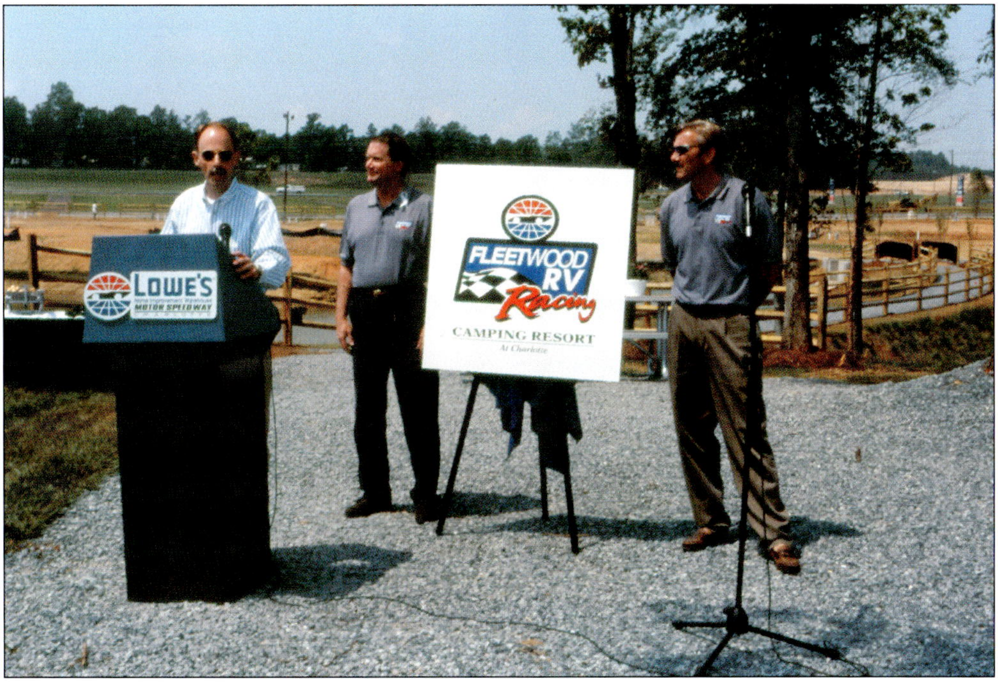

With the number of race fans camping on racetrack property growing each year, speedway officials decided to construct a year-round campground adjacent to the Tom Johnson Camping Center on Bruton Smith Boulevard. The campground is a short walk from zMAX Dragway and the Dirt Track at Charlotte and easily accessible from Charlotte Motor Speedway.

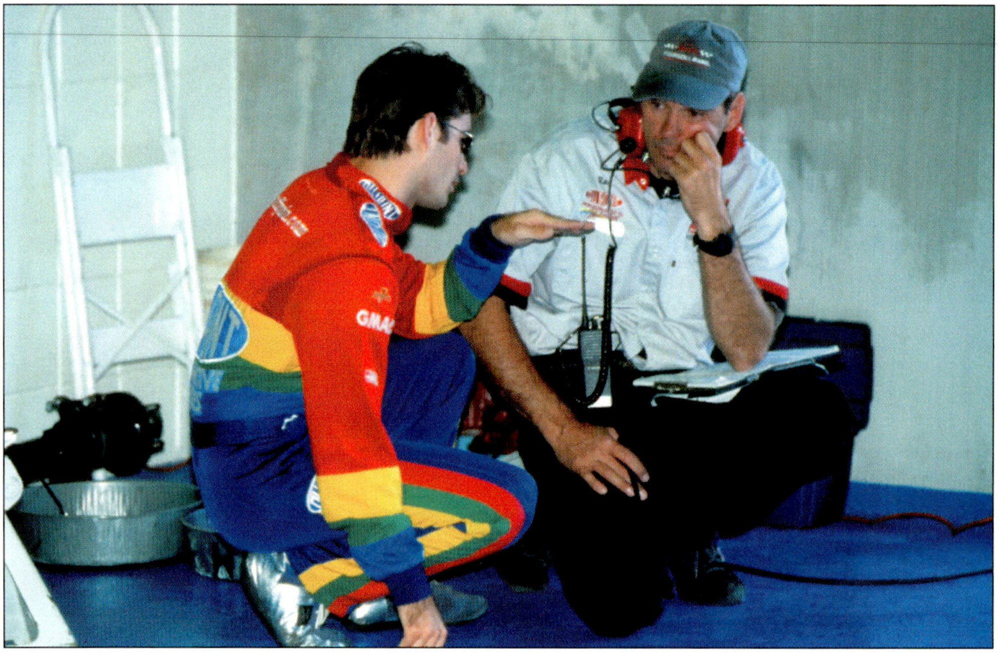

For the 1997 all-star race, Jeff Gordon (above, left) and crew chief Ray Evernham (above, right) brought a Chevrolet to the Charlotte track that became known as T-Rex (below). Gordon collected his second all-star victory with the car, but Evernham had a great deal of new technology on it that was not covered in the NASCAR rule book. After examining it, NASCAR officials told Evernham never to bring the car to the track again.

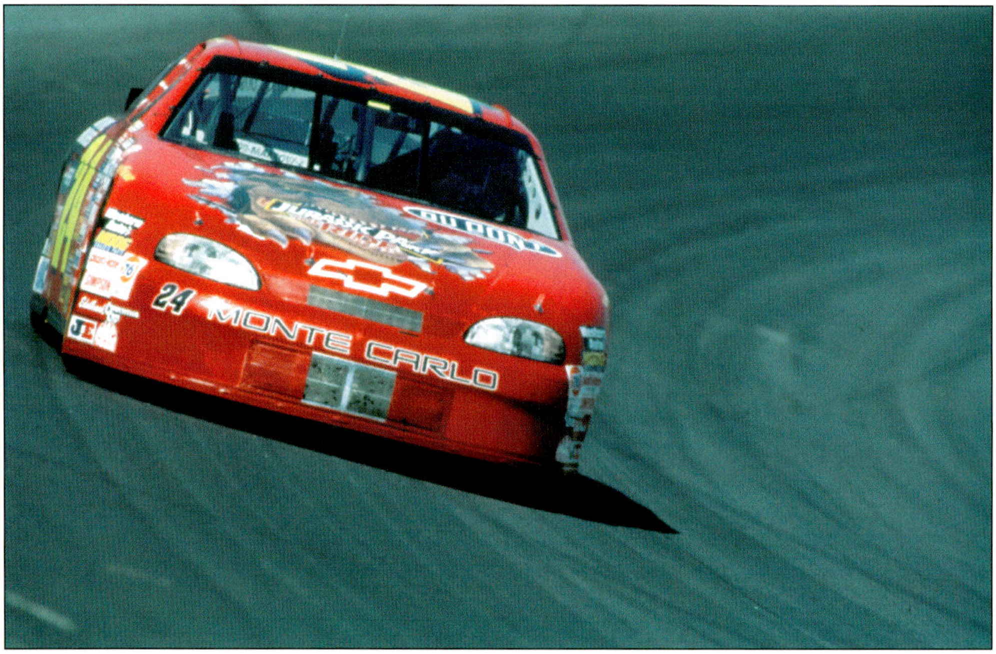

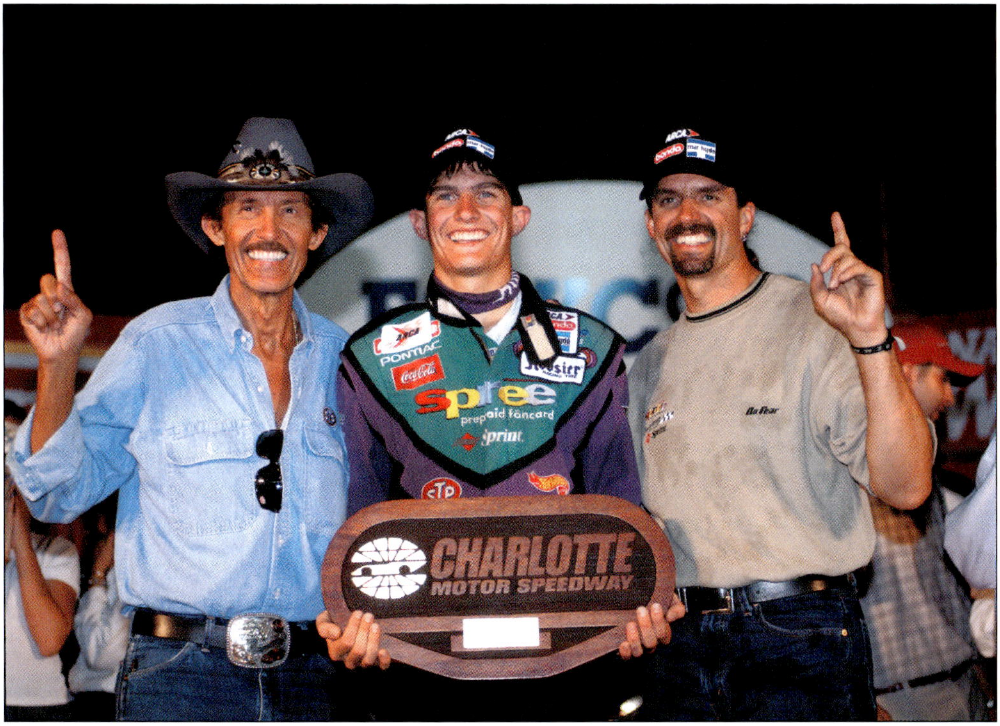

On September 30, 1998, Adam Petty (above, center) got to celebrate his victory in the ARCA EasyCare Certified 100 with his grandfather Richard Petty (left) and his father, Kyle Petty (right). Adam's victory made him the fourth-generation Petty to win a stock car race. To emerge victorious in the event, the 18-year-old Petty had to defeat veteran Mike Wallace, a feat he accomplished by 0.100 second.

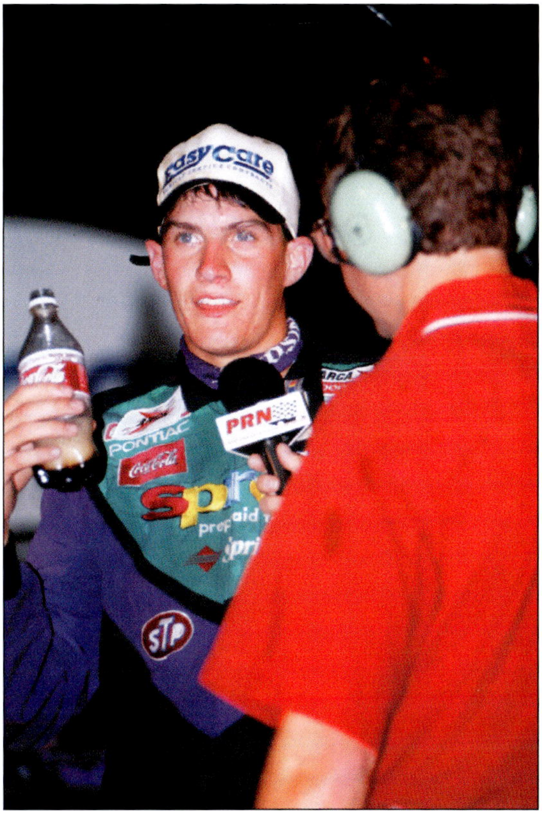

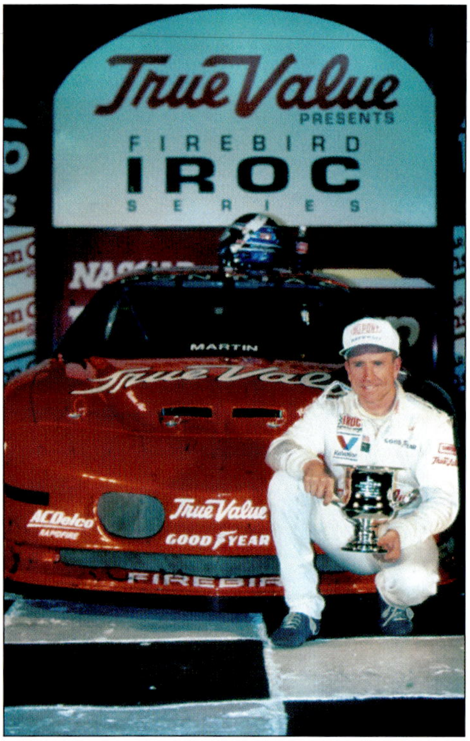

Charlotte was one of four tracks that hosted the International Race of Champions in 1996 and 1997, and it proved to be very beneficial for Mark Martin. The Batesville, Arkansas, native won both Charlotte IROC races en route to two of his five IROC championships. Charlotte was the third of the four races in 1996 and the second in 1997.

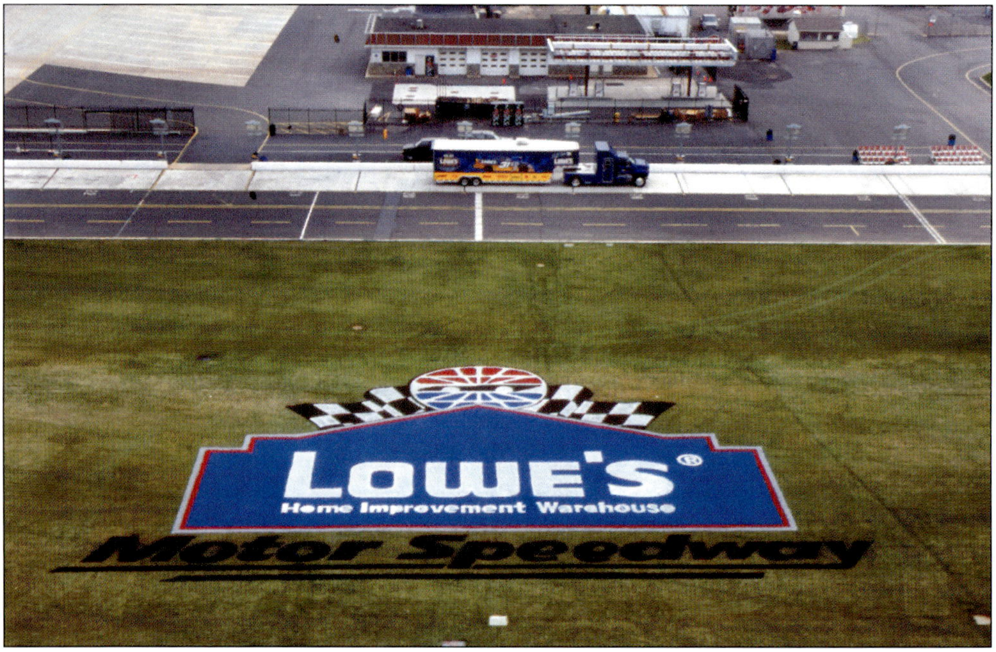

Speedway owner Bruton Smith surprised the racing community in 1999 when he announced a 10-year naming rights deal with Lowe's Home Improvement Warehouse. The track that had been known for 40 years as Charlotte Motor Speedway would now carry the name Lowe's Motor Speedway. Smith's deal, however, did not set a new trend in the sport. Only one other track sold its naming rights to a corporation and that was Smith's Sonoma Raceway.

Five

A Changing of the Guard

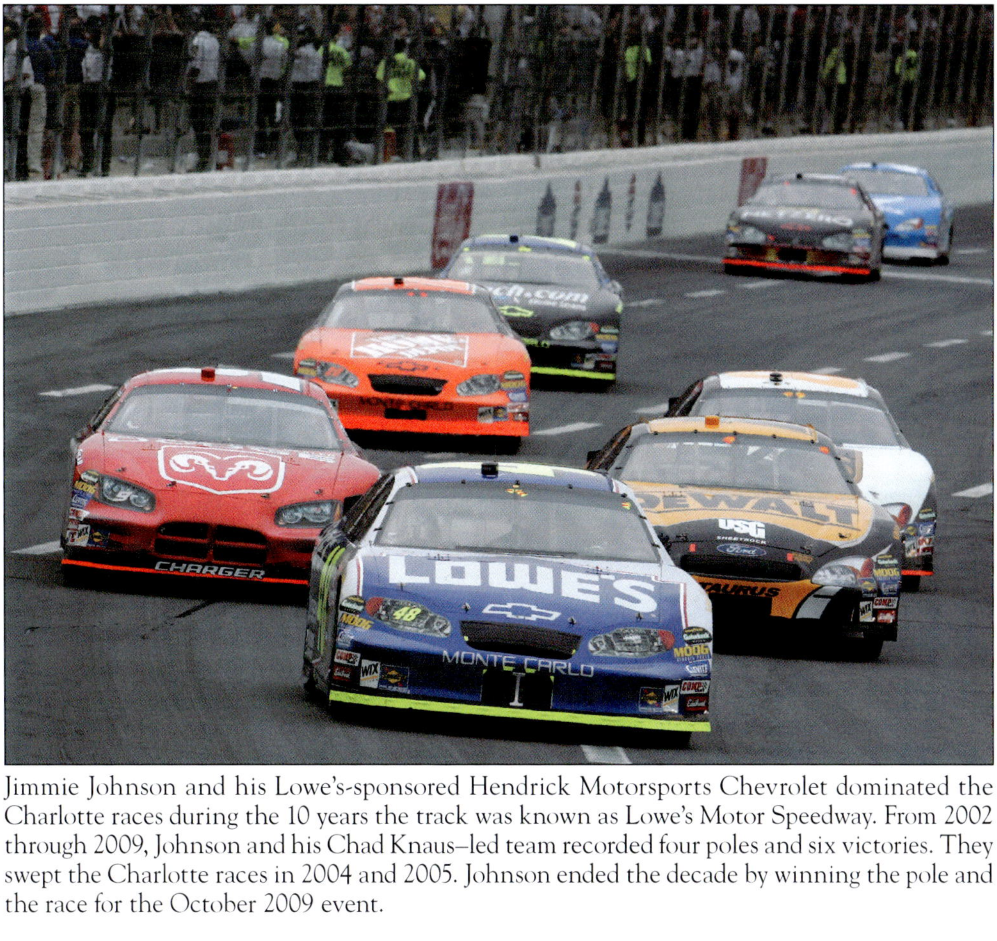

Jimmie Johnson and his Lowe's-sponsored Hendrick Motorsports Chevrolet dominated the Charlotte races during the 10 years the track was known as Lowe's Motor Speedway. From 2002 through 2009, Johnson and his Chad Knaus–led team recorded four poles and six victories. They swept the Charlotte races in 2004 and 2005. Johnson ended the decade by winning the pole and the race for the October 2009 event.

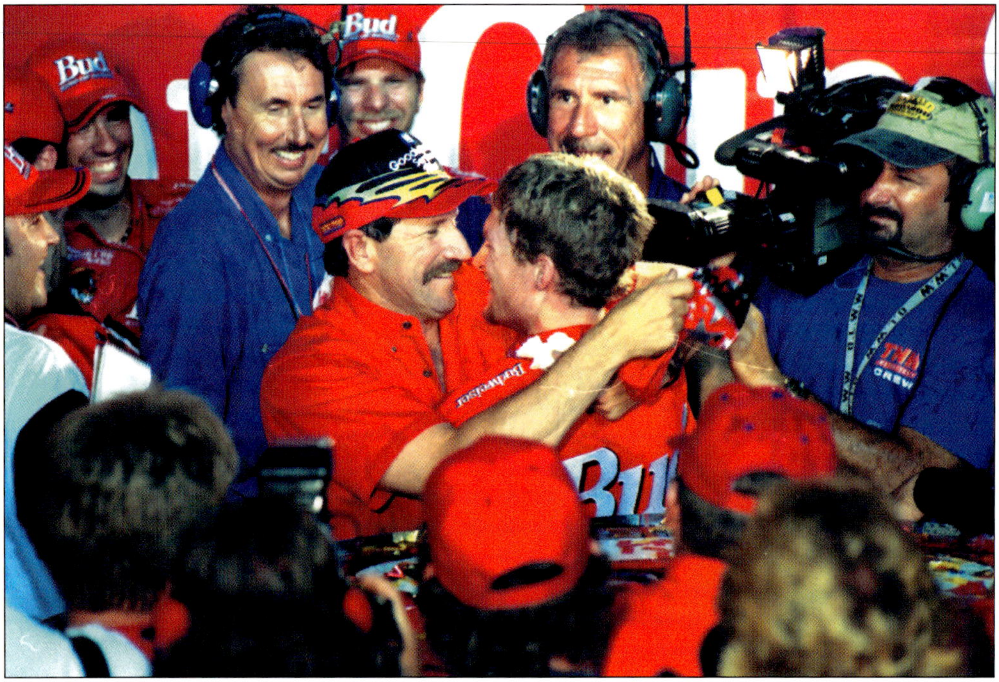

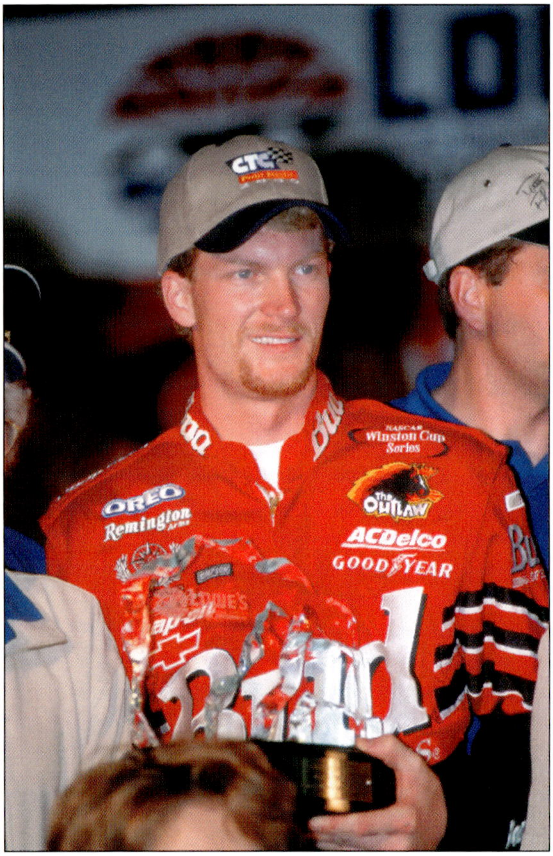

Dale Earnhardt Jr. (above, center right) became the first rookie to win the all-star race in 2000, and his father, Dale Earnhardt, could not have been more proud. After changing out of his driver's uniform, he rushed to victory lane and grabbed his younger son in one of his famous bear hugs. In the race, the younger Earnhardt snatched the lead from veteran Dale Jarrett with two laps remaining in the 70-lap event and held on for a 1.295-second victory. His father finished third in the race. At left, less than a week later, Dale Earnhardt Jr. earned the pole for the Coca-Cola 600 with a speed of 186.034 miles per hour.

Matt Kenseth recorded his first-ever victory in NASCAR's premier series in the 2000 Coca-Cola 600. Driving a Ford fielded by Jack Roush, the 28-year-old Kenseth acquired the victory in his first full-time season in the series. Pit stop strategy during a caution period that began with 40 laps remaining provided Kenseth with the opportunity he needed to challenge for the victory. He took the win by a half second over Bobby Labonte.

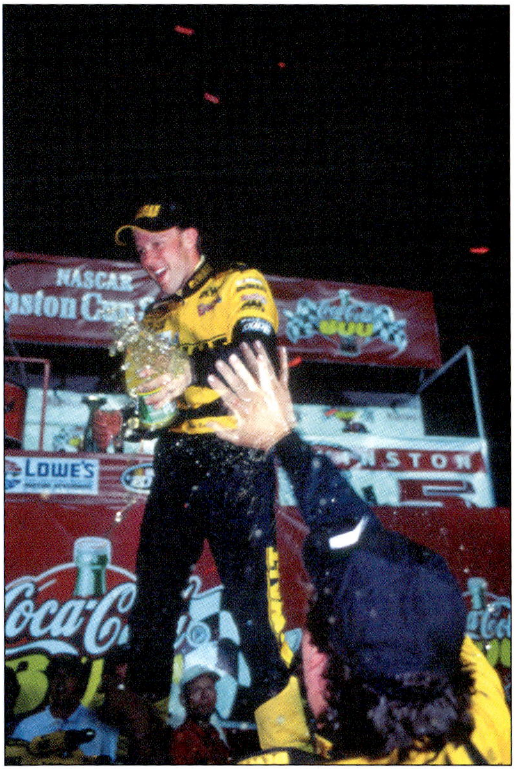

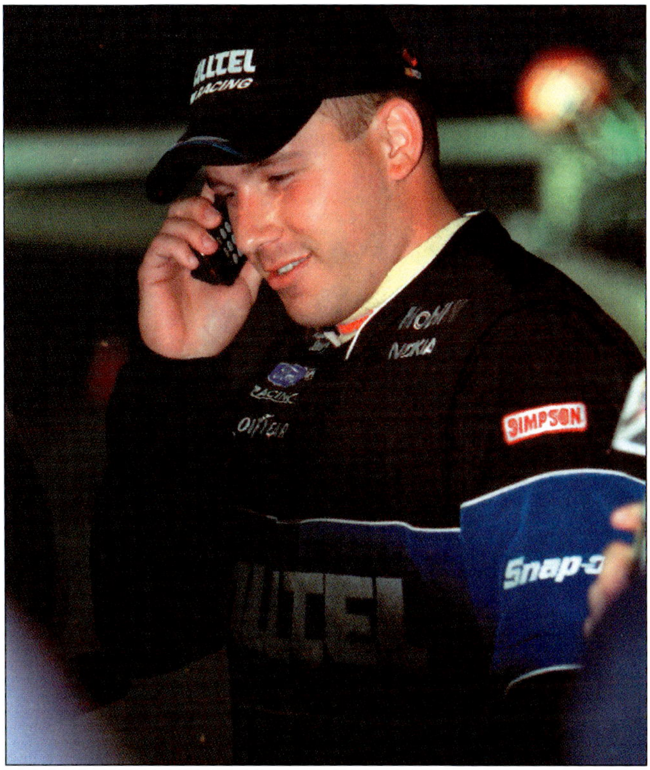

Ryan Newman earned his first-ever pole in NASCAR's premier series during qualifying for the 2001 Coca-Cola 600. That year, the 23-year-old Newman was driving a part-time series schedule for Roger Penske. In 2002, he moved into a full-time role for Penske and went on to capture seven more Charlotte poles during the 21st century's first decade. Newman also won the 2002 all-star race, making him the second rookie to accomplish that feat.

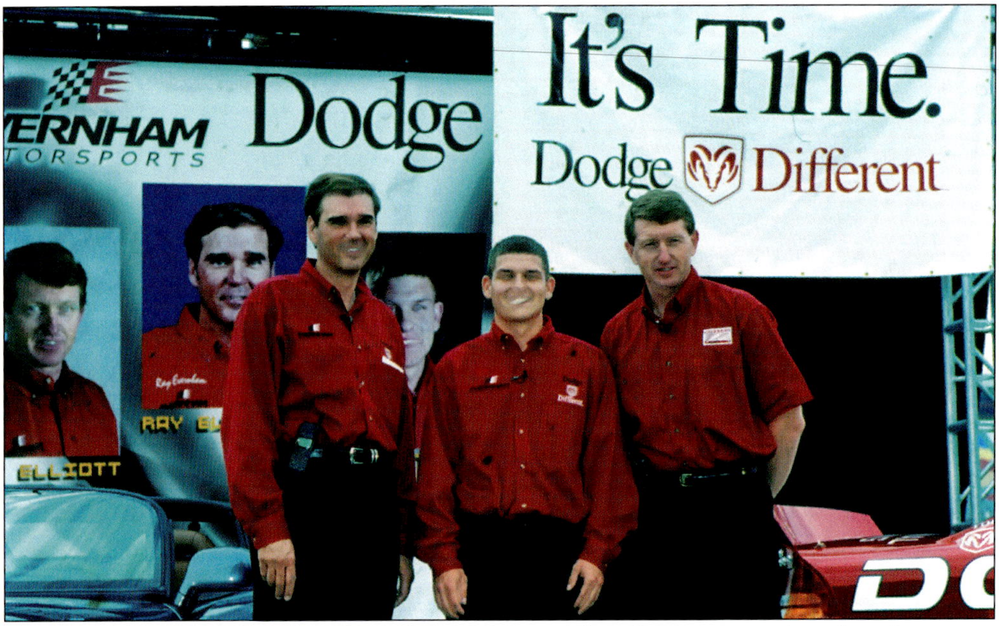

Charlotte Motor Speedway has always been a favorite place for race teams based in the area to hold press conferences. Ray Evernham (left) used the track's victory lane area as the locale for his press conference announcing the drivers for his new Dodge team—Casey Atwood (center) and Bill Elliott (right). Dodge returned to NASCAR's premier series full-time in 2001 with Evernham Motorsports.

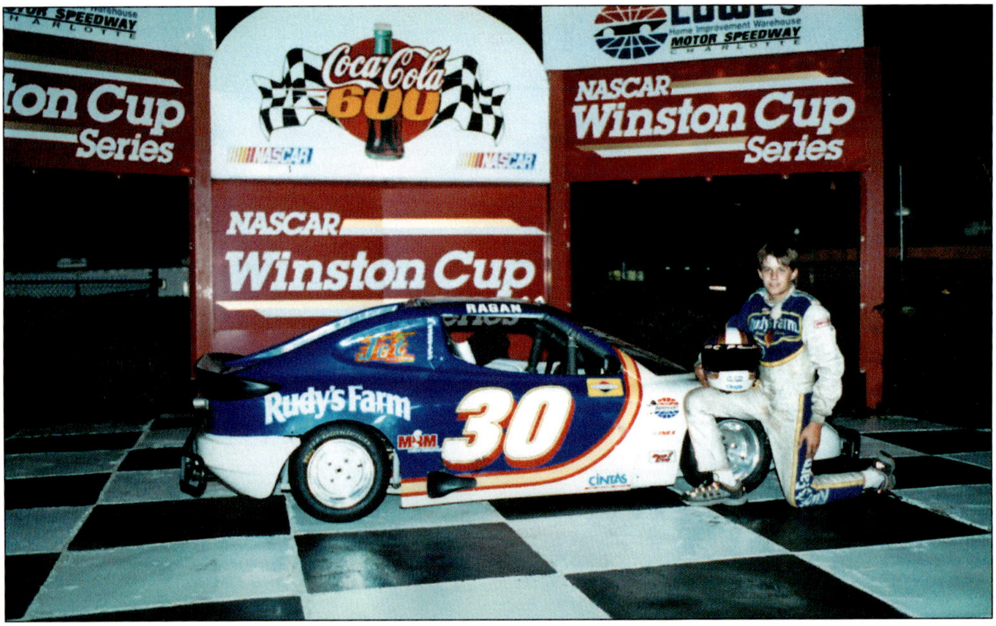

The Legend and Bandolero cars developed at U.S. Legend Cars International under the supervision of Charlotte executives became a popular way for families to introduce their children to racing at a manageable cost. NASCAR premier series driver David Ragan (pictured) was one of those who piloted a Bandolero early in his career. Other NASCAR drivers who have raced either Legend or Bandolero cars include Joey Logano, Chase Elliott, and Daniel Hemric.

Jeff Gordon captured his third and final all-star victory in 2001, but he accomplished the feat in an unusual manner. Just as the green flag waved, it began raining in turns one and two. The wet track caused a multicar crash that involved Gordon. NASCAR gave the drivers with damaged race cars 15 minutes to acquire their backup cars and prepare them to race. Using his backup car, Gordon defeated Dale Jarrett by less than a second.

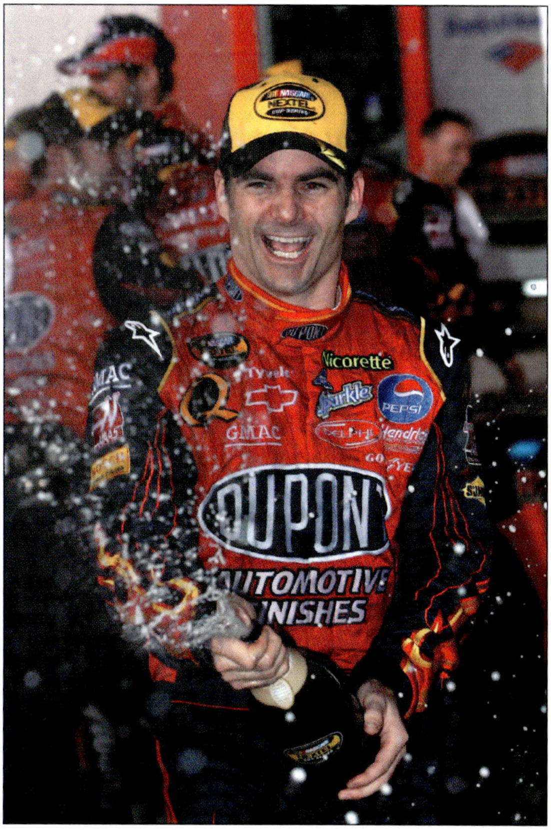

Jamie McMurray shocked the motorsports community in October 2002 when he won the UAW-GM Quality 500 in only his second race in NASCAR's premier series. McMurray was substituting for an injured Sterling Marlin and in only his second race with car owner Chip Ganassi when he secured his first-ever NASCAR victory. McMurray led the final 31 laps and defeated Bobby Labonte by less than a half second.

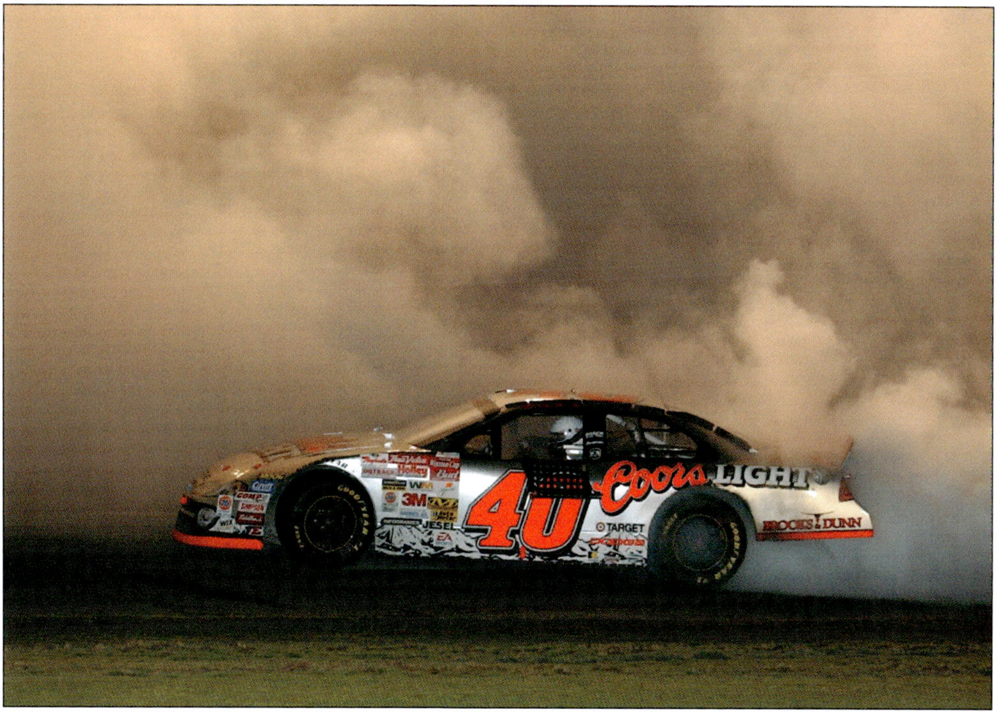

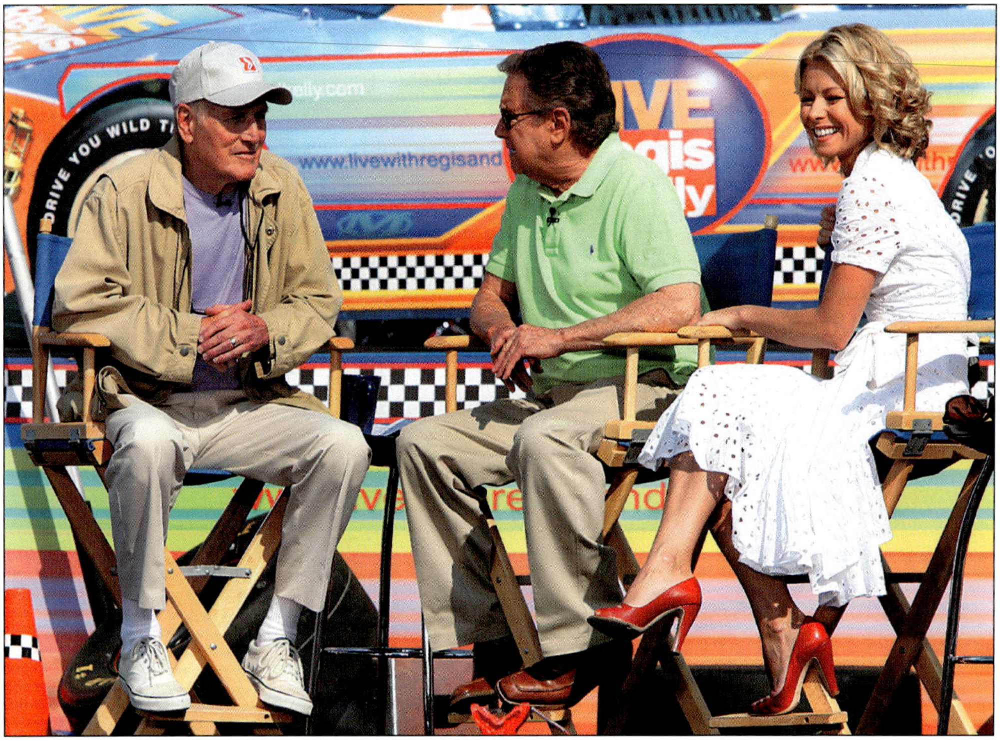

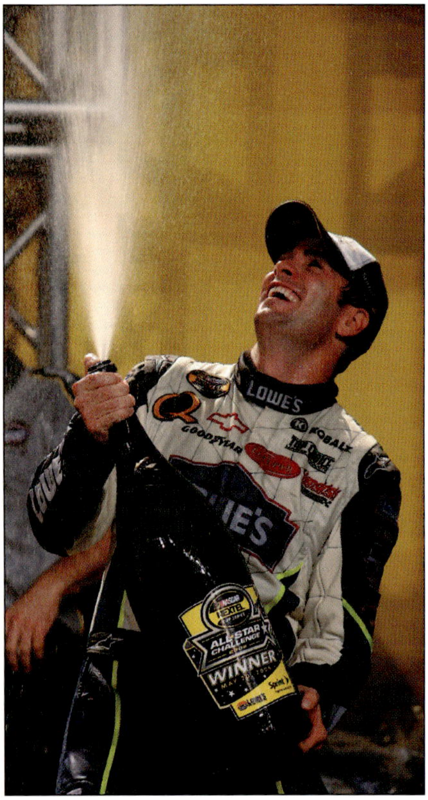

Live with Regis and Kelly originated one of its television shows from Charlotte Motor Speedway in the spring of 2006 when the world premiere of the movie *Cars* was held at the track. It was the first time a motorsports facility had ever hosted a major motion picture world premiere. Paul Newman (left), who was the voice of the character Doc Hudson, was a guest on the show that day.

Jimmie Johnson celebrated his second all-star victory in 2006. That night, the Hendrick Motorsports driver led 33 of the 90 laps, including the final 19. He was not seriously challenged in the race's closing stages as he took a 1.729-second victory over Kevin Harvick. Johnson's first all-star victory came three years earlier in 2003.

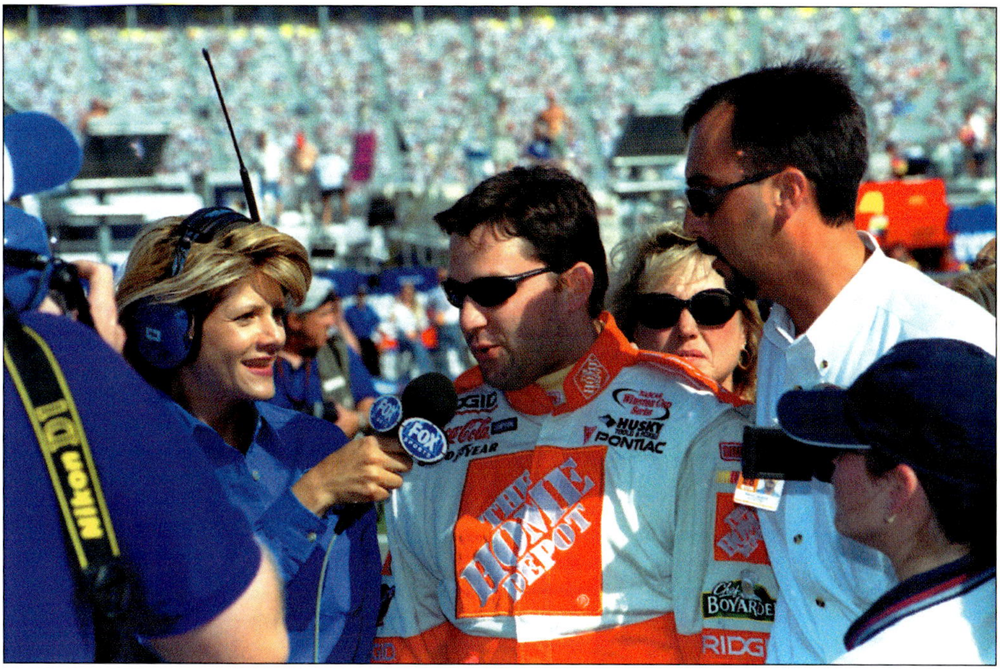

Above, Tony Stewart arrives at Charlotte Motor Speedway for the 2001 Coca-Cola 600 after competing earlier that day in the Indianapolis 500. Of the four drivers who have competed in both races on the same day, Stewart is the only one to have completed the entire 1,100 miles. On May 27, 2001, of Memorial Day weekend, Stewart finished sixth in the Indianapolis 500 and third in the Coca-Cola 600.

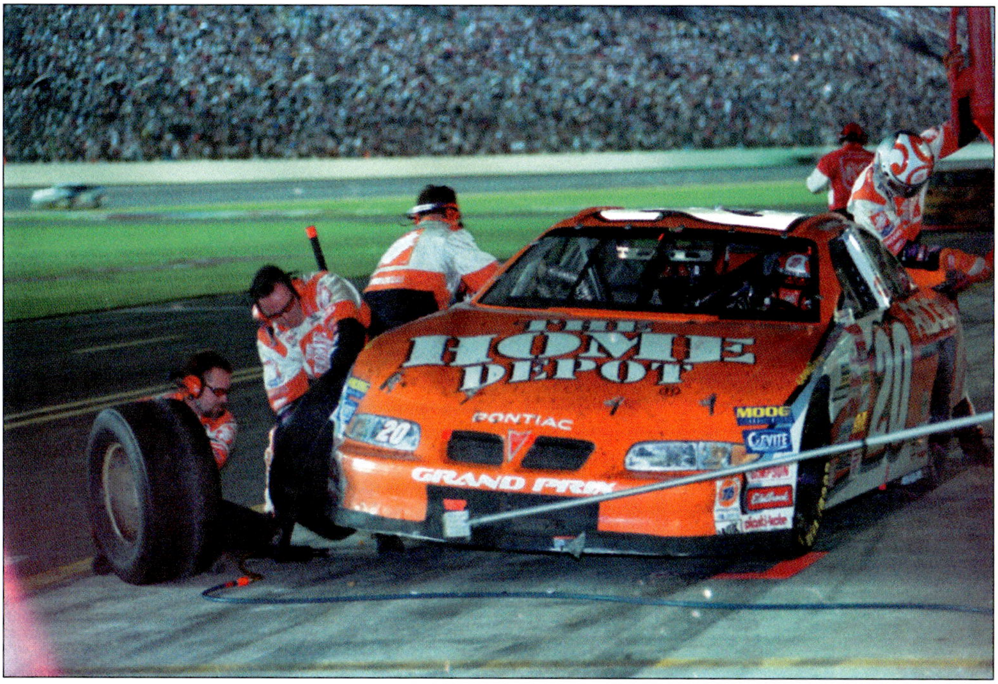

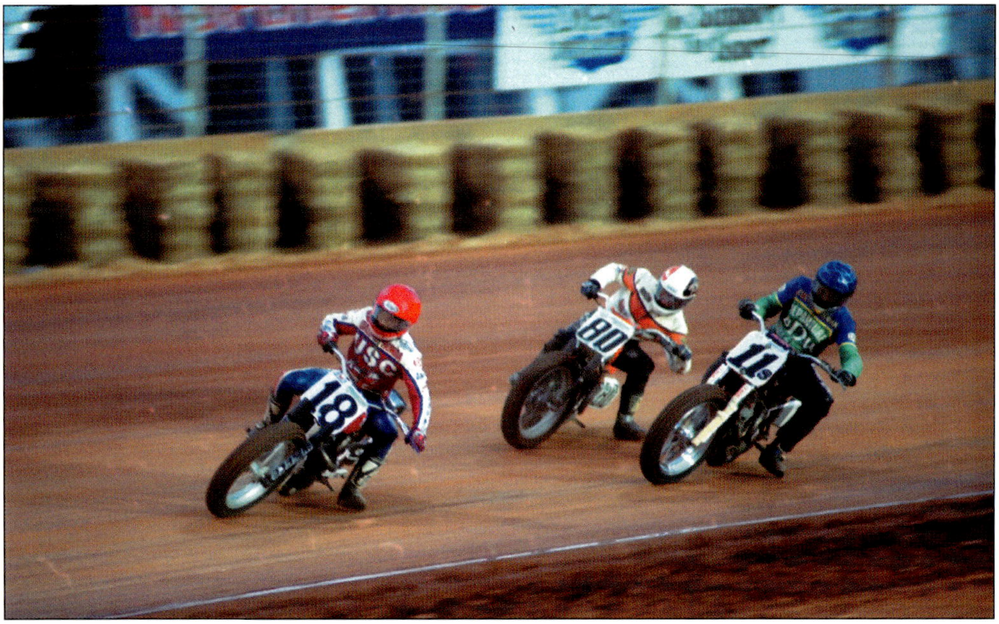

The Dirt Track at Charlotte provided the ideal place for flat-track motorcycle racing to return to the Charlotte area. In racing's early days, it was not unusual for the dirt tracks to host both motorcycle and stock car racing. In fact, many of those who became NASCAR officials or competed as drivers had at one time raced motorcycles. Joe Weatherly, NASCAR's 1963 premier series champion, won three American Motorcyclist Association (AMA) national championships.

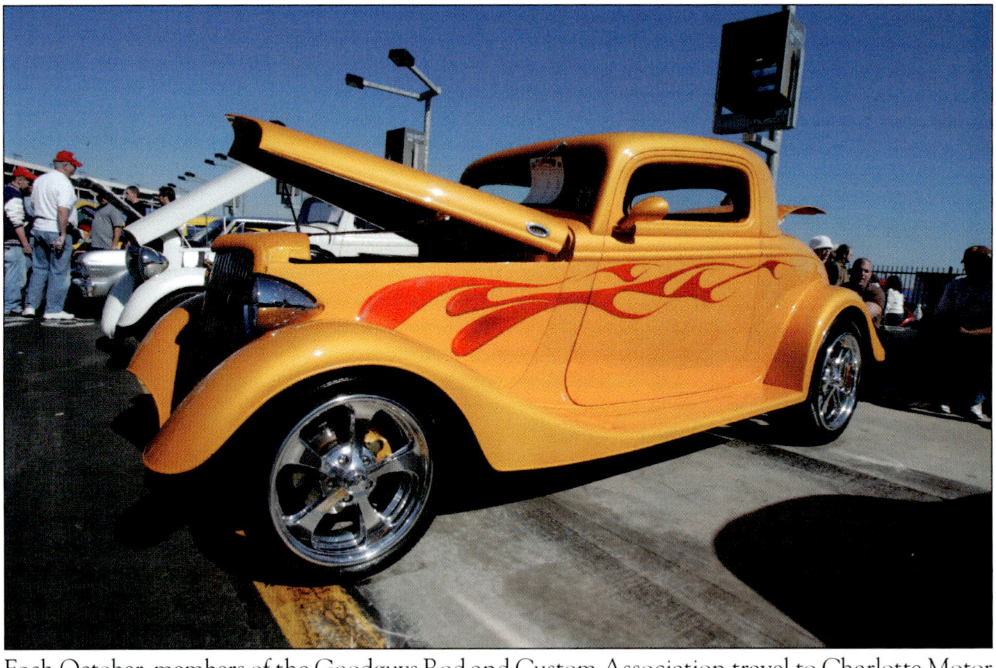

Each October, members of the Goodguys Rod and Custom Association travel to Charlotte Motor Speedway for their Southeastern Nationals. The three-day car show features hot rods, custom cars, classics, muscle cars, and trucks built through 1972. There also are vendors, a swap meet, cars for sale, and a track cruise.

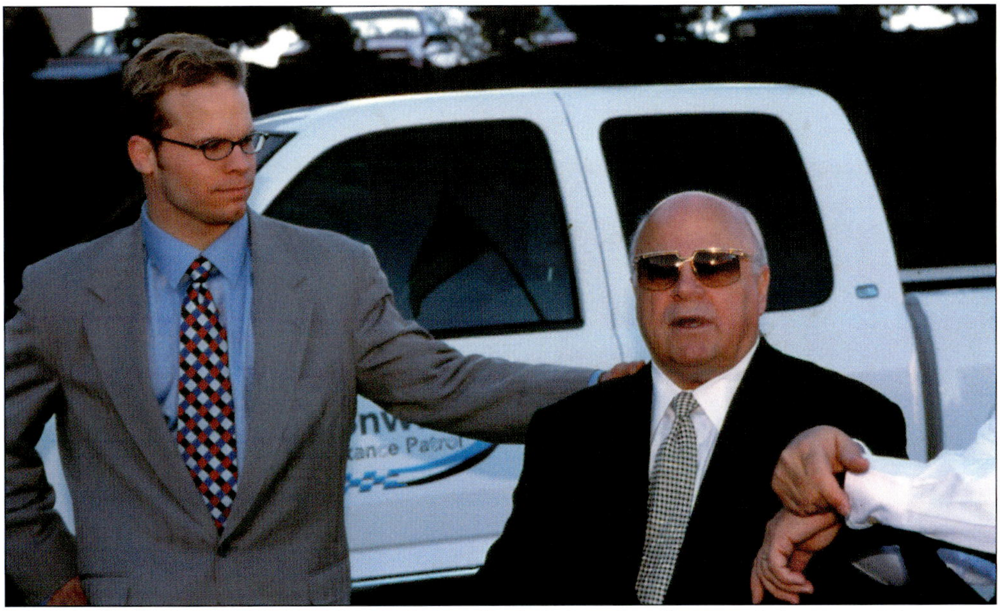

Marcus Smith (left) was named president, chief operating officer, and director of Speedway Motorsports Incorporated when H.A. "Humpy" Wheeler retired in 2008. Smith, who has worked at Charlotte Motor Speedway in various positions since junior high, also assumed the duties of president and general manager at the track. His father, Bruton Smith (right), is SMI's chief executive officer.

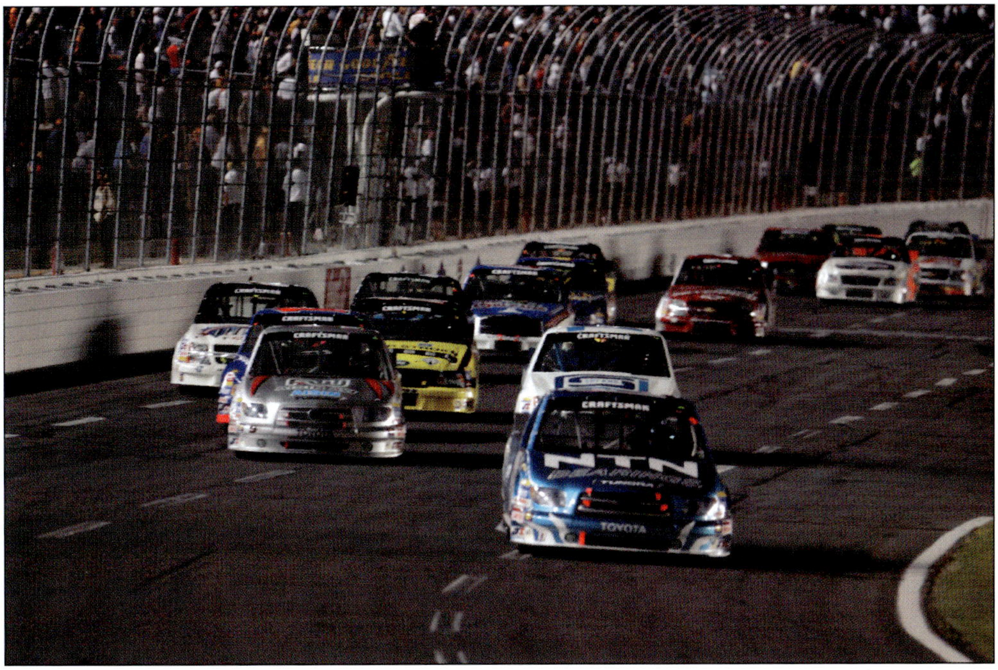

NASCAR's Camping World Truck Series made its debut at Charlotte Motor Speedway in 2003 as part of the all-star weekend festivities. In the inaugural truck race, Ted Musgrave emerged the victor, defeating Brendan Gaughan by less than half a second. The truck race has been held on the Friday of all-star weekend ever since.

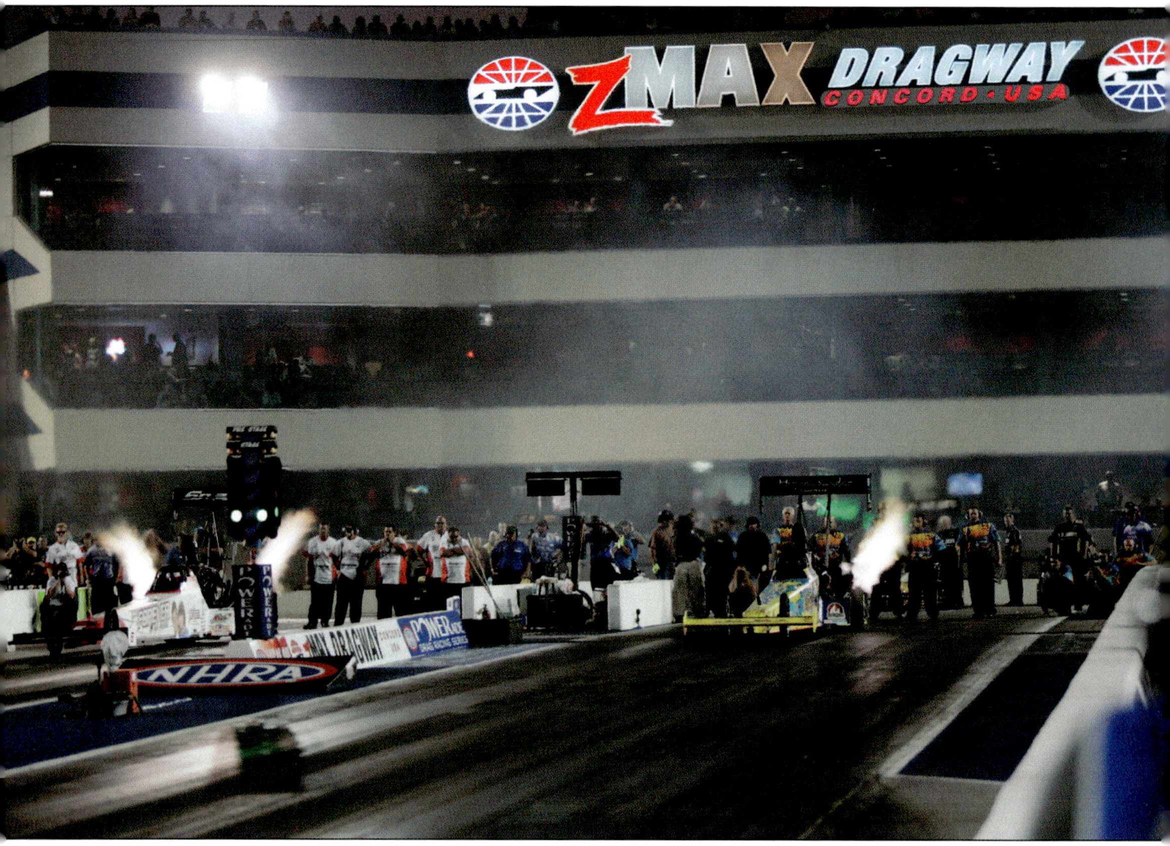

zMAX Dragway, nicknamed the "Bellagio of drag strips," opened in 2008 to rave reviews by competitors and fans. A sellout crowd of more than 30,000 attended the inaugural National Hot Rod Association (NHRA) Carolina Nationals in September 2008, which included a nighttime qualifying session. The winners for the inaugural event were Tony Schumacher, Top Fuel; Jack Beckman, Funny Car; Justin Humphreys, Pro Stock; and Steve Johnson, Pro Stock Motorcycle. Sixteen-time Funny Car champion John Force was honored with the reserved seat grandstand being named for him. When the NHRA initiated its Countdown to the Championship, the Carolina Nationals became the opening event for the six-race title run. The three-day weekends are not confined to the NHRA professional categories. Various sportsman classes also compete.

Six

The Innovations Continue

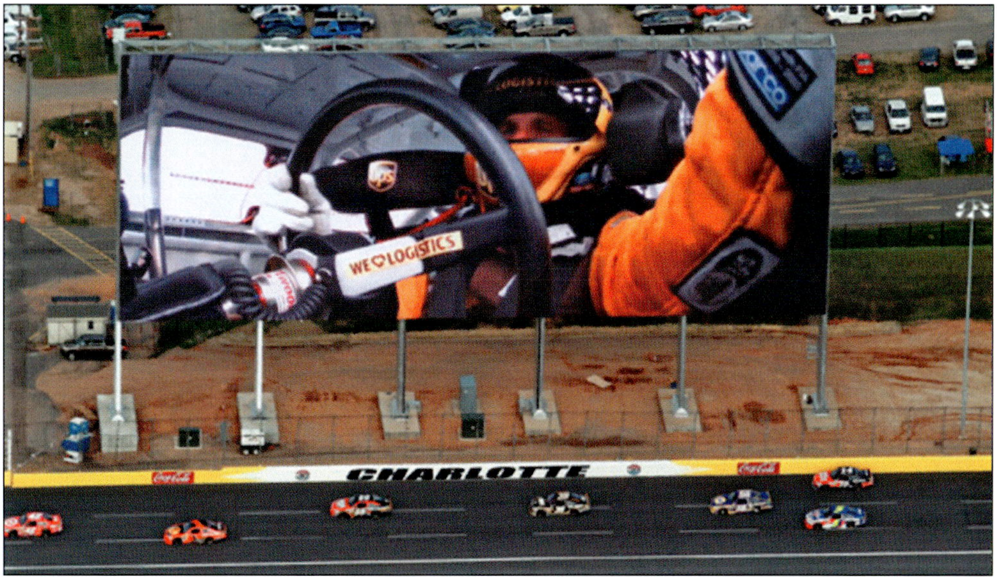

In 2011, the world's largest HDTV was installed on Charlotte Motor Speedway's backstretch. The video screen covers 16,000 square feet and is easily visible to fans seated throughout the frontstretch from turn four to turn one. It is 80 feet tall, 200 feet wide, and weighs 165,000 pounds. During each race, the telecast is featured on the huge screen. Movies also are shown on it during the summer months and the Christmas season.

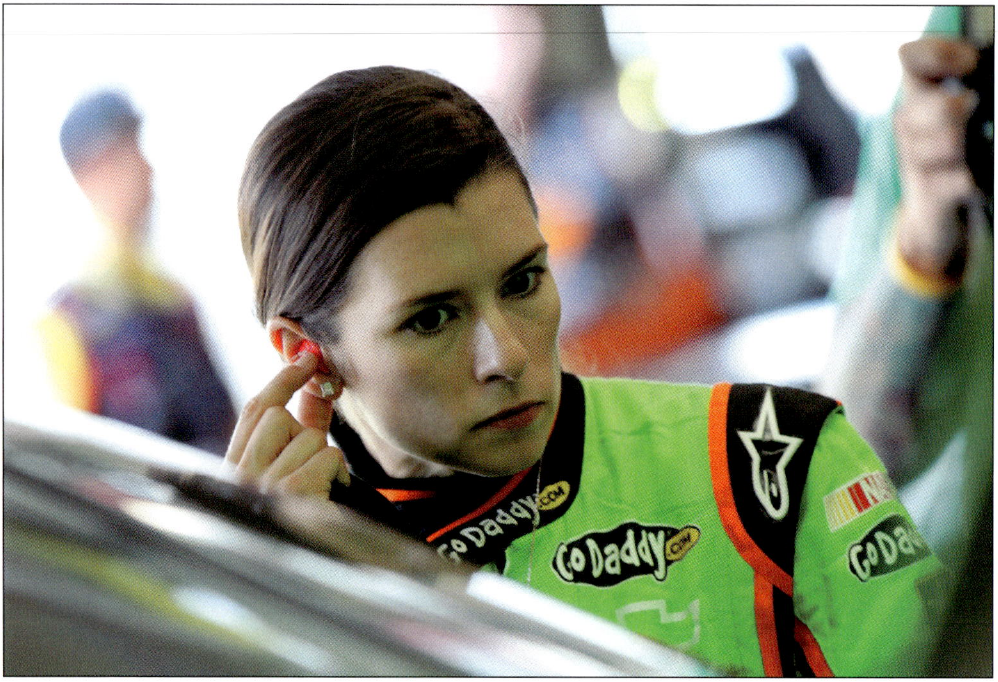

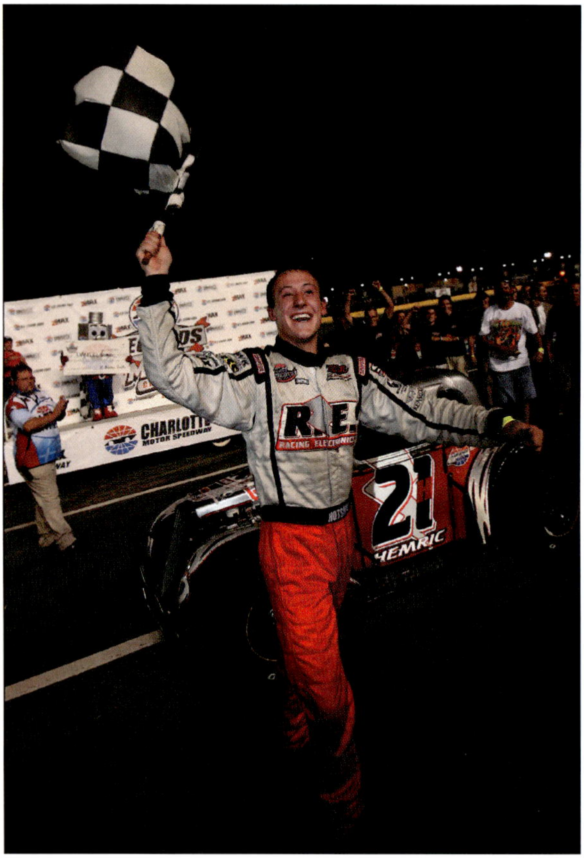

Danica Patrick became the first woman in 36 years to compete in the Coca-Cola 600 in May 2012. In her first venture into stock car racing's longest race, Patrick finished 30th after starting 40th in the 43-car field. Patrick moved to NASCAR from IndyCar, where she won one race and placed third in the 2009 Indianapolis 500.

Daniel Hemric shot into the racing spotlight in 2010 when he won Charlotte Motor Speedway's Legends Million. The Kannapolis, North Carolina, native points to that accomplishment as the boost his career needed. He secured a full-time ride in NASCAR's Camping World Truck Series in 2015, and in 2017, advanced into NASCAR's Xfinity Series with Richard Childress Racing.

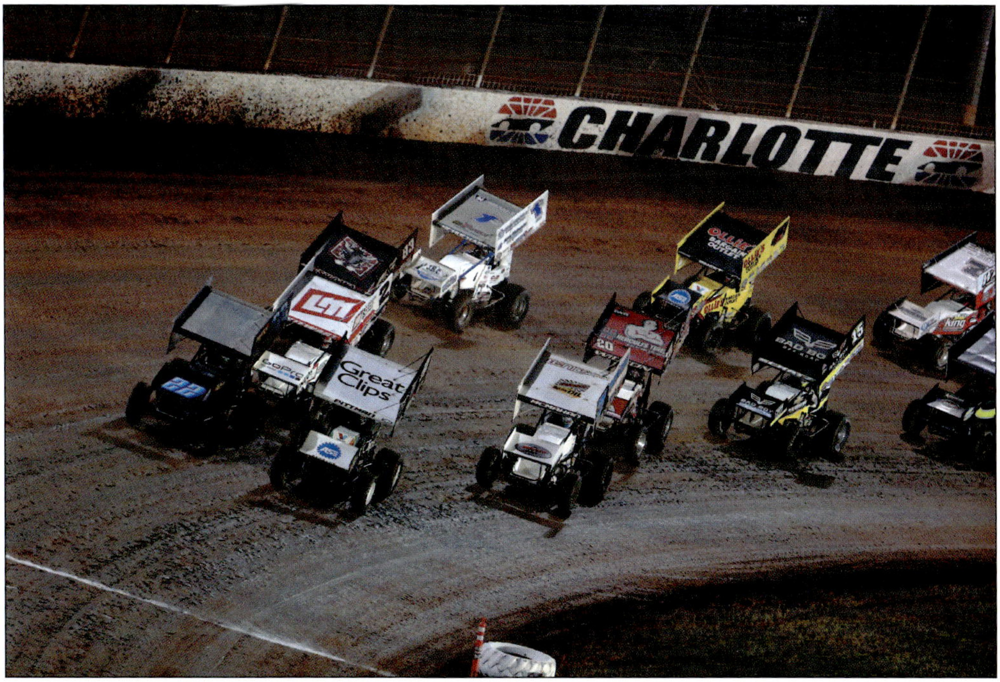

The Dirt Track at Charlotte has become quite popular since its opening more than a decade ago. Above, the World of Outlaws races are always a favorite on the Friday night before the Coca-Cola 600, and the World of Outlaws World Finals are a sellout in the fall. Below, the Dirt Track at Charlotte also makes returning to school a little easier for those who like monster trucks. Every year in mid-August, the track hosts the Circle K Back-To-School Monster Truck Bash. Other events that have been held at the Dirt Track at Charlotte include off-road truck racing, Global RallyCross, and AMA Pro Racing American Flat Track motorcycle racing.

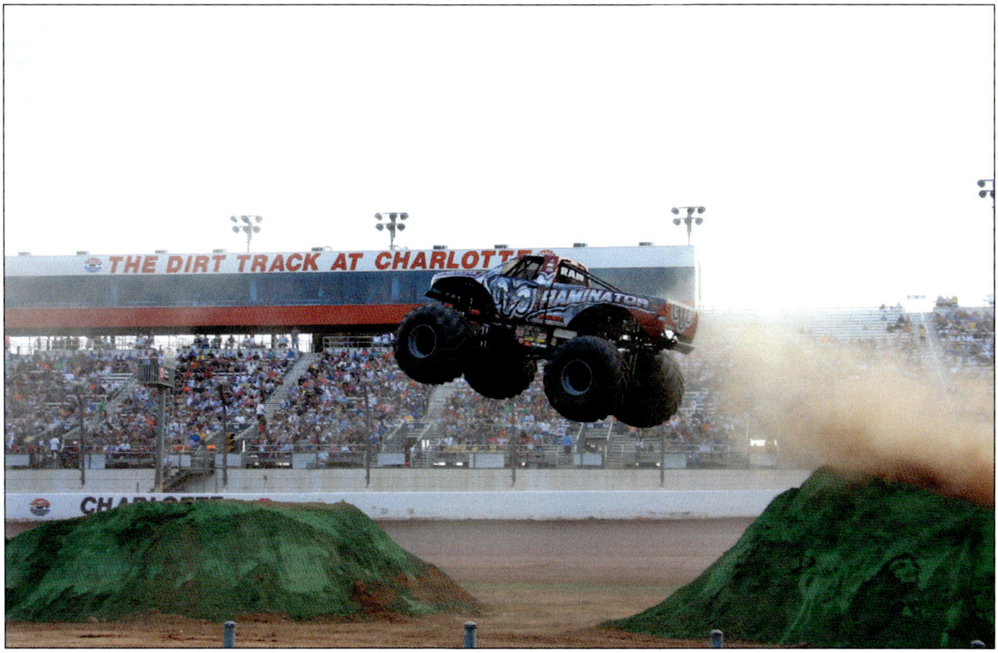

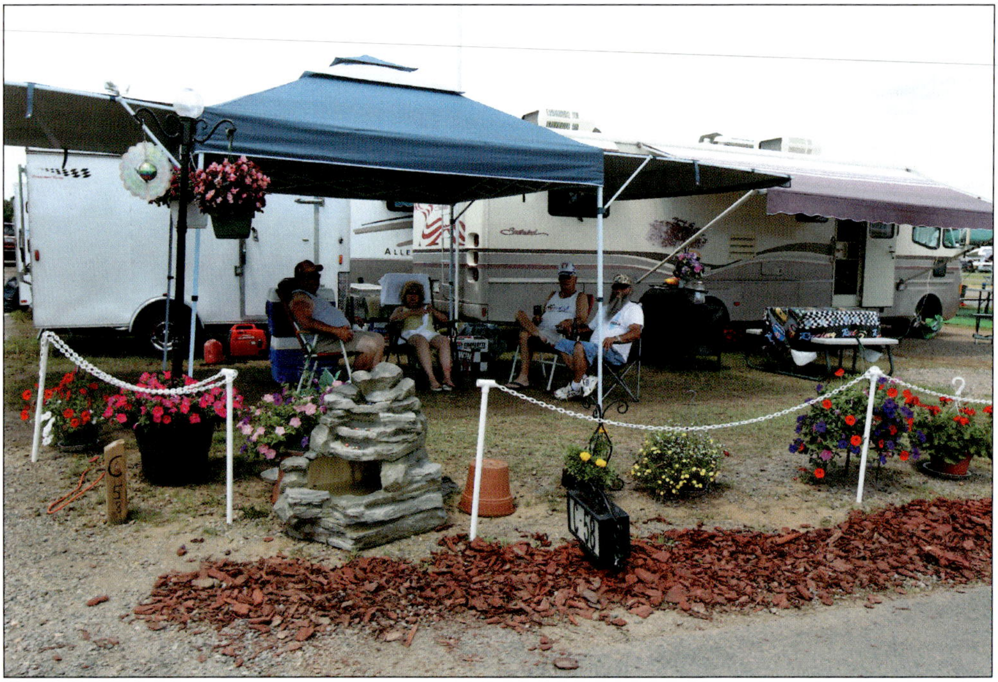

Camping at Charlotte Motor Speedway has become extremely popular, but unlike the sport's early days when most fans slept in tents, comfortable travel trailers and motor coaches are now the home-away-from-home of choice (above). Fans often meet friends for their annual campout and set up miniature neighborhoods complete with flowers and fencing. Trackside camping is also growing in popularity (below). Anyone choosing to watch a race this way has a reserved parking space a few feet from the fence. When it is race time, the motor coach residents only have to step outside to be at their own private sitting area.

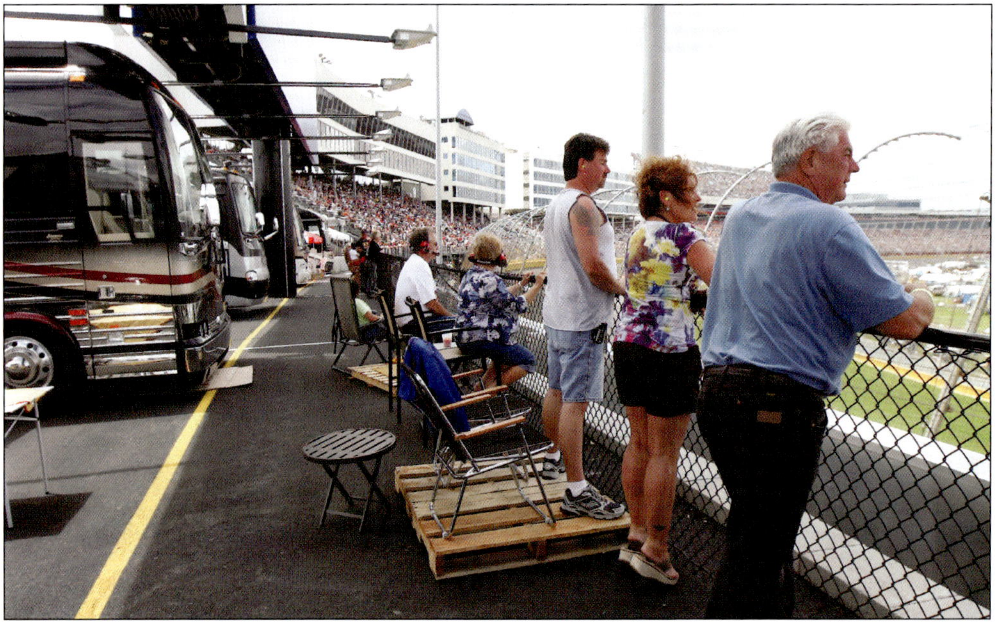

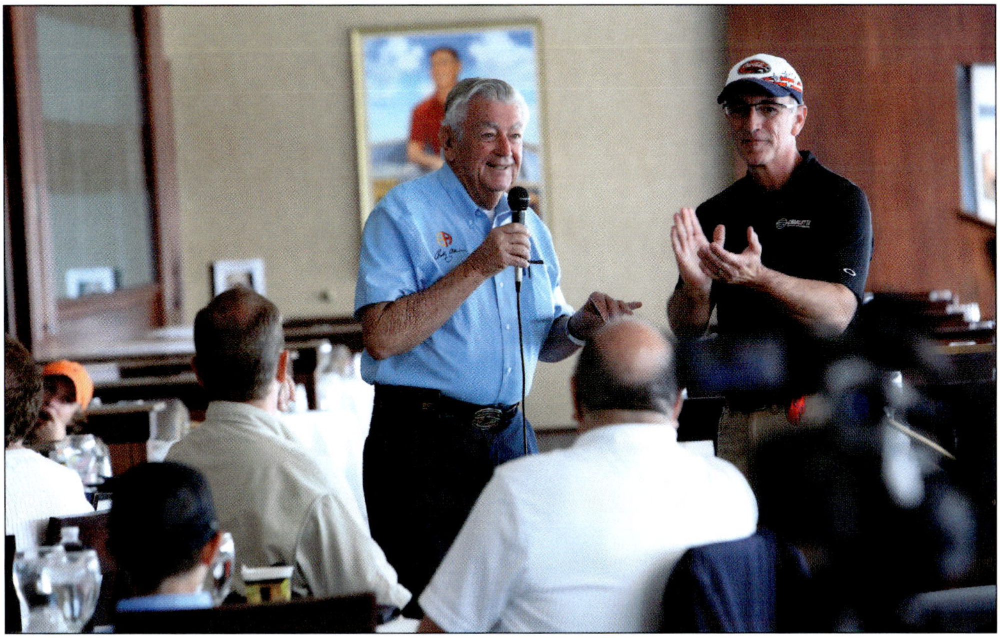

The Speedway Club has become a popular place for fans to meet the legends of the sport. On this particular day, Speedway Club members were treated to breakfast with Bobby Allison (above, left). In addition to hearing stories from the six-time Charlotte winner, the fans were able to participate in a question-and-answer session with the NASCAR Hall of Fame member and 1983 NASCAR premier series champion. On specific days during race weeks, several former drivers, many of whom are members of the NASCAR Hall of Fame, will gather in the Speedway Club and sign autographs for its members. Below, Charlotte has given fans a new experience with six elevated, open-air infield suites. Located between the back of pit road and the entrance to the Xfinity Series garage, the suites, the first of their kind in corporate hospitality, opened in 2012.

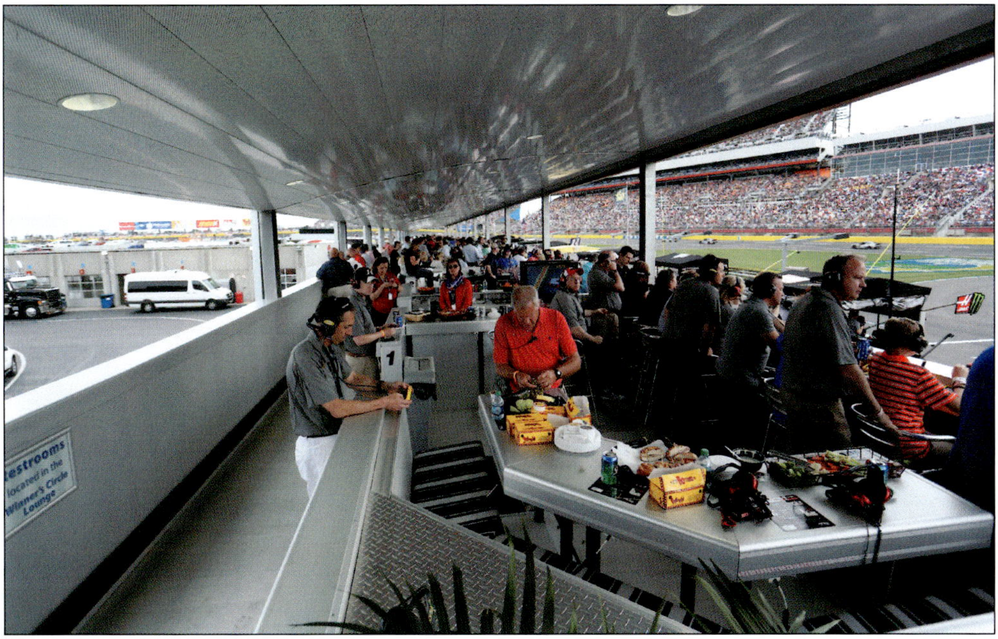

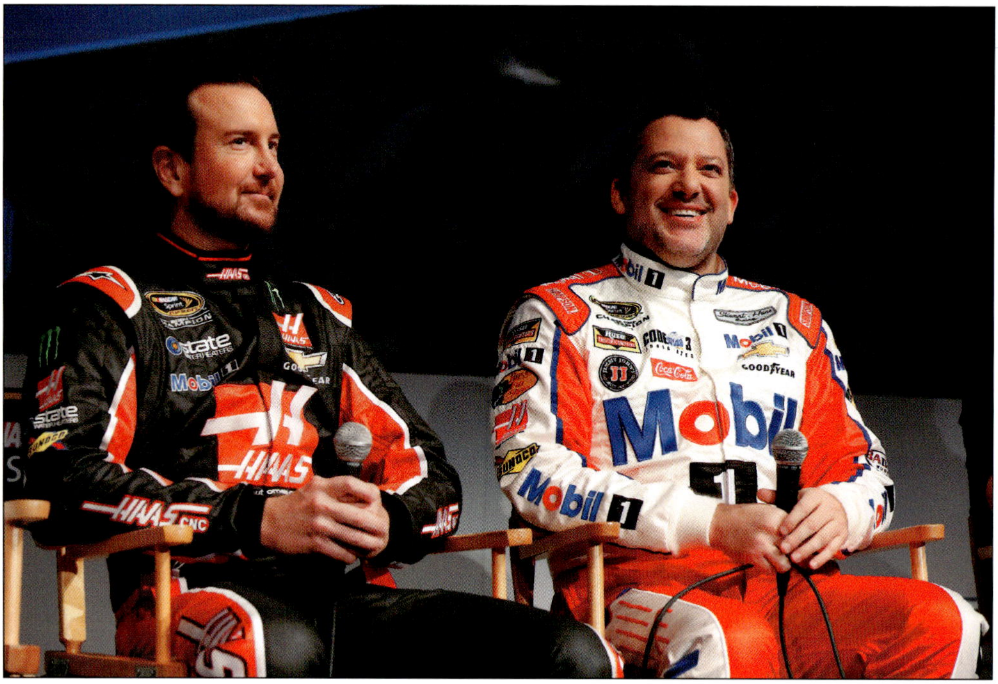

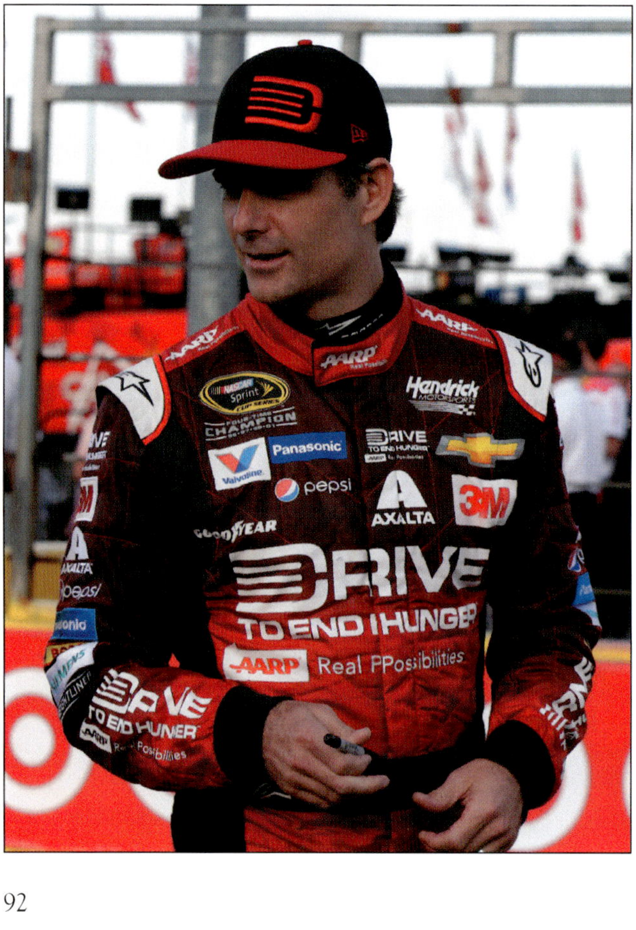

Two drivers who have played a significant role in Charlotte Motor Speedway's history retired in two successive years. Tony Stewart (above, right) walked away from NASCAR as a driver at the end of the 2016 season. During his driving career, he captured one victory, one all-star win, and two poles at the speedway. He failed to finish only one race in 35 starts. He also collected two IndyCar poles at the facility. Stewart's involvement in the sport will now be confined to one of team co-owner, with Kurt Busch (above, left) as one of his drivers. Jeff Gordon (left) decided to move from a full-time ride into the television booth at the end of the 2015 season. In 46 cup point races at Charlotte, Gordon recorded five victories, three all-star wins, and nine poles. In seven Xfinity races, he secured two victories.

No one in NASCAR history has conquered the Coca-Cola 600 with as much ease as Martin Truex Jr. in 2016. En route to the fourth victory of his career and the first of the 2016 season, Truex set a NASCAR record for the most miles led—588. The previous record was 502.5 miles, set by Jim Paschal in the 1967 World 600. Truex also led 392 of the 400 laps at the 1.5-mile track. That broke the record of 335, also set by Paschal in 1967. Two more records set by Truex Jr. involved the time of the race and average speed. It was the quickest Coca-Cola 600 in the race's 57-year history. It took 3:44:08 to complete. Truex's average speed also was the fastest at 160.644 miles per hour.

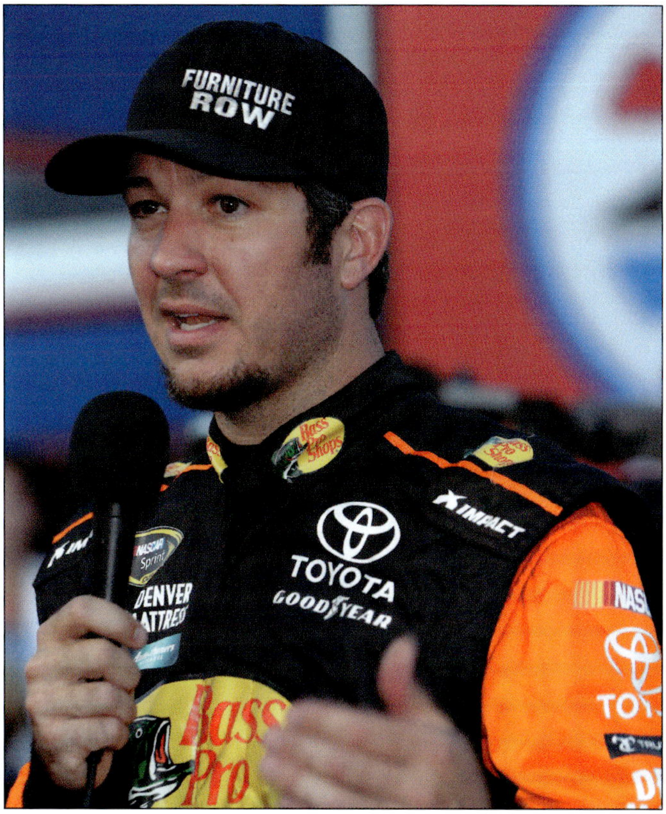

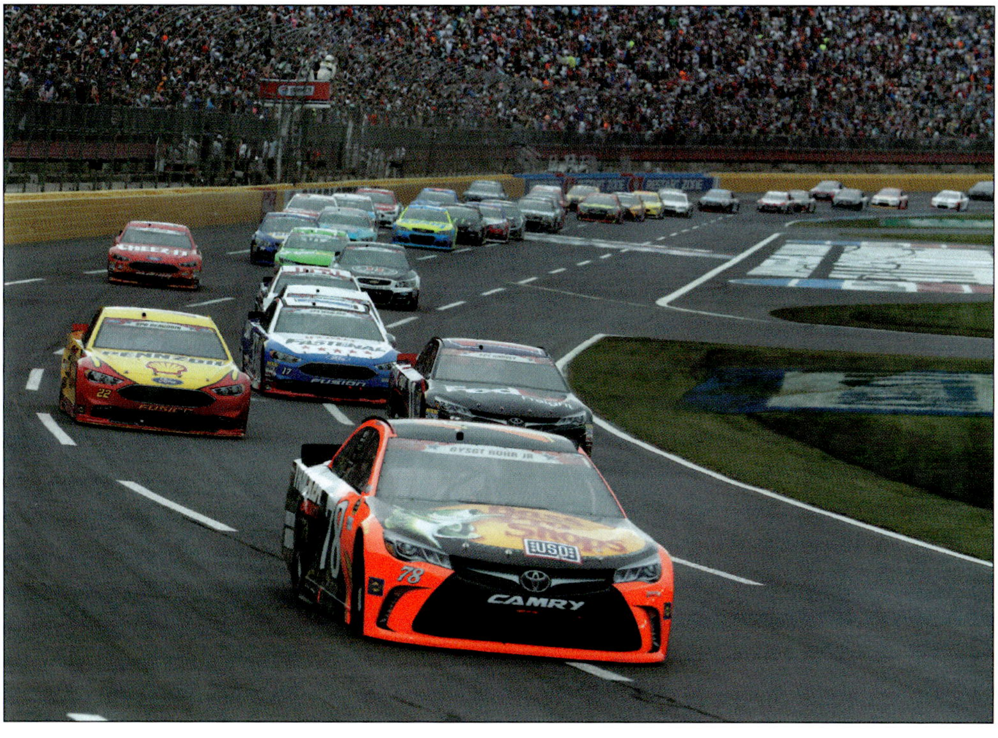

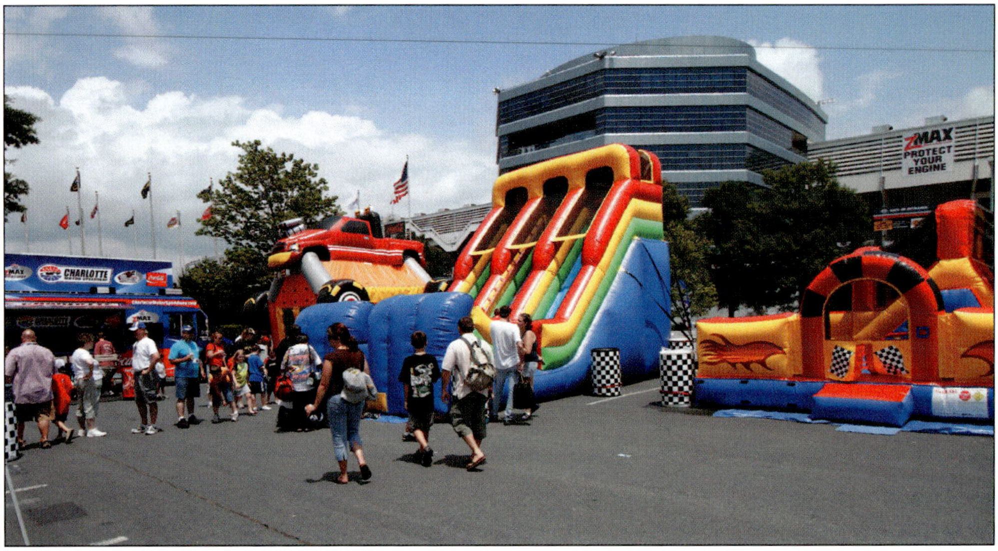

A revamped Fan Zone opened in 2011 (above). Located on a paved 10-acre area near the speedway's main entrance, it includes a Play Zone for children. The kid-friendly area includes bounce houses, face painters, and a petting zoo. Also located in the area are interactive games, displays, and the Fanatics NASCAR merchandise tents. In recent years, the track has added Speedway Christmas (below). The holiday-themed light show covers three miles over the speedway's infield, grandstands, and concourse. From mid-November through December 31, 2016, the light show spectacular attracted a record 120,000 cars. With track rentals and events, the speedway is now used more than 300 days annually.

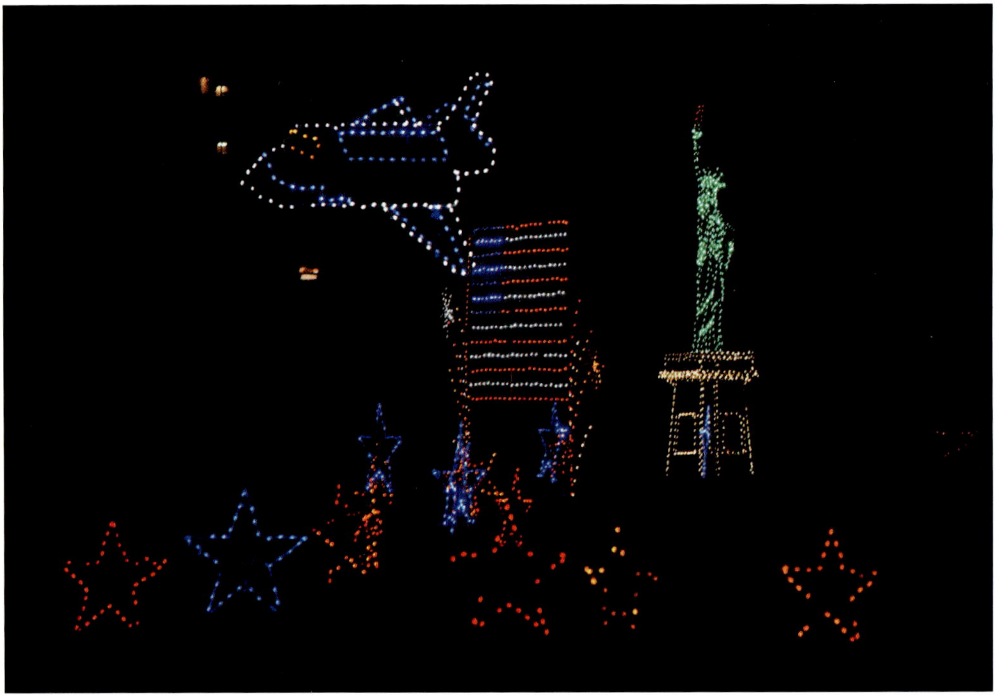

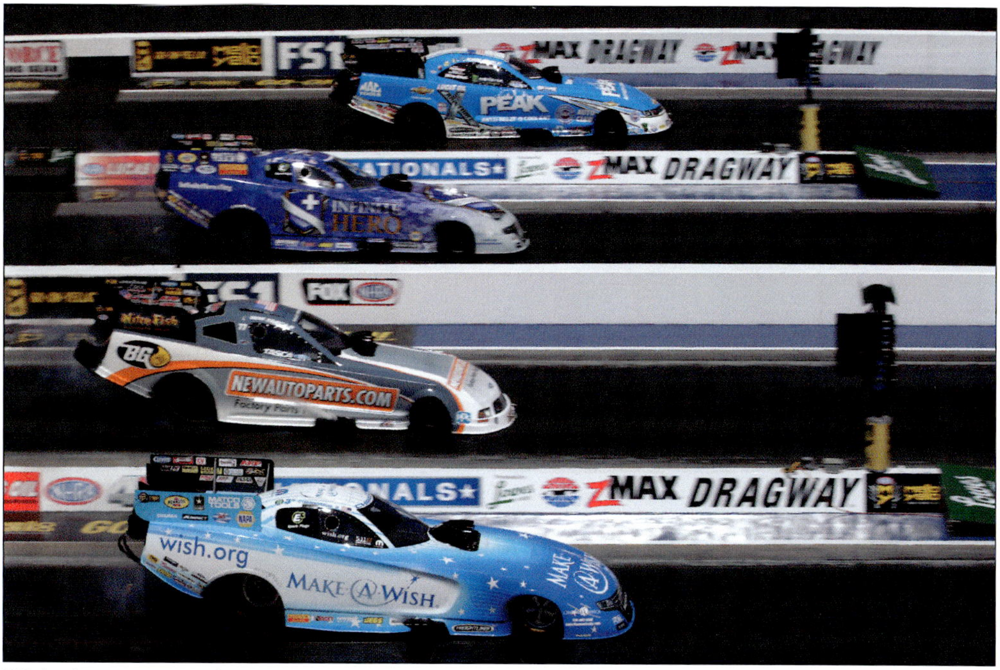

With the opening of zMAX Dragway, a new era in drag racing began with its unique four-wide event. The only race of its kind, the NHRA Four-Wide Nationals are held in April and present a new challenge to the competitors with two, instead of one, advancing after each elimination round. The four-wide event involves all of the NHRA's professional classes—Top Fuel, Funny Car, Pro Stock, and Pro Stock Motorcycle. Shown above are, from the top, the Funny Cars of John Force, Jack Beckman, Bob Tasca III, and Tommy Johnson Jr. Below, Charlotte Motor Speedway's quarter-mile track located on its frontstretch has become the site of the season finale for NASCAR's Whelen Southern Modified Tour. The event is held in October after pole qualifying for the Bank of America 500.

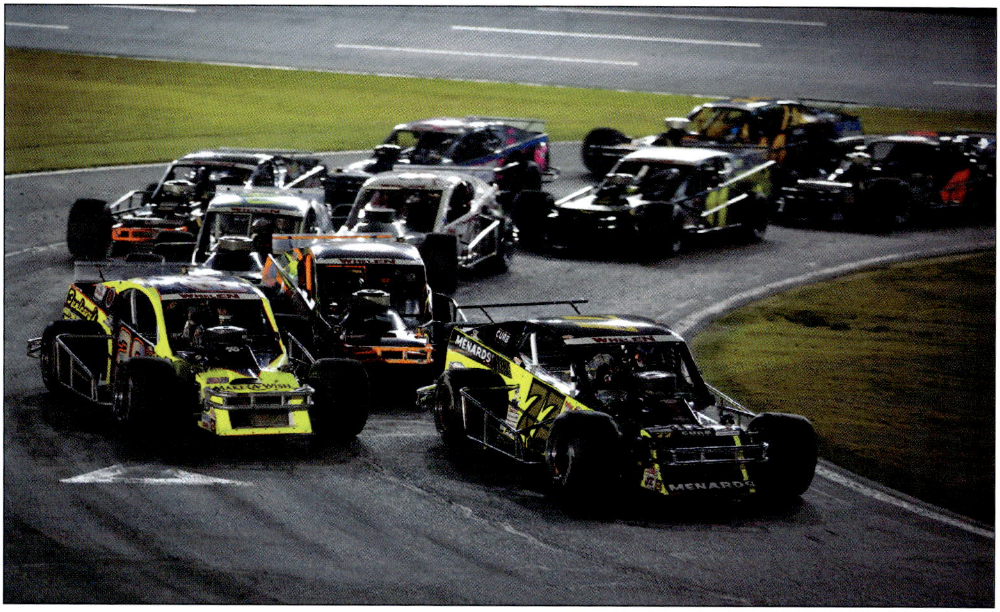